What people are sa

The Spirituality of th

Myth is where soul and spirit intersect with intellect. That is why myths are one of the most integrative, healing forces we know anything about, as Peter Fritsch shows in *The Spirituality of the Holy Grail*. In this insightful book, Fritsch rescues myth from its unfortunate reputation as "nothing but fiction." He restores to the Grail legend the restorative, guiding function it has served for centuries. Mythless cultures are without direction; they may be dying cultures. That is why *The Spirituality of the Holy Grail* is an antidote for the deadening effects of a soulless materialism, the greatest threat to our future and our world.

Larry Dossey MD, author of *One Mind: How Our Individual Mind Is Part of a Greater Consciousness and Why It Matters* and *The Power of Premonitions: How Knowing the Future Can Shape Our Lives*

Peter Fritsch's book is a treasure. It will appeal to a minister, a therapist, or the average reader interested in growing in Christ. It touches theology, philosophy, and rational thinking. It will enhance your life no matter where you are on life's journey. It is full of gems you will want to linger over and digest slowly. It flows well with worthwhile examples of rich personal and professional experiences. Fritsch's writing comes across as humble and knowledgeable at the same time. He forges complex issues into the readable and understandable. Personally, Fritsch gave me words to express the growth and pain of others as well as my own. His practical and applicable thoughts at the end were adaptable for any who are open to their own interior growth. The bibliography is worth the price of the book. In the end, Fritsch conveys that there is more than we can ever perceive and in that there is hope.

Pamela Walden Taylor, Minister of Pastoral Counseling and Spiritual Director at Friends United Church of Christ, Indianapolis

The Spirituality of the Holy Grail

Restoring Feminine Spirit
in the Western Soul

The Spirituality of the Holy Grail

Restoring Feminine Spirit
in the Western Soul

Peter L. Fritsch

CHRISTIAN ALTERNATIVE
BOOKS

Winchester, UK
Washington, USA

JOHN HUNT PUBLISHING

First published by Christian Alternative Books, 2021
Christian Alternative Books is an imprint of John Hunt Publishing Ltd.,
No. 3 East St., Alresford, Hampshire SO24 9EE, UK
office@jhpbooks.com
www.johnhuntpublishing.com
www.christian-alternative.com

For distributor details and how to order please visit the 'Ordering' section on our website.

Text copyright: Peter L. Fritsch 2020

ISBN: 978 1 78904 771 4
978 1 78904 772 1 (ebook)
Library of Congress Control Number: 2021930343

A CIP catalogue record for this book is available from the British Library.

Design: Stuart Davies

UK: Printed and bound by CPI Group (UK) Ltd, Croydon, CR0 4YY
Printed in North America by CPI GPS partners

We operate a distinctive and ethical publishing philosophy in all areas of our business, from our global network of authors to production and worldwide distribution.

Contents

Acknowledgments   viii

Introduction   1

Section I. Why the Fisher King Story?   13

Chapter One: Finding Our Souls Again: My Story   15

Chapter Two: Historical Background to the Fisher
King Story   22

Section II. What Is Our Soul?   35

Chapter Three: The Nature of the Soul and How
It Functions   37

Chapter Four: Healing the Wounded Soul   65

Chapter Five: The Soul Contains Our Opposites and
Then Helps Us Heal by Integration   81

Chapter Six: Balancing the Need for Stability of Outer
and Inner Needs Is Essential for Our Healing   105

Chapter Seven: Love Is Behind All Reality   122

Chapter Eight: Trusting and Using Our Intuition for
Guidance and Rich Experience   138

Chapter Nine: What Is the Ontological Purpose of Our Life
    Expressed in the Soul?   146

Chapter Ten: The Fool Who Saves Us   159

Chapter Eleven: The Soul Helps Us Face the Death of
    a Vision as Well as Our Physical Death   168

Chapter Twelve: Our Choices at Mid Life   178

**Section III. The Nature of Evil, and How We
Understand and Overcome Its Influence**   **191**

Chapter Thirteen: Where Does Evil Originate?   193

Chapter Fourteen: The Nature of Sin and the Proliferation
    of Evil Lies in the Acts of Unconscious Living   209

Chapter Fifteen: What Steps Can We as Individuals Take
    to Deal with Evil Effectively?   221

Chapter Sixteen: The Basis of the Evil of Narcissism and
    Keeping the Soul Wise   240

Chapter Seventeen: Having Done All, We Stand   256

Chapter Eighteen: Finding Language about Evil: Creating
    a Container for the Questions   263

Section IV   **275**

**Conclusion: Spiritual Disciplines to
Practice to Nurture the Soul**   **277**

Summary   341
Bibliography   344

Acknowledgments

Fifteen years ago I read for the first time one of the most helpful books in my library. It was written by Jungian analyst Robert Johnson of San Diego and titled, *The Fisher King and the Handless Maiden: Healing the Feeling Function in Men and Women's Psychology*. I found myself returning to the slim volume repeatedly, each time finding new nuggets of truth speaking deeply to my soul.

Ten years earlier I had studied Emma Jung's and Marie-Louise van Franz's scholarly volume, *The Grail Legend*, alongside Robert Johnson's classic, *He*, about masculine psychology, using the same motif. The story of the Fisher King, or Perceval and the Search for the Holy Grail, took hold of my imagination and I found the symbolism of the story speaking to dark reaches of my forgotten self and spirit.

The stories spoke to me not only because of my own hero's quest, conquest, confrontation, demise, burial, and transformation, but also called me to examine aspects of Self which were long forgotten, neglected and unloved.

Over the past decades of inner work, lost aspects of Self have slowly been renewed and given honored space in my awareness. A sense of movement towards wholeness has been the result.

Within the last decade, Cynthia Bourgeault's and Elaine Pagel's writings about the Wisdom Gospels, which elevate the feminine figures of the Jesus story and the feminine spirituality of early Christianity, helped restore my belief to a semblance of reality in the balanced person of Jesus of Nazareth. Labeled and grouped together with more Gnostic writings declared heretical by the patriarchal institutional church of the Third Century and excluded from the canonical New Testament, the Gospels of Thomas, Andrew, and Mary Magdalene were the most helpful to my developing thirst for a balanced theology that made sense of the behavior and teachings of Jesus.

Also John A. Sanford, my mentor for more than a decade, wrote about the balance of masculine and feminine energies in the person of Jesus in his book, *The Kingdom Within*. Each of these writings has helped develop a more holistic understanding of the person of Jesus, who is the One through whom I relate to God.

Incorporating the personal body work of Tantric traditions has also had a formative effect upon my own theological practice, as within this eastern teaching I found the ever-present work of the Holy Spirit as I have always known Him/Her as an intimate, speaking, moving force working in conjunction with my intuition and insight. Tantric teaching brought incarnational reality into my life in a deeper way than known before. I experienced a profound healing of compulsive eating, and a removal of somatic pain in my body which had been trapped within all of my adult life due to extreme abuse accrued in childhood.

Each of these paths of knowledge helped me look for themes and stories that honored the oppressed feminine of God that I have always instinctively known existed, but failed to find words and images to convey. The symbolism of the Holy Grail, as a vessel and chrysalis symbol of transformation, has given me a rich, inner relationship to the reality of the love of God known within my soul since my adolescent spiritual awakening.

I wish to acknowledge the influence of my primary mentor in Christian spirituality and Jungian psychology, John A. Sanford of San Diego. Also, along with Sanford has been the profound inspiration of Sanford's friends Robert Johnson and Dr. Morton Kelsey.

Writers who have greatly influenced my journey in helping transform my images of God and understand my experiences of the holy are the Hungarian theologian Boros László (Ladislaus Boros), Laurens van der Post, Anthony Bloom, André Louf,

James Frazier, Agnes Sanford, Carlo Carretto, Watchman Nee, Elaine Pagels, Mircea Eliade, John O'Donohue, Rainer Maria Rilke, Kyriacos Markides, Josef Pieper, Simon Schama, Paul Tournier, Marie-Louise von Franz, Marion Woodman, James Griffiss, Catherine De Hueck Doherty, Rees Howells, Baron von Hügel, Irene Claremont De Castillijo, Romano Guardini, Ferenc Máté, Paul Yougni Cho, and last, and most profoundly grateful, C. G. and Emma Jung.

I give thanks to my wife, Dr. Mónika Farkas, whose gently powerful spirit introduced me to the ways and means of integrating my soul and body through her own spirituality and medical background resulting in a truly Christian honoring of my body and soul together, as a temple of the living God.

Introduction

Mircea Eliade – Myth expresses the absolute truth, because it narrates a sacred history, a trans-human revelation which took place at the dawn of the Great Time in the holy times of the beginnings. Through the myth we detach ourselves from profane time and magically re-enter the Great Time, the sacred time.
(Eliade, Mircea. *The Sacred and the Profane*. Harcourt, NYC, NY, 1959)

C. G. Jung – The crisis of the modern world is in great part due to the fact that the Christian symbols and myths are no longer lived by the whole human being, that they have been reduced to words and gestures deprived of life, fossilized, externalized and therefore no longer is any use for the deeper life of the soul.
(Kelsey, Morton. *Myth, History and Faith: The Mysteries of Christian Myth and Imagination*. Element Books, Rockport, MA, 1974)

Rollo May – Surely Nietzsche is right: our powerful hunger for myth is a hunger for community.
(May, Rollo. *The Cry for Myth*. Dell Publishing, NY, 1991)

This introduction includes an apologetic for the use of mythology to teach about the nature of the soul, an explanation of the format of the book, and a short personal overview of the story of *The Fisher King Myth*, also known by the title, *Perceval and the Search for the Holy Grail*. The story has many versions. Having read as many accounts of the myth as I could research over the past two decades, I am choosing the aspects of the legend that most speak to me personally about the nature of the soul. I am using this eleventh-century myth to write about the need for the twenty-first-century seeker of God to understand one's predicament, and to find solutions for the healing of the soul.

Episcopal priest Dr. Morton Kelsey taught that myth describes in words a pattern of images that have important meaning. Ritual is a way of expressing this pattern by acting it out. Through myth and ritual, we are given understanding, new insights, and new knowledge of spiritual powers, realities and ways to relate to them. This releases new energies, new springs of energy within us. The religious approach to soul work also provides protection from maligned forces around us by the surrounding helpful forces.

Mythology is a language in words and ritual that provides a way for us to connect with spiritual realities. Mythology helps us to express what our souls experience within us, outside of us, in our past, and as we dream of our future.

Kelsey wrote that the main difficulty modern people have about myth is that our view of our humanity is too restricted, as we continue in the world view of Logical Positivism which modern Philosophy has debunked, but our culture continues to emulate and hold up as supreme. Polányi Mihály (Michael Polyani) and other great thinkers demonstrated repeatedly that the concept of the scientific method of reductionism is not objective, as the observer has a set of presuppositions through which he/she pushes, like a grid, all the information coming to a person. Our observation also effects the behavior of the observed, so that there is no such thing as objective dissimulation of facts.

Truth is always in motion, and changes depending on how we perceive reality. The materialistic view of reality continues to dominate, especially the Western Church world view, thus excluding the more sophisticated and insightful perspective of reality of earlier brilliant philosophers and scientists. In our arrogance, we leave out more than half of all intelligence, the right hemisphere of the brain's intuitive, instinctive intelligence and knowledge. Only as we learn to synthesize and balance right- and left-brain intelligence can we arrive at conclusions that come closer to our outer and inner experiences.

Myth is not simply stories that are fanciful based on perhaps a historical event or person. Myth speaks of another realm of reality and experience than the physical one. Myth is a succession of narratives that describe our contact with the spiritual world and how it interacts with the physical world. As Kelsey eloquently said, "Myth is where spirit and matter touch each other. They are not opposites [*myth and history, myth and prepositional truth*], each gives a review of the facts from their own point of view." Myth speaks from the spiritual dimension and cognitive historical prepositional story touches us from the historical, sensual perspective.

In my observation, this is why Biblical Fundamentalism intellectually and practically fails "to hold water." Its world view tries to make myth describe prepositional, historical truth instead of emphasizing that myth speaks from the spiritual divide to the events of history. Thus, Biblical Fundamentalism tries to force mythological narrative to fit into the restrictive box of Logical Positivism. This doesn't mean, in my view, that a particular biblical story is not historical, but that historical truth and myth complement each other. By trying to force historical criticism and mythology together as identical, instead of seeing them as complementary, the biblical literalist misses out on the richness and value of both and thus starves the soul of much needed spiritual nourishment.

Thirty years ago, when I discovered Jungian psychology and the mythological realm of images speaking to me in my dreams while I slept, I uncovered a renewed vitality and love for Holy Scripture. The sacred text came alive for me without the nagging inner conflict arising from an earlier viewpoint that restricted me as a young man. For me, the mythological, allegorical approach to sacred text created a balanced and holistic use of both right- and left-brain intelligence.

In the very early Christian Church, the School of Antioch was one of the two major centers of the study of biblical exegesis and theology during Late Antiquity; the other was the Catechetical School of Alexandria.

I returned to my earlier seminary studies to read about the conflict between the more "rational," (read, left-brain) approach to the Bible of the Antiochian Schools of the first few centuries and the more allegorical approach of the non-rational, allegorical (read, right-brain) Alexandrian movement. Both are right and truthful, but separate. If held in a one-sided viewpoint, they give only a partial understanding of the spiritual and material world. Together, they give deep insight to integrate the spiritual with the physical world, both of which we live within.

Christian Fundamentalism is a fairly recent phenomenon, less than two hundred years old in the West, and has no basis in early church history or Jewish approaches to sacred text. The early church used stories and mythology freely to talk about how people interacted and experienced the spiritual dimension and how this experience influenced and often directed their outer everyday living. The early church didn't use the word "myth" but that is what they did. They told stories, they listened to the allegorical symbolic language of their dreams just as their ancestor did for centuries before them. When they used sacred text, both the Old Testament writings and the New Testament gospels and letters, they used them symbolically and applied the truths within them to the practicality of daily life. They did not push to prove the objective historical data of the stories. They trusted their inner intuition influenced by how they experienced God's indwelling Spirit and discovered power, hope and inspirational love which empowered them to live very interesting and vital lives.

We can do the same today. Mythology, properly understood

as speaking to the inner world of truth by narrative, can help us connect with deeper realities within our souls.

I will never forget something a friend studying to be a massage therapist told me once. He said that his massage professor quoted a study in which medical doctors discovered that the human heart responded to words, sounds and touch to the body, a fraction of a second before the brain registered the information and was able to respond.

To me this means that words have power and are creative, and can be intelligently understood at a biological and instinctual level even before the cognitive thinking of our brains has time to respond to the data. I find this fascinating and true to my experience as a priest and a conduit of Christ's healing. Words, music, and all kinds of "non-rational" stimuli touch us at our core in ways that our left-brain thinking cannot either penetrate or catch up to within the right-brain intuitional and instinctive intelligence.

This need to integrate the paradox of opposite ways of processing information is what I mean when I stated above, our world view is too small. What we think human intelligence and experience are, must be expanded.

This is why, as a writer, teacher, counselor and priest, I emphasize the importance of learning the symbolic language of our dreams. They help us connect our outer and inner world in an intricate balance which gives us energy, connection and deepest joy.

I will be using both the eleventh-century Grail myth mentioned above and additional stories from the New Testament teachings and life of Jesus to illustrate how the soul gets damaged, or restricted, and how it can heal and grow again.

Men and women usually have different types of soul wounds, but the healing process is almost identical, with a few differences. As a Christian and Jungian, I enjoy the belief from the Genesis Creation Myth that states we are created as balanced, androgynous beings, with masculine and feminine aspects of body and soul within each of us. The work of C. G. Jung and his brilliant followers has shown the important value of viewing human psychology and spirituality using this androgynous option for describing and understanding human nature.

I will attempt in this book to teach what I have learned about how the soul is wounded, and subsequently experiences healing using the Fisher King story, which may appear on the surface as primarily a story of the wound in men. However, because it speaks to the wounded feminine spirit of both the inner and outer cultural life of the West, I will be using the story to illustrate how both men and women are hurt, and how they can restore wholeness. I have taught this topic in many seminars and discovered that the story speaks to both men and women, thus the need for the writing of this book.

I, like John A. Sanford, Jungian analyst and Episcopal priest, believe that the soul, of both men and women is a she. As he writes, in *The Kingdom Within* (*The Kingdom Within: The Inner Meaning of Jesus' Sayings,* J.B. Lippencott, NY 1970, p. 122).

I have called soul "she," sexist language this. But soul herself resists being thought of in masculine terms, or, worse yet, known by neuter designations. Yes, soul is she. Soul is Yin. Spirit may be masculine or neuter, but soul, like Mother Nature, to which she is akin, will forever remain unalterably feminine in her essence no matter what our objections. So in man or in woman, our deepest essence is soul, a feminine reality.

He prefaces these statements by stating that the soul is subjective, experiences things, suffers and rejoices. The soul is very reflective, and receives psychic impressions and creates them, which are all feminine characteristics. The soul fashions and participates in both psychic and spiritual life. We find our fantasies, imagination, true values and meaning in the feminine qualities of our souls. Most of all, our souls yearn to give and receive love, and understand where our sense of belonging is, in God. It is in our souls, that faith is born, recognized and used to bring about new changes in relationship with God and others. Relationship is a feminine quality, as opposed to the masculine characteristic of competitiveness.

Jungian analyst and writer Irene Claremont de Castillejo also acknowledged the need to re-value feminine writing before her death in 1965 and published later in the early seventies in her book *Knowing Woman: A Feminine Psychology*:

The so-called emancipation of woman has resulted in women invading what was hitherto man's world in every branch. In other words, they are living the life of the animus [Jung's word for the masculine energy within a woman's soul]. There would be nothing wrong in that if it were not that in going over to man's world, women's essential values so often get thrown overboard.[...] Hovering over this now familiar situation I see an enormous menacing question mark: has woman's libido gone so far over to the masculine world of ideas and mechanics that the feminine passionate concern with life is actually denuded of the libido which it needs in order to hold the balance between the opposites? Is this imbalance perhaps one of the deep-rooted causes of the most devastating wars the world has ever known?
(De Castillejo, Irene Claremont. *Knowing Woman: A Feminine Psychology*. Shambala Publications, Boston, 1973. pp.82–83)

I am aware that some people may take objection to this generality, but hopefully these statements above, as images, will be helpful to others to think of their soul as a feminine quality. This is why the Grail is such an important symbol of both the nature and structure of the soul. The Grail shows us how the soul creates unity out of division and relationship out of individualistic endeavors and attitudes.

It is not only the Grail as a stone, cup, bowl and chalice that provides a symbol of the feminine valuing of life. There is also a strong, rich tradition that has been almost completely ignored until recently, which has survived in the southern French province of Provence for close to two thousand years. This is the story, in my opinion quite probable based on historical fact, that after the death and resurrection of Jesus, his lover and wife, Mary Magdalene, their daughter Sarah, and Joseph of Arimathea traveled by boat across the Mediterranean to the coast of southern France.

The church in this area for two thousand years has honored Mary Magdalene as the wife of Jesus and the mother of his child, whom are believed to have lived and brought the teachings of Jesus to this place. This tradition has believed that the Grail is not a mythological artifact that has become a symbol. Instead the Grail was the person of Mary Magdalene, the wife of Jesus. In either case, the Grail as symbol of cup or of a very special woman, the chief apostle and follower of Jesus, are carriers of the balanced feminine of God.

This is important because Mary Magdalene does not represent the maternal, or eternally virginal aspect of feminine values that are held in the figure of Mary, the mother of Jesus. Moreover, as the wife of Jesus, a fulfilled man, the archetypes of lover, and husband and wife, make Jesus fully human, even as the Christians later understood him as fully incarnate God.

This means that sexuality, passion, virility and much more is part of who God is, and a very essential aspect of who we are as fully integrated human beings. This is in direct opposition to the institutional church which pitted devotion and passion as antagonists against each other.

We will be discussing the archetypes portrayed by this prospective historical mythology of Mary Magdalene and

Jesus as husband and wife later in the discussion about the nature of the soul and prayer. For now, I suggest the reader refer to Margaret Starbird's *The Woman with the Alabaster Jar: Mary Magdalen and the Holy Grail* for more historical insight and scholarship about this ancient story.

There are many excellent scholastic books available discussing the probability of this position and I recommend the reader to investigate. Several of them are listed in the bibliography. Suggested additional reading regarding Mary Magdalene can be found in the bibliography under writers Elaine Pagels, Michael Baigent, Karen King, and Cynthia Bourgeault.

The structure of this book is divided into four sections

The first is a short overview of my life story to give the readers a sense of my own soul journey, and why this myth has been so helpful to its healing and continued desire for growth. This is followed by a historical background to the Myth of the Holy Grail and my paraphrase of the story itself.

The second longer section will address how I have come to understand the nature of the soul itself; how the soul functions, communicates to the conscious mind, and its intimate connection to the body. Indeed, the soul and body are one unity. I will not be addressing metaphysical theories regarding its origin, reincarnation, and other hypothetical conjunctures usually associated with a book of this kind. My focus in the first section is to remain on how we *experience* a sense of soul.

This second section also speaks to the problem of the major wounds of the soul, how they happen and can be understood, how they affect our inward and outward relationships, and how they can be healed. I will teach about how psychological and spiritual projection occur and damage our self-awareness and keep our relationships with those we love in constant turmoil and dysfunction.

This section will talk about how the Inner Critic finds its origins in the Negative Father and Mother archetypes constellated in early childhood, and continues to create the tyranny of black and white thinking and a hopelessly deficient, dualistic view of reality. Both the addiction to the Hero/Heroine archetype and other characteristics of an unhealthy soul will be discussed and show how one can move forward, get unstuck from repeating patterns of unhappiness, and progress into a more mature aspect of the inner journey. For an in-depth discussion of these primary archetypes I encourage the reading of C. G. Jung's *Man and His Symbols*, especially the seventh and eighth chapters.

We will also look at some of the paths of healing for the wounded soul, including the redemptive role of the Fool, the Old Man/Woman, King/Queen and the Old and New God archetypes which can provide for us insights to inner peace and joy. In this section, the reader may discover value in the teaching about recognizing one's spiritual family and ancestors and their role in bringing inner community and a sense of continued belonging.

The third sector, also longer than anticipated, will speak to the problem of evil, the various possible means of understanding its origin, function, and ultimate purpose in the life of the individual and societal soul. This discussion of evil is something that has been lacking in the literature of healing and the soul but strongly needs to be addressed. There are no easy, pact answers to the questions of evil but hopefully this book will address some of them in enough depths for the reader to find more hope for their own lives. The bibliography will also provide some helpful reading I have discovered on the subject that has helped me remain steadfast in faith, and not overwhelmed with despair due to the presence of evil in my life and in our corporate society.

The Fourth and final section is the Conclusion where I share ideas of practical tools one can utilize in both the healing of the soul and its continued renewal and health. These ideas come from centuries of spiritual writings as well as my own observations which have proven helpful in my own life and in the lives of those with whom I work in spiritual direction. Dream work, active imagination journaling, fantasy writing, body work, and other useful implements will be taught as well as a bibliography provided to give the reader additional resources to explore. I trust this book will inspire and give hope to people who are seeking greater peace within, which can allow a greater calm regarding life's outer challenges.

In place of footnotes or endnotes, I am placing the information from where I quoted in parenthesis so the reader can see immediately where the quote is from, and not have to look it up at the end of the chapter. Where an idea expressed is found in a particular text, I am referring to the author and book from which it came. All books referred to can be found in the bibliography.

We begin now with an overview of my own life story's experiences which have shaped my world view and spiritual orientation.

Section I

Chapter One

Finding Our Souls Again: My Story

I am not a psychologist nor a scientist, but I am an active observer of human behavior and a healer of the soul, which is my calling as an Episcopal priest, writer, teacher and counselor.

It may be helpful to first introduce part of my own story of soul searching, wounding and healing process, to give the reader the assurance that I am not just quoting what others have written or said, which has been very valuable, but what I share in these pages also comes from my experience.

All of us have a journey from original wholeness, to extreme brokenness, and now, hopefully, on the path to renewed and conscious wholeness, as I believe God intends for us to know and trust. However, this is not the place for an exhaustive autobiography, only an overview of the issues I had to work through, in hope to give the readers some sense of relatedness to my story, and hope for the affirmation of their own.

I was born in the early fifties in the San Francisco Bay Area, into a highly educated family whose roots were in New York City, German speaking Switzerland and Austria-Hungary, respectively. My father, an only child, was born in New York of immigrant Hungarian parents. His father was a highly respected mechanical engineer with over two hundred patents to his credit while working for Otis Elevator Company. My father's mother was a Hungarian peasant, a passionate lover of cooking, her husband and son, and of a dark, "Bleeding Jesus" type of Roman Catholicism. Yet she maintained a sweet, earthy personality and courage. My maternal great-grandmother was from the ancient Hungarian medieval home of the Hungarian kings and queens, Székesfehérvár, an hour west of Budapest, between Lake Balaton and the capital city.

My mother was the middle child of three, her father a fourth-generation inventor; a brilliant, coppersmith (owner of Burkhard's Kettles for candy manufacturing, Brooklyn, NY) of German Swiss peasant stock. My maternal grandmother was a highly refined teacher and musician. Her brother was head of Psychiatry for the State of Connecticut and held his administration at the famous Danbury Mental Hospital. Her roots were English-Scotch, with strong Celtic mysticism tied in to the family line which expressed itself in the American phenomenon known as Christian Scientist.

Music, travel, concerts, art galleries and literature were the influx of my childhood environment, along with the wide open spaces of undeveloped land among the hills behind Redwood City on the San Francisco Peninsula. I had one brother, a mere thirteen months older than I, but as different and opposite a sibling as I can imagine. He was a natural athlete and a strong extrovert. I was a bit more reserved, quieter, introverted, uncoordinated, and intellectual.

My mother was in the first school of Physical Therapy in the world at Columbia University in the late 1940s. Upon graduation, being among the first thirty certified physical therapists, she immediately secured a very high paying position at the Children's Hospital in Honolulu working with polio survivors. My father's first management job with American Can Company put him on the assembly line in the same city making sure the pineapple cans they made kept out botulism.

Three years later, and after my first brother died at birth due to Hydrocephalus in 1950, my parents moved to the San Francisco area where my father continued his work in quality control for American Can and my mother gave birth to my brother and myself. She never worked professionally outside the home again.

My mother suffered from a lifetime of brittle diabetes, and was insulin dependent since her twelfth year. As an adult she suffered blackouts and sugar or insulin-overdose comas on a regular basis. After her death from the dreadful disease at age forty-seven, I would learn from her closest friend and early Redwood City neighbor, that I was trained at age two, to cross the street where we lived to fetch help from this neighbor (the autopsy performed on my mother showed a virus had lodged in her pancreas, suffering it to not function when the virus was active and then to be capable of functioning when the virus cycle was dormant. Thus, doctors were never able to adequately monitor her insulin intake level. Her body responded to this constant flux of high and low blood sugars by aging very prematurely, resulting in devastating strokes which caused her death at an early age).

Whenever my mother would collapse into an unconscious state, which according to the friend was an average of once a month, I, at age two, would cross the street, ring the doorbell and get the neighbor's help; the ambulance would take my mother to the hospital.

Why I, as a toddler was given this responsibility and not an adult hired to care for my mother, I will never know. Adequate family finances was a non-issue. What I do know is that I have no memory of not being responsible for the life and death of an adult whom I loved and depended upon to live.

Due to diabetes, and possible bipolar disorder, her severe mood swings meant that home was never a safe place. My father was at work during the day, and by my grade school days, was traveling for weeks at a time for his company. Mother was alone to raise two boys. I found some respite from the drama at home by spending every free moment year round outside in the fields, forests and a lake in the summer. Nature was my nurturer in the best sense of the word.

My family lived within walking distance of a recreational complex called Emerald Lake. Membership and participation were affordable for many families. It was small, hedged by tulles, filled with fish, snapping turtles and other creatures of dank, wet places. It was a child's paradise, allowing children over five years old to spend the day from eight in the morning until ten at night supervised by professional lifeguards, without the presence of their parents.

Freedom. I relished in the wet, sunny, sandy, emerald green waters. The diving platforms, the giant swing and floating rafts were great playgrounds for the large groups of children who played together seven days a week.

As a strong introvert, I also found places among the trees and a sandy knoll on a level above the main beach where I could be alone and yet hear the sounds, and see the sights of the lake activity. The lake was a safe haven away from home. When I started psychotherapy in my mid-thirties, dreams of Emerald Lake taught me about the inner dampness and feminine watery world within my own soul. I would come to realize how grateful I was for this innocuous anchorage as a child.

To make matters a bit more complicated, I was born a blue baby, unable to breathe properly on my own. This story was told to me when I was sixteen by the doctor who assisted at my birth. He said my lungs were not functioning correctly as I was born with a depressed sternum, pushing the heart and lungs into unnatural positions in my chest. The labored, barely breathing newborn was immediately incubated and my parents were advised I would not last the night. Having lost one son at birth already, my parents prepared for the worst.

My father said that word got out of my condition to the small group of young couples who had formed the basis of a new Methodist congregation in Redwood City. An elderly woman member of the fledgling group called and gathered most of them and their sleeping children into her small living room at midnight and led them in prayer over four hours for my healing.

My doctor continued his version of the story saying that the morning after my birth he arrived at the hospital expecting to have to tell my parents of my death. Shocked, he checked me out thoroughly. He found my sternum, for reasons unknown, had changed to a normal position and my heart and lungs were functioning just fine. My parents were overjoyed, and excerpts from my baby book kept diligently by my mother, show a deep affection and attentive care I received from her for my first two years.

However, due to the lack of oxygen at birth, my coordination and especially my inner ear had been badly damaged. No one ever told me I was nearly deaf. As a child, I was taken to Stanford University hospital numerous times for hearing tests. I was given almost daily speech therapy sessions at my local public schools from kindergarten until high school. However, I had no idea why. I played high school football and was successful at knocking people down, but throwing or catching or running skillfully with a football was out of the question.

I would learn of the extent of my hearing condition for the first time after graduating university while teaching elementary school myself. Parents told the principal that the classroom children suggested that I might have a severe hearing condition and I might be unaware of the problem. Gladly I made an appointment with a PhD audiologist at the local university and had my hearing tested.

The doctor came out from the prolonged, sophisticated testing with a grim, white look on his face. He sat me down, leaned forward and said, "Did you know that you understand no consonants at all? All you can decipher is vowel sounds. You cannot distinguish the beginnings or endings of syllables. How in the hell did you make it through university?" Perplexed, I asked, "Well, how bad is it?" He stated something that would shake me to my core, "If this were an eyesight problem, you would be legally blind."

Shocked, things slowly began to fall into place. No wonder I daydreamed my way through school activities, and became the class clown out of boredom. If instructions or questions were written on a blackboard, I was fine. But if I had to listen to the teacher talk or professor lecture, I was soon tuning them out, not because I didn't want to learn, but because it was exhausting to try and understand what was being said. I had assumed either I was lazy, my parents' estimation throughout my growing up years, or I was stupid, the opinion of my brother and most of my classmates. No wonder I preferred to be alone and hated school!

Reading was my salvation.

As you can imagine, the adult *soul issues* that I would have to work on were confusion, mistrust, fear of rejection, abandonment, low self-esteem, a negative mother complex, a lack of a sense of belonging and the disease of codependency as the only means of feeling valued.

I would need to unlearn many old patterns of self-destructive thought and recreate my original innocence, but consciously, not naïvely. I would have to learn to give myself tremendous self-nurture and not look to any relationships to provide for me what I must do for myself.

Along with this challenge, I would learn to value my being as a vast, mysterious and beautiful creation of a loving God, whose very nature is Mystery, yet intimately relational. I would learn to withdraw all projection of the feminine energy, both positive (creative) and regressive (destructive) from people in my outer life. I would learn to manage these energies within where they could be transformed and balanced to bring forth life through death, burial and the resurrection of my psyche.

I would learn to be my own best friend and to know that belonging is not an outer, but an inner reality that has always been. I would acquire the intuitive knowledge that the loneliness I have felt all my younger years was an illusion, and thus has no power to continue to isolate me from myself, and thus others.

I would learn and still continue to learn that my value is not determined by my usefulness to others (codependency), but my feeling about myself, my valuing, was intrinsic to who I am, unique, individual, and owning a great capacity for joy and happiness.

I'm sure there were and are many more issues! But that was enough to keep me busy with inner work for the past forty years, and so the inner work continues.

Chapter Two

Historical Background to the Fisher King Story

The story of *The Fisher King*, or *The Search for the Holy Grail*, arose almost simultaneously in multiple countries in eleventh-century Europe, as a spontaneous reaction to the cultural turmoil and catastrophic decadence of the religious and civic dysfunction of the times. The Church Crusades attempting to control Palestine resulted in the wholesale slaughter of Jewish and Arabic people not only in the Middle East, but also the first known European-Jewish holocaust in Worms, Germany, enacted by Crusaders on their way to Jerusalem. The Church put chests in the entrance of churches demanding that people provide the finances to sustain the war effort.

There were three different "popes" claiming to be the only pontiff in Rome, France and Germany. Clerical abuse was rampant, and the moral decay of power was at its worst in the thousand-year history. The masculine attributes of patriarchal power, domination and control was one-sided to the complete exclusion of the feminine principles of caring, listening and relationship. Certainly, Western Europe was at a tipping point of self-destruction and spiritual poverty as the rich got richer and the poor, more destitute.

As Jungian analyst John A. Sanford wrote in *The Kingdom Within*, whenever the streams of living water have dried up within a culture, God provides water for the people who are hungry and thirsty for holiness. History has shown that usually it is outside the religious institutions the holy water of truth and sustenance spring to provide balance and hope for the people of God, regardless of their religious or non-religious orientation.

It is my belief that the emergence of the Grail Myth at this point in history was an offering of counter-intuitive spiritual life to balance the destruction and hopelessness of the culture. This is why I believe the story can speak to us in the modern Western world. We need the truths of this myth to speak to us today about who we really are, why we are so wounded individually and collectively, and what we can do to find our intrinsic wholeness as human beings in relationship with one another again.

The symbolism pertained in the story is vast and all consuming, so I have carefully picked those motifs and symbols that most speak to me about the nature of the individual soul and how we find peace within, in order to begin finding conflict without. I emphasize the individual for a reason.

C.G. Jung spoke a great truth during an interview with the BBC shortly before his death in response to the all-pervasive question, "Dr. Jung, do you think we [Western Culture] will make it?" Jung smiled quietly and softly said, "If enough individuals do their inner work."

This is my focus. I don't believe that we as individuals can help causes by group participation unless each of us is willing to do the hard work of healing our own souls. Perhaps once we are in the individuation process of healing, and continue to make this the highest priority of our time and energy, then there can be a more collective healing in our societies. If we do not do the required inner work, all causes will simply be targets for our own unconscious, unhealed and projected inner pains.

Sir Laurens van der Post, close friend of Jung and thinker extraordinaire, said in the early nineties near the time of his death:

Don't look for leaders. The age of leaders is past. Be your own leader and do your inner work. As the new Twenty First Century comes to pass, God is bringing together other like souled persons throughout the world to be your community.

You will find one another.

(Van der Post, Laurens. *A Walk with a White Bushman*. Chatto and Windus, London, 1986, p. 68)

Thus, the importance of the Grail story at this time in our history.

I will now give a short overview of what I find to be the most important aspects of a varied story with multiple nuances and emphases due to the various versions that swept Europe from Celtic, Teutonic, Briton, Arabic and Persian/Indo-European Eastern sources.

The Fisher King Story

Long ago an adolescent King was hunting in a forest with his companions and got separated from them by the chase. As the evening drew near, a delicious aroma drifted to his nostrils and he followed the scent to an unoccupied camp with a fire, containing a roasting salmon on a spigot glistening hot oil and ready to be consumed. Glancing right and left, he saw none of the occupants of the camp, and he presumed they were still hunting somewhere in the forest.

While he was aware that he was trespassing, the aroma and sight of the roasting salmon was too great a temptation to his famished stomach and appetite. He reached to the spigot and tore off a piece of the fish bringing it to his open mouth, only to realize belatedly that it was too hot. He burned his tongue, his lips, and fingers, the meat fell from his astonished hand to burn through the cloth on his breeches, horribly scorching his genitals and thigh, before falling to the ground.

In the German version, as he is attempting to reach for the salmon, the owners of the camp and the salmon return and one of them lets loose an arrow at the King, piercing him through his testicles. The arrow cannot be removed.

In severe pain, he leaves the camp to return to his castle, too painful to be able to do anything but lie on his bed, but not too wounded to die. Thus, the Fisher King's wound becomes known throughout the kingdom and the legend arises that one day, a wonderful Fool will

24

arrive at the castle and ask the question, "For whom does the Grail serve?" and the King will be miraculously healed. At the same time the wound began, the whole kingdom suffers a type of death. The fields do not yield their crops, the grass does not grow, the abundance the kingdom once knew has evaporated, and springs of water become dry. Only the legend of the coming Fool gives the King and his people hope.

However, there is one activity the king can do on his own that relieves his suffering for a moment. He can fish in a river or lake. Therefore he spends much of his waking hours finding solitude fishing, hoping to alleviate the terrible suffering he endures until the appointed time.

Many years later in the forests not too far away, there lives a young boy being raised alone by his mother. Unbeknownst to him, his father and seven brothers have all been killed as knights in duals with other knights in battle. To protect her remaining son and herself, the mother takes him far away from civilization into the woods in hopes of keeping him from following the same destructive path of his father and brothers. The boy's name is Perceval, which means, Holy Fool. She tells him nothing of the doom that befell his father and brothers.

One day, while Perceval is out in the forests collecting wood for the home hearth, he meets in a meadow, five magnificent, shining-in-armor knights, gleaming brightly in the sun. He has no idea who or what they are, and he asks them. He learns they are knights of King Arthur's Round Table. Excitedly he runs home to tell his mother what he has experienced, and declares on the spot, that he too wants to become a knight.

Broodingly, his mother realizes the time has come that she cannot keep him with her any longer, and she tells him for the first time the fate of his father and older brothers. Undaunted, Perceval puts things together to leave, his mother reluctantly helps him pack and asks of him one favor. "Please continue to wear this homespun underwear/garment I have made for you, as a reminder of me, your mother, whose heart you are breaking. Also, one word of advice, as you go out into the world, do not ask of people too many questions. It is not polite."

He hurriedly agrees.

As he is crossing the bridge over the stream that separates their home from the rest of the forest, his mother follows him weeping; as he looks back from the edge of the forest he sees her fall and assumes that she has fainted with grief. The truth is, she has died of a massively broken heart and lies dead, with no one to care for her body or burial.

Impetuously, Perceval goes to King Arthur's castle, approaches the King and his Knights of the Round Table and demands to be made a knight on the spot. The court is in disarray because the Red Knight had rudely thrown a chalice of red wine in the face of the Queen recently before departing on his massive steed amidst the turmoil. Things are in upheaval in the court because of this unexpected and dastardly act.

There is an empty chair at the table next to the King. Perceval naïvely sits in it, not realizing it is reserved for the knight who would find the Lost Grail. The empty chair was known as the Judas chair, reminiscent of the Last Supper of Jesus and his disciples, after the moment when Christ gave Judas the piece of bread, leaving him to his evil devices to betray the Son of Man. As the opposite of Christ, the absolute Good, and Judas incarnates the principle of Evil.

When Perceval sits in the empty Judas chair there is an extremely loud cracking sound that permeates the castle. All look at the chair and beneath Perceval the stone seat is cracked in two. A huge spiritual violation has occurred and the Holy Fool is lucky not to have been swallowed by the earth beneath the chair.

There is a spiritual connection between the eventual One who would be honorable enough to sit upon this chair, thus nullifying the evil that humanity has done through the betrayal of Christ by Judas long ago. But of course, Perceval has no idea what piety he has breached with his immature behavior.

Gazing at Perceval, Arthur, remembering the prophecy of his advisor Merlin, that one day a knight would appear who would be holy enough to seek and find the Holy Grail, gives Perceval his request, knights him, and bids him farewell as Sir Perceval. Just as he abruptly arrived, Perceval now hastily departs.

Perceval goes on a lifetime series of adventures. The day immediately after his knighting in King Arthur's court, he is moving through a forest, and comes across a knight in shining red amor. Naïvely, Perceval asks the knight to give him his armor. The Red Knight has just come from Arthur's castle where he has stolen a chalice and tossed the wine contents in the face of the queen, causing utter chaos and turmoil. He laughs deridingly and tells Perceval that if he wants the armor, he must take it from him by force.

Amazingly, Perceval throws a stone (in some versions, the Red Knight throws his javelin and misses Perceval, who returns the affront with the Red Knight's spear) that kills the knight on the forehead, then takes the knight's sword and cuts off his head, removing the armor and putting it on himself. It is way too big for him, but he doesn't care. After sending the chalice back to Arthur's castle dismissively with the page accompanying him from the court, he mounts the Red Knight's horse as his own and sets off on his adventures. Little does he know that the chalice that he lightly dismisses to be sent back to Arthur with the page will later become the center of his meaning and life's purpose.

Perceval then goes on his way, and eventually meets Gornemant. This old man mentors him in the ways of a true, noble knight. He learns to battle, to seek out fair maidens in distress and deliver them, and he becomes, eventually, the epitome of the ideal knight: brave, truthful, and forthright in every way. However, as he leaves his mentor for more adventures, Gornemant instructs him with Perceval's repeated mother's admonition, "When you encounter experiences with others, don't ask too many questions, as it is not polite." He thanks his mentor and rides off wanting to find his mother and share with her all that he has learned and experienced.

But first he comes to a fair maiden named Blancheflor (White Flower), a girl close to his age, whose fiancé knight has left her for a while to do battle somewhere else in the kingdom. Perceval is attracted to her, and she is his first real encounter with a flesh and blood young woman. They talk, and then spend the night in a chaste, strange embrace, face to face, shoulder to shoulder, hip to hip, and feet touching feet. They do not interact sexually, but platonically, like a brother and sister. In the morning, he dresses while she continues to sleep, he reaches out and steals her knight's ring of promise from her finger. He doesn't know why he does this. He does it impulsively. Perceval tells himself that he wants to introduce Blancheflor to his mother, but in his haste to keep moving, he leaves her behind to her fate.

When Blancheflor's fiancé returns and finds the ring missing, he treats her cruelly and leaves her destitute.

Perceval comes to a river in the forest. The road he has been traveling ends at this point. It is near evening, and he is concerned about finding a safe place to spend the night. On the river is a boat with a man hunched over in silence, fishing alone on the water. Perceval cries out to him a request for information about where he could lodge. The fisherman replies, "Go back the way you have come, turn left and you will come to a castle. Enter therein and spend the night."

Surprised, as he saw no other road in the forest except the one he was on, Perceval thanks the fisherman and returns, following his instructions. Sure enough, Perceval finds a road to the left, takes it and immediately comes to a fantastic castle. He goes across the drawbridge, his horse's hoofs clipping the wooden bridge as it is drawn up quickly behind as he crosses.

Inside he is warmly greeted by pages who take his horse for care and remove his armor, promising to clean and furnish it for him later. They lead him to a beauteous room where fine clothes are laid out for him to wear and help him dress. He is brought down to a brilliantly lit banqueting hall, illuminated by a vast array of candelabras and torches. The room is full of people looking at him with happiness and expectation. He is awed by the luminosity of the room and wonders what this place is and what his role may be participating in the events about to unfold.

Then a man is brought in by four others carrying him on a litter bed and placed in the center of the hall. Perceval is amazed to recognize the man as the same fisherman he encountered earlier that afternoon at the riverside. The man explains that he is the Fisher King and this is his kingdom and castle, and that Perceval is his guest. As he stands next to the Fisher King, a maiden brings to Perceval a broken sword and tells him to put it on. He sees that it is damaged and lays it to the side of where he is standing. Feeling a bit confused and self-conscious, he doesn't put the sword on his belt.

Then from the side of the hall enters a strange procession led by a page carrying a tall, white-handled lance, the sharp point dripping with dark, red blood. Following the lance are four men carrying a four-legged table with dark black cherry-wood posts and a white gleaming, square-shaped top. The table is escorted by four pages bearing tall candlesticks. Following the table in the procession is a beautiful young maiden carried on a green pillow, a magnificent chalice, known as the Grail, encrusted with precious stones set in gleaming gold. A brilliant light emanates from the Grail as if it is on fire with energy. Following her are more pages and maidens carrying a set of knives and a round platter.

The procession first comes to the Fisher King and stops. He struggles to lift himself to be able to partake of the cup, but alas, he cannot, and sadly lays back on his litter. The procession moves on to each person in the banqueting hall. Each thinks of a request of the finest food and drink they can desire and magically the Grail provides exactly what they want.

As all of them partake of the abundance of the Grail each person looks longingly at Perceval, hoping that he will address the group with the question that will set their King and, thus, their kingdom free. While Perceval is very curious to know what the procession is all about and what it means, he remembers the words of his mother and his knightly mentor, and decides to be safe and not embarrass himself or anyone else with questions. He ponders that he will ask a page privately later in his room what the meaning of the evening's event might be.

To the left of the hall, Perceval notices for a moment another doorway partly open, and behind a curtain he gets a glimpse of another very old man sitting on a wooden chair with a crown on his snow-white head. This old man makes eye contact very briefly with him and Perceval sees both sadness and hope mixed together in the old man's countenance.

Quickly, the room empties and the procession returns the way it had come. Perceval is taken to his room to retire for the night. When he asks the page attending him what the evening's event was all about, the page looks away with embarrassment and says nothing. Perceval goes to sleep in the guest bed and sleeps a deep longing sleep, only to awaken in the morning light finding himself on the forest floor, his armor and horse next to him and with no people or castle anywhere to be seen at all.

Confounded, he picks himself up and sets out on his journey again. He has much to learn and much to experience. Many days after his encounter with the Grail Castle he comes to another young woman in the forest and sits down beside her. She holds the body of her beheaded, dead knight in her lap.

She somehow knows who Perceval is, and his name. He tells her about his encounter several nights before in the castle of the Fisher King. She asks him what he saw. Where did the procession come from? Where did it go? Did he ask the question of the people about the procession and about the Grail?

When he replies he did not, she chastises him with vigor and explains to him how the King was wounded long ago and how this situation has created the stifling of all creativity and productivity in the kingdom. She tells him how awful it is that he didn't ask questions.

She tells him about the broken sword, how it needs to be repaired, and how he must not only repair it but not put too much confidence in it, even after the repair. She tells him that he is responsible for the death of his mother in leaving her destitute and alone in the forest. He is humbled by her rebuke and instructions, and promises if he ever gets the chance again he will do the right thing for the Fisher King. He gets up and leaves her a wiser and more grounded individual.

Perceval then spends the next twenty or more years roaming the country, fighting dragons and rescuing fair maidens, challenging every knight he meets to a dual, and wins. His reputation is spread far and wide as the greatest knight of all.

After a long time he begins to lose his enthusiasm for knighthood. There seems little to do that he has not already done. One might say he is burned out. His armor is now a bit tarnished, his horse tired and worn, and he finds himself wandering in the forest without much awareness of his surroundings, pondering the next step in his journey slowly in his mind. In between all his adventures and activities he has searched for the Grail Castle, but to no avail. The homespun underwear of his mother has long since tattered and fallen away unnoticed by Perceval.

In another version of the story, he returned to Arthur's court wherein rides the most ugly old witch-type woman riding upon a hideous donkey. She confronts Perceval with his multitudes of sins, both of commission and omission. She chastises him for being such a fool as not to ask the question about the procession in the hall of the Fisher King. In front of King Arthur and all the people, he is humiliated and shamed. This encounter will help him begin to own his own shadow, which up until this time he has been extremely unconscious of.

He leaves the castle and while continuing his wandering stumbles upon some pilgrims who have just left a hermit priest living in the woods to whom they have confessed their sins and received absolution. The day is Good Friday, they wanted to be prepared to receive the Blessed Sacrament on Easter Sunday. They admonish Perceval as they meet him, stating, "Why are you wearing your armor on this most holy day and not covering yourself in ashes and penance? Don't you know this is Good Friday?" Perceval replies gloomily, that no, he didn't know. They tell him about the priestly hermit and admonish him to go make his confession and prepare to take communion on Easter.

He agrees. It has been many years since he has received the Blessed Sacrament; because he is unsure of what to do next, he goes and finds the priest in a stone hut deep in the forest. The old man looks sternly at Perceval and declares him a lost sinner of the worst kind. He reminds him of all the knights he has killed in haste and also how he has stolen the ring from Blancheflor destroying her life and her relationship with her fiancé knight.

The hermit is very hard on Perceval and tells him that his refusal to follow his intuitive instinct and ask questions about the meaning of the Grail procession has increasingly damaged the Fisher King and his kingdom. His pride wounded, Perceval listens attentively and repents of his sins of commission and omission. Perceval makes his confession, receives absolution and gets ready to continue on his journey. As he leaves the stone hut of the hermit, the priest says to him, "Go now. Go back the way you have come, turn left and see where it leads."

From long ago, Perceval remembers the exact words spoken to him when he was a young man by the Fisher King while fishing upon the waters. With increased inner anticipation, he returns the way he came through the forest, and finds to the left a road that was not there earlier. He takes it and finds himself again at the Grail Castle at last. He enters, is happily recognized by the pages, escorted to his room, bathed, and dressed for dinner.

In the banqueting hall he greets the Fisher King, now much older, with salt and pepper hair, but still mortally wounded, lying on his litter. The Grail procession begins and comes to stand in front of the King lying on his side. Perceval, with a quiet calmness, loudly asks the essential question, "For whom does the Grail serve?" He realizes he doesn't have to have an answer to the question, however, his responsibility is to ask, which he does.

Immediately, the King rises on his own two feet, receives the Grail in his hands and drinks of the contents freely. His wound is healed and the whole hall is filled with loud, celebrative cheering. The trees outside in the countryside transform their leaves from winter deadness to spring renewal and the crops suddenly appear full bloom in the field; the original glory has been restored to the kingdom.

Perceval is the guest of the Fisher King and introduced to the Older King behind the door to the left, who is the Grail King. Both men are close relatives of Perceval, being his uncles, brothers of his father and of his mother. The two Kings tell Perceval that the old hermit priest is also a brother of his mother. He is in the home of his ancestors whom he never knew.

After three days the healed Fisher King dies and is buried. Perceval becomes the new Fisher King and required to protect and guard the Grail.

For many years more he holds court in the Grail castle, until finally, in advanced age, he retires into the hills of the forest taking the Grail with him to spend the rest of his days in quiet reflective prayer and solitude. The grail is now hidden, until a time when it will be needed again to bring restoration and life.

In other versions of the story it is hoped that Perceval would return with the Chalice to Arthur's court, indeed Arthur expects this. But Perceval's desire to retreat into the world of composite and complete spiritual seclusion overrides whatever his conscience may have dictated to him regarding the need to bring the spirituality of the Grail publically to the world. Instead, he retreats into hiding and secrecy.

Section II

Chapter Three

The Nature of the Soul and How It Functions

A recent dream revealed more of what I feel must be said in this book.

I dreamed I was in a church start-up environment in an office building. A young woman was teaching children about their spirituality.

Two old, stuffy acting English men, brothers and professional writers, were criticizing the teacher saying that she didn't speak eloquently, and didn't use the "King's English" properly. Their attitude was condescending, arrogant and rude.

In working with the dream in active imagination, I first confronted the English writers in my dream with their arrogance and got their cooperation to stop their criticism and start helping the teacher by mentoring the children, at her direction.

Then I asked the teacher what she was teaching the children, as I was curious. She replied:

"I am teaching them that they are extremely special, unique, that no other person has their soul, and that they do not possess another person's soul. I am teaching them that no two souls are alike, just as no voice, fingerprints or snowflakes are alike. So, God has created each child a unique and individual soul."

She continued explaining:

"I am teaching them to value and know their own souls, its likes and dislikes, what gives it pleasure and what does not. Once they know more of who they are, they will be able to honor and appreciate themselves at the deepest level of knowing. With this healthy self-awareness they also will be able to see the Divine in others."

When I asked her about ego inflation, regarding children

knowing they are unique and highly valued, she answered:

"Inflation occurs in people who are unaware of their own beauty, and thus have identified their sense of Self with their ego. These children (in the dream) will not be egocentric simply because they will be able to relax into who they really are. Their relationships with others will be infused with this deep, non-egocentric love for Self, thus extendable to all others."

This message from the Active Imagination exercise reminded me of Jesus' words, "Love your neighbor as yourself." Jesus continued by telling the parable of the Good Samaritan to illustrate his point. The ability to love one's self, and not identify one's Self (the center of the human being) with the ego, allows us to love others freely without an ulterior motive.

Children, assured and self-aware of their original goodness, when allowed to separate from the oneness with the mother gradually, learning that she is a human being and not perfect, are able to accept their own humanity. The idea that children are born sinful, in the sense that they are morally bankrupt or a blank slate, in my experience is absurd. In my view, original sin can only be understood to make sense as a lack of self-awareness and a state of unconsciousness.

Personally, I don't think that children are born with such a lack of self-awareness. I define sin as a disconnect with Self, occurring when the soul and distinctive value of a child is ignored, rejected, repressed, or cruelly treated in the name of conformity and correction. Alice Miller and many other prominent writers have demonstrated repeatedly that harshness with children creates a deeply wounded soul. In the worst cases such abuse hinders the ability of the child to become highly conscious because much of this ability has been shamed into silence.

The Genesis story of creation, the older version in chapter two which follows the newer one in the Genesis prologue, states that God created the first human being, Adam, which means "of the earth" from soil. Then God breathed the "breath of life" into the earthling and this being became a Living Soul. To me, this wonderful myth describes the reality that we were originally created as inspired, breath infused bodies and souls, and together, the physical aspects of our being are fully instilled with spiritual reality. Our bodies and spirits constitute the human soul in wholeness.

The Body, Instinct and Archetypes

What do I mean by the human body, the physical aspects of our bodies? Just as in the example earlier of the human heart giving off electrical impulses, signifying the ability to "hear" stimuli before the brain electronically has registered its reaction to the sound, I believe neuroscience and biology have shown that each cell, organism and organ in the body has the ability to store memory. Medical personnel and psychologists who work in somatic healing have researched this phenomenon for decades and proven its reliability. My work in healing prayer has shown me that spoken words release healing energy that can set free specific areas in the body that are trapped in traumatic memory, and healing often occurs when prayer and words are addressed to the different places in the body. The study of chakras has been shown to be extremely valid regarding these realities.

We all contain instincts as part of our physical body. Instincts were defined by Jung as "physiological urges and are perceived by the senses of sight, sound, touch, smell and taste. But at the same time instincts show themselves in fantasies and often reveal their presence only by symbolic images." Jung called these images that appear in our dreams and in our folk tales archetypes.

According to Wikipedia "Instinct can additionally be understood as innate behaviors that have an inherent inclination within a living organism towards a particular complex behavior.... and should be distinguished from reflexes," which are responses to specific stimuli.

Webster's dictionary says that in everyday language, "the word *instinct* is often used to refer to intuition, and even clairvoyance."

The Cambridge dictionary states that instinct is "the way people or animals naturally react or behave, without having to think or learn about it."

Thus, I use the word instinct to discuss an innate, intrinsic aspect of our physical bodies, as created and given to us as a gift by God, which contains natural complex behaviors which are at least morally neutral, if not intrinsically morally good. These natural complex, natural behaviors influence the activity of our consciousness.

Jung wrote in his book *Man and His Symbols* that:

If the unconscious contains too many things that should be conscious, then its instinctive functions become twisted and prejudiced; and motives appear that are not based on true instincts, but owe their (twisted motives) existence and psychic importance to the fact that they have been consigned to the unconscious by repression or neglect.

An example of such a behavior might be racism, which some might perceive as having its basis in instinct, but in truth exists because true instinct, acceptance and enjoyment of diversity and the natural ability to connect spiritually with others has been repressed or neglected. My observation is that racism, for example, is not always a learned behavior modeled by an authority figure but often occurs when emotions, trauma, vulnerable experiences are not processed, but pushed down in the unconscious by shaming or other repressive actions.

Jung wrote that our basic instincts have not disappeared from civilized consciousness but often have separated consciousness off from basic instincts where the instincts are forced "to assert themselves in an indirect fashion.... through physical symptoms, unaccountable moods, and unexpected forgetfulness such as mistakes in speech."

In working with trauma victims, sexual abuse victims, and Post Traumatic Stress Disorder situations with veterans of war, I have observed the repression of instincts may cause physical illness, psychotic disorders, sick co-dependency issues, and many other illnesses. Only with excellent therapy, and most important dream work and prayer, healing of the repressed emotions allows healing of the natural instincts. Dysfunctional behaviors such as racism, rage, denial and emotional instability can be healed when the repressed memories are allowed to surface given a container to hold them within the soul. This allows the soul to give freedom to the repressed parts of the body to heal.

We are not taught how to manage suffering in most of Western culture, and the result is a concentration and centralization of pain in the soul and the body. This can be healed with steady, mature and patient guidance and companionship on the inner way.

These natural instinctive behaviors may include such realities as physical pleasure, sexual joy, a balance or dance between human interaction and needed solitude, spontaneous expressions of great joy and ecstasy, or a reverent introspection and tranquility.

The Unity of Body, Instincts and the Soul

Most Westerners have a bit of trouble with the word instinct, having been flavored with negative connotations by Christianity and other religious influences that repress the human body and sexuality. But if we accept that the human body and soul are a unified whole in creation, we can open ourselves to view the body and soul as containing wonderfully complex instincts that provide vitality, fullness and great expression to our unified life. Spirit and physical body act as one, not split into two or more separate entities or categories of being.

It is my belief, because of my work in spiritual counseling, that negative behaviors that could be attributed to bodily instincts may be expressing themselves as unattractive because of the drastic split between the body and soul.

For example, we might look at compulsive eating and accompanying obesity as being a result of a person not controlling their instinct to eat and drink. In this case the field of healing eating disorders has shown the opposite. We know that eating disorders can be a direct result of emotional trauma repressed and trapped in the body. Healing occurs when both the emotional soul issues are addressed in therapy, prayer, and body work. Such prayer can be directed to specific chakras, for example, the power chakra, the area between the belly and the anus, (root chakra) along with gentle body work.

Jung wrote in *Man and His Symbols* that many Early Church writers, mostly of Greek thinking, were looking for ways to describe the Christian experience in Greek thought forms. Many of these leaders described the human anthology as threefold, or Trinitarian: body, mind and spirit. But in the Old Testament Jewish anthology, *pneuma* (Greek), *ruah* (Hebrew) breath or spirit, was something that God infused in special persons at specific times for particular purposes (prophecy, or divination, preaching, ecstatic dance and others).

Body and soul were united and seen as one, and sometimes were overtly filled with spirit, which was a Hebraic way to understand the ecstatic behavior and to symbolize spiritual authority. The Greeks had no concise or positive view of the soul and spirit after death, but a dreary, gray existence for most in Hades, a drifting, depressing reality with no content. This is certainly not what the Early Church trusted was the experience of life after mortal death. Yet this Greek Trinitarian view of human beings continues to be used, and I feel it is grossly insufficient to explain the phenomenon of the soul as we experience it.

I want to encourage the reader, if they have not done so already, to write out their personal history and get a grasp of what their main life issues are. This first chapter will take a deeper look at the purpose and design of our souls, and how we can better understand who we are, and how we can appreciate our own mystery and brilliance. We are made in the reflection (image) of a most beautiful and loving Being/Other/God/Goddess/Higher Power/non-name, whatever distinctive word image works for us most effectively.

One View of the Purpose and the Nature of the Human Soul

I want to remind the reader that this book is not attempting to analyze the multitude of metaphysical concepts about the human soul that history has given us. Instead, I will use my own experience of inner work and the observations I've had from working in the counseling of souls of many people over forty years as a businessman, teacher, priest and spiritual director. My writing is based on how people experience their souls and a sensing of soul in their everyday lives not based on concepts which can never been proven as fact one way or the other. We will focus here on what seems to make a healthy soul distinguished from an unhealthy one!

To begin, I would like to talk about the purpose and meaning of the soul. To do this, I will introduce characteristics of the Grail itself in the Grail Myth, which can be understood as a symbol of the soul, or at the very least the feminine principle which engages the soul and brings her to life.

The Grail, foremost is a vessel, a feminine container in most versions of the story, a type of Chalice (Communion Cup). The vessel is the oldest known symbol of this ability to contain attributes, such as life-giving water, or after the invention of fire, the ability to cook food in a transformative way as illustrated in the cooking pot of the sign of the covenant story God made with Abraham in Genesis chapter fifteen.

The different versions of the Grail Myth describe the Grail as a cup, an animal horn, a stone bowl, a metal or wooden bowl, even a spherical round stone. In all cases the Grail was a container of life-giving, overflowing spiritual and material power. Modern American Thanksgiving dinner tables are decorated with the Horn of Plenty, a rarely perceived symbol of the Grail from antiquity.

The Grail is a spherical stone when often portrayed by the medieval alchemists. They perceived the Grail as their philosopher's stone, that which is Matter, or Mother, Earth, soil, the ground of being. The alchemists used fire and pressure to transform base metals such as iron or lead, hoping to transmute them into valuable gold. Simultaneously they secretly communicated that their chemical experiments were really an illustration of an inner, spiritual, transformative process. They understood what God had given to us within the soul in creation, and they observed that the bringing of insight, the fire of illumination, and the opening of self-awareness to God was intrinsic to the nature of the soul's capacity and purpose.

In the Christian myth of the Grail, it was said to have been the cup used by Jesus at his Last Supper with his closest chosen disciples in which he performed the Passover Seder meal. During the meal Jesus stated that the wine in the container of the Grail was his Blood which was given for the life of the World.

Tradition states that three very important persons of the New Testament church in Jerusalem, Nicodemus, Joseph of Arimathea, and Mary Magdalene, protected the Grail during and after the crucifixion of Christ. Nicodemus was said to have caught and scraped the blood from Jesus' body, and from the lance wound in his side, conserving this blood in the Grail. The three of them were believed to have crossed the Mediterranean with it and landed on the southwestern coast of France. As mentioned earlier, there are churches in this area to this day that revere the Grail and keep this story alive and well.

The emphasis of the theology of these French churches where the Grail is revered is not on the sacrificial nature of Christ's death for the forgiveness of sins. Their theological focus is on the life-giving source of spiritual love poured out from the four-chambered, mandala-sacred heart of Jesus. Christ's love is emptied out in the blood and made available to all who partake of it, just as the Grail provides a loving abundance of whatever one needs and desires to all who receive from the Grail in the Fisher King castle. Indeed, the Grail is a dispenser of God's love in a powerful feminine, nurturing manner and consistency.

Ancient church people understood the belief that life itself, the very essence of that which is aliveness, is contained in the blood. Thus, the blood of Jesus saves, not because of Anselm's emphasis on Christ as sacrificial payment for the sins of humanity, but the sacrificial love poured out in giving life and abundance to all who receive of the blood. We come alive spiritually by the infusion of the love of God in the life blood of Jesus within us appropriated by our souls, which are both the recipient of the substance within and the container itself, the Grail.

The Grail is not only a symbol of the contained, transported and now available love of Christ for all persons who partake of it willingly, but is a symbol of the original, primitive mind (Jung), or the original human soul. I view the soul as a container which brings forth and spills over with the needed love and affection of God for us, individually and corporately.

My understanding of these ideas is based on my experience. I have found personally that the soul is both the organ that contains the life of Christ, and the organ which dispenses this life to the whole person; the conscious and unconscious mind and the physical body. The body and soul are intimately interconnected in our very physiology. Thus, the primitive mind, the conscious and unconscious and the body are closely in continuous interdependence and active association, therefore they function as a whole in a unique and wondrous oneness.

The Grail is able to provide such sustenance because of its feminine ability to balance conflicting opposites, and to contain the tension of these opposites bringing forth new vitality, life and creativity.

What do I mean by opposites?

Jungian analyst Robert Johnson, in his book *Inner Work*, teaches that our vitality and ability to live creatively is the result of balancing opposites, not in a seesaw back and forth manner, but as a manner of feeling the tension between opposites and then using that tension as creative energy. This is similar to Hegel's idea of the thesis finding its opposite in the antithesis, and creating a new synthesis. Yet my experience does not fully support Hegel's theory as a way to understand what I discover in my soul, as much as being aware of the conflict of opposites there and not running in denial or fear of the tension I feel. In my opinion, Hegel's thesis keeps every process stuck in rationalism, and ignores the non-rational intelligence in each of us. I am learning to be a quieter, non-anxious presence to the tension. I am allowing the eventual new thoughts, feelings, and intuitions to arise from the murky waters of the tension. This brings a new clarity, direction, or focus. Movement forward is possible.

An example of a popular expression of our modern inability or discomfort to remain in the tension of the opposites, is found in the third movie of the Indiana Jones trilogy, *Indiana Jones and the Last Crusades*. In the final scene we view the pinnacle conflict in the Grail cave between the American Nazi traitor, the shooting of Jones Sr. (Sean Connelly), and the subsequent healing of his gut-wrenching bullet wound. We then watch the tragic death of the only feminine voice in the film, that of Elsa, the German blonde (Elsa, who, reaching to try to grasp the falling Grail, herself falls to her death in the abyss of the cave). The four men (the number four representing finality and completion) Indiana, his father, Dr. Marcus (the museum curator), and Sallah (the Arabic friend), ride off on their horses out of the narrow canyon into the desert sunset as if true victory has been achieved. The hero myth lives on like the end of a serial with anticipation of the next adventure.

However, in my observation, there is no true triumph in the end of this story, only a pathetic, continued immaturity of the one-sided masculine energy at the expense and destruction of the only feminine principle in the film.

I find in this ending to the movie scenario mentioned above, a deep dissatisfaction, and a remaining tension. There is no final resolution at all. The feminine has been lost, sacrificed, cut off, destroyed, and only the masculine foursome are renewed to pursue justice another day. There is no balance, only a triumph of the masculine rationality. This is a good example in my mind of modern western humanity. A false bravado that believes there is triumph when the reality is that the tension remains because the feminine is sacrificed and regulated to the abyss, hidden, repressed and forgotten.

For true renewal and integration of opposites, one would think the movie would also have redeemed the lost feminine, as well as renew the hero's quest of Indiana Jones and his friends. The film portrays the deep chasm of dysfunction in Western culture, the continued dominance of the masculine at the expense and death of the feminine energy.

John Sanford writes:

The masculine aspect of personality may be variously described as logos, or outgoing reason, active creativity, controlled aggressiveness, psychological firmness, the capacity to strive for goals and overcome obstacles en route.

The Feminine aspect of personality comprises eros, or the capacity for friendships, understanding, awareness of others, creativity through receptiveness, an indirect way of attaining goals, patience, compassion, and the valuing and nourishing of life.
(Sanford, John A. *The Kingdom Within: The Inner Meaning of Jesus' Sayings*. J.B. Lippencott, NY. 1970)

These general principles may be helpful in discerning opposites. It is also important to know that opposites are not just generalized and collective in all humanity, but individualized as well. Each of us has our own set of primary opposites that we can bring together in harmony that are particular to our personal history, personality and uniqueness. This will be discussed in a later chapter.

Other Archetypal Opposites Contained in the Human Soul

The soul is a storehouse of both collective and personal images. Sanford points out that many of these are buried in the unconscious. Our dreams can reveal these deepest images within us to our conscious mind. These images are described poetically in the New Testament Letter to the Hebrews where it describes their presence as an abiding in the pierced place between our marrow and our bones, the cradle of our life source; the place where our blood is developed. King Nebuchadnezzar was informed in the Old Testament story by the prophet Daniel that his dreams containing these inner images should allow him to understand the inmost thoughts of his heart. The same is true for all of us.

I perceive that the Positive Mother archetype is given to each of us by God in creation. The biblical psalmist writes that "[We] are fearfully and wonderfully made" within the darkness of the mother's womb. Many writers use this sacred text to describe the physical body in all its intricate wonders and amazing capacities to overcome adversity and thrive. But few, in the Judeo-Christian tradition apply this same viewpoint when speaking of the human soul.

In my view, to be created in the likeness or image (essence) of God/Goddess is to know that the human depths of beauty, wonder, and our capacity for love is a way for us to understand who we intrinsically are. As a businessman and priest, I have witnessed unbelievable beauty, love, forgiveness and strength in human souls I have known. I have recognized many cases of profound love, acceptance and forgiveness toward others from people who had every right to be vengeful or vindictive, without mercy and ruthless.

I have spent most of my work as a parish priest working in counseling and healing for severely abused people who desired to work through their self-rejection and denial (in order to survive) to conscious awareness of the abuse. These people have held on to the anger long enough to work it through and own it, not letting go of it prematurely. Then when all is said and done, there came a time for them to make a decision to practice letting go, to stop trying to fix the abuser, to accept that God is just and loving, to acknowledge the reality of Evil and to move on with living one's life. This ability to rebound from such abuse is found by assimilating the energy of the Positive Mother archetype.

I think of one case involving a classmate of mine in seminary. This woman, in her late forties, had come to me while I lived in student housing and asked me to be a witness and prayer partner to her healing process. She had experienced a meltdown type of severe panic attack at the beginning of the class regime. She sought out and found excellent therapeutic and medical help from outstanding professionals in the city and began treatment of a long overdue healing for severe abuse.

My classmate was a highly intelligent, effective writer and

teacher. She would make an excellent priest. She was having flashbacks, long buried memories of some of the worst abuse I have ever heard, read or seen in any sadistic movie or novel. Her father was a leading citizen of her city in a rural agricultural area. He was the head lay leader of the local aristocratic church and highly respected in the community for his philanthropy and graciousness.

Unbeknown to others, he was also, in secret, a practicing black witchcraft warlock of a coven of active witches. He began to force his daughter, starting at age seven, through age seventeen, to be the coven's ritual abuse victim during their weekly Black Sabbath Rituals. I cannot imagine the devastation this would bring to a sensitive, intelligent soul such as my classmate.

For three years of seminary, after each session with her psychologist or medical doctor when she began the slow process of regaining her sense of self and healing the traumatic wounds of her childhood experience, she would knock on my dormitory door and ask for prayer for healing of the memories. In our senior year, during one of these healing prayers for her wounded soul, she experienced a fantastic inner healing that affected her body as well.

As I prayed for healing of her latest memory that has surfaced, within thirty seconds or less, her spine straightened, scoliosis of the spine disappeared, her legs became the same length and her pelvis turned in two distinct jerking motions so that her torso was straight in line with the rest of her body. She would later tell our homiletics class about it in a public sermon.

She would have to buy a new wardrobe because of the straightening of her legs and torso.

This woman, by all considerations, should have been dead. She should have died from the trauma, or a fatal accident, or suicide. Yet she would tell me how each week during the Black Mass while she was sexually abused, she would see the face of Jesus somehow before her and this image would allow her to disassociate enough from the pain and trauma to survive.

She went on after seminary to live her life as a whole and unique individual. Her soul was beauteous. That is the only way I can describe her strength and courage. It was profound. It was lasting and it was authentic. She would die ten years later in her late fifties, due to complications from another illness that was not healed, but her spirit remained strong, vibrant and alive, carrying her into the next life.

This friend was an example to me of the resilience to heal, and the unfathomable depths of the soul to renew herself and to stay open and continue growing. I believe this capacity lies within each of us. My friend appropriated the Positive Mother Archetype in extraordinary depths and learned to nurture her soul to health again.

Are There Limitations of the Soul's Ability to Grow?

I knew a counselor many years ago that believed that only a very few people carry their inner work forward to their full capacity. She told me repeatedly that this was because a person's background limited their ability to grow. For many years I found myself agreeing with this professional but a few years ago I changed my mind.

I am aware that a person's background, education and their world view that was formed as a young child may in many ways limit a person's spiritual capacity. But I think this limitation is still within the dictates of the individual will. This sense of mine is not just a stubborn insistence on the idea of free will being intrinsic to my world view. It is a result of my experience in being a pastor, and in observing human behavior. Time and again I have seen people rise far above what seems to be their capacity for spiritual growth and become truly, completely new people.

Conversely, the people I worked with who seemed to grow to a certain point and then stop, seem to have this determined by an inability or unwillingness to continue to choose the more difficult paths. I don't say this in judgment at all, just in observation. Even within the therapist who held this belief in limitations by family background, I could see in this person their unwillingness to continue growing. I think it may be because of the deep hurt this person experienced in life, and as they grew older, the fear of losing what they had or being hurt more was too strong.

Thus, the need to say that others are limited by their background may have been a projection of the therapist's own need to stop growing. I really don't know. I do know, however, how important it is not to judge another person's progress or lack of it. We all must honor the mystery that each of us are. No one knows the heart of another except that person and God.

The Grail Myth teaches that the soul, symbolized by the Grail itself, is a container that can not only contain, but mix, integrate, and transform the opposites listed above in human behavior, thoughts and feelings. The soul, like the Grail, is an open vessel, open to receive into itself the life of God and open to dispense this same life energy. Only that which is alive, thriving and growing can give life. The Grail is matter, earthen, made of clay, metal, wood, precious stones and base rock material. Yet it receives and dispenses, and pours out that which is heavenly.

The soul is also intimately connected to the body which is earthen, made of specific elements found in the earth's soil. Yet the soul as part of the body has been infused with the life of God. The breath of God has filled the soul to overflowing, thus its ability as a living reality to receive and to give, to expand and contract as needed, never static, never an immobile "concept."

As Orthodox bishop Anthony Bloom teaches in his book, *Living Prayer*, "The body, from the very first day to the last, has been the co-worker of the soul in all things and is, together with the soul, the total human being."

I like to think of the soul as the womb of the Great Mother, the uterus, and the place where new life is constantly coming forth where it can become conscious, recognized, honored and cherished. While most people suffer terribly from the destructive aspects of the Negative Mother Complex, also available to all is the abundance of the Great Mother, the giver of life.

How Do We Experience this Abundance?

Many self-help books teach the need to change our thinking with self-affirmations of truthful quotes, sayings, and proverbs. Certainly, the effectiveness in helping others by reading inspirational stories has created the insatiable demand for the *Chicken Soup for the Soul* Series of multiple subcategories of persons (veterans, youth, seniors, etc.). Unquestionably, such affirmations help us change our thinking in many ways that open us to new possibilities of abundance.

Faith also seems to be a key for many people. However, it is important how we interpret the concept of faith in relationship to experiencing the abundance of life giving us energy. Many Americans believe in a faith that says God rewards people who work hard and who are kind to others. The American version of the Judeo-Christian ethic may appear to teach many people that God rewards the good and withholds blessings from those who are not good enough. Many Eastern philosophies teach the same dynamic under past lives and reincarnation views, karma and other popular ideas. The idea is that if we are good and upright we will be rewarded with abundant energy.

As a Christian priest, I take a different slant on these teachings found in many self-help books while at the same time knowing that they are sufficient aids for many people. I find in the teachings of Jesus a different viewpoint on how we can experience the abundance of the Great Mother Archetype.

I am not an animist, nor simply a Nature thinker. I see the destructiveness and brutality of Nature as much as the next person. Yet I see something deeper, perhaps more subtle in the teachings of Jesus regarding the moral necessity for abundance.

When he was asked whether a blind man's disability was the fault of his own sins or the moral imperfections of his parents, Jesus rebuked his disciples and said something very different from the Jewish thought of his day (which said the above, the good are rewarded and the sinful, or unclean, are punished with calamity and poverty by God). He taught that God's glory was the purpose of this man's disability.

I have heard countless teachings along the lines of "the man was born blind so that Jesus could heal him and this would prove that Jesus was the Messiah." I don't like this idea at all. I do not think Jesus tried to validate anything about himself or his mission. I believe Jesus did what he did because he loved people, and for no other reason.

Nor do I adhere to the concept that the man was responsible for his condition due to his behavior and moral character in his "past life or lives." Certainly, that teaching is attractive to many people; all but the one carrying the burden of the disability.

Instead, I believe Jesus was speaking to a different reality when he said the man was born blind for God's glory. On one hand, I can understand the story allegorically. The man being blind was unenlightened. After his encounter with the holy man, Jesus, he could see, and thus was now "enlightened."

But I think there is a deeper reality going on that Jesus is speaking to and this belief of mine is due to being close to several people as they work through their "fate" of an inherited, or birth-determined disability or disease.

I have observed in a few people *an innate ability to stand still in the disability.*

By this I mean to not perceive it as a loss, but simply as something *that is,* which cannot be explained. From this position of standing there is a type of acceptance of one's fate which is not fatalistic, nor static; just the opposite. I have witnessed in others a deep acceptance, and with this attitude or faith a standing in reality; to perceive a deeper reality of possibilities. These few people see expanded potentials beyond rational human endeavor to visualize and create openly, a feminine receptivity to God. This openness goes to the depths of their souls to an interconnection with their bodies that causes them to soar.

With this soaring sometimes comes partial or complete healing of the disability, but the physical healing is not the focus. The freeing of the soul, the release and healing of hampering condescending limits of thoughts and actions is the focus. Physical healing may be a byproduct because of the interconnectedness of the soul and body.

This release of binding limitations of how one views their reality is what I would call the glory, or the *doza*, of God. It is a going past the obvious to the most obvious that is very rarely seen or even considered of value.

I believe, based on my experience that the abundance of the Great Mother, the Glory of God that Jesus spoke about is an inner reality of a lavishness of thought, intuition, and instinct, given to each of us in creation. This gift empowers us to use our imagination to soar wherever soaring is needed in our lives to create beauty, appreciation and a reverence for that which is holy.

This abundance allows us to perceive God in one another, and not just in people we know well, but also in the stranger. Perhaps even more importantly, this abundance helps us recognize our own value and God's presence within.

A Personal Experience of *Doza* in Another

Many years ago when I was a young, self-employed business man, I took a morning walk in my neighborhood. Coming toward me from the other direction across the street was an elderly woman dressed in an Indian sari, bangles of bracelets on her arms, and the single eye painted on her shining forehead.

My neighborhood, as most of my suburban town, had few, if any nonwhite minorities at the time, and the sight of this old woman with her dark, glistening skin and colorful garb was unusual and wondrously unexpected.

Without any premeditated thought, I put my palms together in a prayer type of gesture, held them to my breast facing her from across the street and bowed my head slightly.

I will never forget her face. She returned the gesture with the grace of an angelic being, her broad smile and gleaming white teeth visible even at the distance. There was a divine spark between us as she and I ritually honored the God/Divine/Christ/Goddess/Mary Magdalene within each of us.

The sense of connection was one of the deepest I have ever known and now, nearly forty-five years later as I write about it, my skin rises in goose bumps. The encounter lasted not more than three or four seconds, but what it accomplished in my soul was eternal. I am so thankful for this and many other experiences of a glimmer of the abundance of the divine energy that the soul, the Grail, contains. Both the woman and I were affirmed by the Third Person Present in that moment, and the only way I can describe the feeling is one of feminine, transcendent abundance.

How sad that so many people restrict the reality of abundance to just wanting material gain. I believe and have experienced that there is a place and time needed for such a material gain, but even that is transitory, and impermanent. The greater abundance is the inner freedom to be all whom God has created us to be.

The Soul Is the Instrument that Asks Questions Allowing *Doza* Discoveries

In the story of the Fisher King and his wound, Perceval is not required to answer the question, but simply to pose it, "For whom does the Grail serve?" Having to answer the question is similar to restricting our souls to have the answers and solutions to our yearnings that could only come from a limiting closed way of being. To simply ask the questions of our hunger is to know we are an open vessel able to contain the tension of the opposites that we feel. We can trust that the opposites we sense will eventually unite and bring forth a new conception, idea, or creative solution. To only have to ask the question can also mean we are only asked to trust. We are not required to have faith for the outcome of that trust. Trust implies relationship, loving relationship. Trust means reciprocal caring.

Like most Americans, I have struggled with the fact that in comparison to the rest of the world, I have had a super abundance of material blessing. Yet most of the time I ask God for more because I am afraid of lack. I have noticed that even when my bank account has more than needed for reasonable financial safety, I continue to worry either about losing what I have, or I choose to be anxious about my health, my aging body, a number of things I have little control over. I am in excellent health, having lost a large amount of weight I carried all of my adult life by reversed insulin-based diabetes. Yet I continue to worry about prostate cancer and other unimaginables. Like an insecure child, I LOOK for things to worry about and feel less trusting of God to provide for all my needs, materially and emotionally.

Jesus taught that there is a glory, a *doza,* available for all of us. His teaching invites *us into that trust* in God for all our emotional, physical, psychological and relational needs. But how do we get to this place of trust? I confess this is one of the greatest challenges of my life, especially now in my final third stage.

To begin, I am finding that my soul already has both the capacity and the ability to trust. I do not have to try to have more trust, it is a gift, already being used within me by God's Spirit that infuses my body and soul. I also learned a valuable tool thought from the twentieth-century Chinese teacher Watchman Nee, that trust is a choice and is *not based on feelings of trust*. In fact, I would venture that trust is a valuing that may not contain any semblance to feelings of security at all. Human beings can decide to trust even if they continue to feel afraid. Trust is a choice of consciousness, and I have learned to step into a mode of trust regardless of whether the pain I feel and fear continues or not.

From this position of trust, Watchman Nee says God often will then infuse us with faith as a gift. Faith cannot be manufactured by us. Once faith is given, we then can speak to our situation. We may or may not find the faith is accompanied by a release of fear. In any case, we can choose to trust, and from this inner place, open our souls to faith which is proactive and can act from within to the outer world of our circumstances.

This trust is based on the reality that God has already provided for us all that we need. The universe is our friend, not our enemy. We trust in what already has been done for us and for all others. From this truth we can often move forward into a living faith in this reality. The trust is not limited by feelings, and can be released by a decision of our will.

In speaking of this trust, it is imperative to mention some ideas about the Providence of God. I found some useful words from the Hungarian theologian Ladislaus Boros pertaining to how we can trust God with every circumstance we may find ourselves facing.

First, some words of context to place Boros in regards to his own need to trust in God's providence in his life. At age twenty-two, with a price on his head by the communist government, Boros narrowly escaped from the brutal regime in Hungary in 1949 with only the clothes on his back. He studied philosophy and theology at various European Jesuit universities. In 1954 he did his Ph.D. in Munich with a thesis on the problem of temporality with Augustine. He was ordained a priest in Enghien, Belgium in 1957 and worked from 1958–1973 for the Jesuit magazine *Orientation* in Zurich.

From 1963 he held a teaching position for religious studies at the theological faculty in Innsbruck.

After leaving the Jesuit order and the priesthood in 1973, he married the love of his life. He spent his last years of illness as a freelance writer near Zug. He was diagnosed soon after his marriage with throat cancer at age fifty-two and died ten years later. As he lost his ability to speak, his writing became his voice. I highly recommend all of his books to thinking persons of all faiths and persuasions.

God's providence can be described as a change of mind, an inner transformation. It does not mean that God will miraculously intervene in our lives and remove all danger of attack. On the contrary, it means that there is no ultimate way out of our difficulties. Everything could stay as it was before. The danger may not disappear from our lives. We may have to go on living with our fear and depression. God's providence means, however, that, despite all this, everything has in fact changed. In and through all our suffering, God's goodness has appeared. We can, therefore, say: This thing is hurtful, but basically, it doesn't really count....

Your ultimate, inner being, the most important aspect of all, can never be taken away from you. It is in God's mercy forever. Even if everything collapses, God promises heaven will always be open to us [for Boros, heaven is now, within us, not just a future event or state of being].

In Christ, God has made a new beginning possible for us. This possibility of a new beginning is always open to us in all the situations in which we may find ourselves. For God, no person is forever lost. That is the essence and the inner promise of our faith in God's providence.

(Boros, Ladislaus. *The Cosmic Christ*. Search Press, London, 1973, pp. 29–31)

The Body Can Respond When the Soul Decides to Trust

Our bodies can respond to this decision to trust which contains seeds of power to transform us. My body responds easily to directions and relaxes when I speak to it words of encouragement. Let me give an example.

I have had pain in my lower back from an injury since I was a young man, dislocating a disk in the lumbar area lifting a heavy object with an attitude of the invincibility of youth. Two years ago, I did a stretch at the gym against the instructions of my trainer as I worked out one day alone while she was on holiday. I tore ligaments and tendons in the lower back area and the sacroiliac ligament where the hip and pelvic join. Since that time, I have had daily and nightly uncomfortable pain. What helps to relieve it is movement, especially walking.

When I begin my daily walk the pain is fairly severe. I have learned, however, that if I speak silently in my soul to my back telling it to relax and for all the bones, ligaments, tendons, cartilage, muscles to go into proper alignment, I can actually feel the pain begin to wane immediately, and soon I am walking pain free.

How can this be? I summarize that my body and soul are already working together in communication, but my conscious mind is somehow fixed on outer things; what I am going to do for the next few hours, what type of workout I need to do at the gym, and many future worries? When I stop myself and simply be conscious in the moment and pay attention to my body, treat it like the friend that it is and speak gently in love to it, there is an amazing response.

My body is not my enemy, it is my closest friend. The pain I feel is not a curse or a punishment for some mistake I have committed in my past. It is a daily reminder that I need to treat myself with gentleness, get enough sleep and rest and to relax my soul into my body, as a lover would sink into his or her lover's embrace.

The only idea that makes sense to me regarding where the soul is located is in the body. Based on experience, and the experiential ability of many people to see auras, I think there is no specific "location" other than the reality that the physical body is contained, enveloped, completely integrated with the spiritual body. To my mind, the spiritual and physical body is the location of the soul in their entirety.

For me, this means that the entire physical body is filled with the complete soul. This may explain why when we are conscious of what we are doing and we speak to the different parts of the body they respond. We can speak harshly with criticism and receive the negative effects of such cruelty, or we can speak and affirm with loving thoughts and words to the body and it responds with positive health and vibrancy.

I have read teachings recommending that we direct our thoughts to "speak" to the soul, encouraging it to "relax" down into the body. On one hand such an exercise seems to work, and bring about a sense of greater calm and feeling of centeredness.

But I discovered for myself another way to think about this that works even better. I give thanks to God and to my soul and body, that my soul *is already* completely infilling and indwelling my body in wholeness, however, I am not conscious of this fact. When I accept this as fact, I discover there is no stress or tension of trying to "get it right" within, it just is right. The soul is relaxed in the body *because this is something God has already done within us through creation.*

I don't know if this is a semantic phenomenon or a shift in awareness that is closer to the truth. Of course there is no way to prove this one way or the other and it may be a personal preference. For me, the point is to accept that my soul is whole throughout and within my body and there is no separation. Perhaps at death the spiritual body which contains the soul leaves the physical body at some point as the physical shuts down.

In any case, the striving that many of us experience in trying to attain a sense of peace does not seem reasonable to me. The idea of the "rest of God" being an aspect of how God has created the universe and us in it, provided not just the capacity to relax the body and soul in conjunction with one another, but the very essence of such a connectedness is ours as a gift that requires only a subtle trust in this verifiable truth.

This perspective changes our focus from being required to "think" a certain way to a relaxing, more intuitive gnosis, an experiential knowing which brings peace and harmony to our conscious awareness.

I often think of C. G. Jung's famous response to the question by the British Broadcasting Company interviewer during a final episode recorded and displayed on British television shortly before Jung passed to the greater life. He was asked, "Dr. Jung, one final question. Do you believe in God?"

Jung's face lit up brightly with a broad smile and tilted his head back, with glistening eyes dancing as he emphatically replied, "No, I don't believe in God, I know!"

I find the need for myself to trust in this Truth as it is revealed to be a journey of process not of belief. It is a shifting over to my observable capacity within my intuition, where I find a similar knowing. This knowing allows trust to flow.

Believing and using suppositional thinking is fine but it doesn't bring me the peace that a more subtle, relaxing-into-intuitive intelligence provides where the knowing resides. As a result of experiencing deep trust in God's creation within myself and in the ever-existent Presence which I sense within, my "faith" is strengthened so that I can articulate it. But the faith is not what brings the peace. It is the intuitive knowing that comes from a deeper place and reality of spirit that brings innermost harmony.

What Is Meant by Experiential Knowing?

Again, I want to use the archetype of the Great Mother the Nurturer as an example of how I experience this knowing. Just as a newborn child of all mammals, including human beings, most often find the warm, life giving nipple of the mother immediately after a successful birth, so I experience instinctively the sense of rest, assurance and peace of God when I listen to my intuition in regards to the body-soul connection that is mine in creation.

It is not something I do. It is something God has already done and provided. The newborn animal doesn't create the milk, nor the vehicle of transport, the nipple of the mother's breast. Yet the pre-birth and post birth process that the newborn fully participates in is part of how the mother's body and hormonal changes create both the warm milk, and the ability of it to flow through the created nipple which provides the source.

In the same way, it is both our desire to become aware of our connectedness with God in body and soul, and the yearning that moves us forward to keep seeking and finally finding the peace that is already provided and waiting for us within to experience.

For me, only what is required is some privacy, some moment of solitude, some stillness, to provide the environment for me to turn, to repent, to compress inward my awareness and discover anew the reality of this loving presence that is both God, and the unity of my body and soul.

Jesus promised in John's gospel, as he encouraged his followers to love themselves and one another with the quality of love which they experienced from him, that the result for them would be an awareness of God's indwelling presence.

"If you love me, then my Father and I will love you and come and make our home in your hearts."

For me, there is no greater truth, no higher spiritual reality than to trust, that in our imperfect and often broken feeling state, God has already come and made a very comfortable home within. God has arranged the furniture, we might say, set up shop others might imagine, providing a true living environment for God and for us to enjoy together with all aspects of our being.

Chapter Four

Healing the Wounded Soul

Transformation Is Easier When We Trust that Our Soul and Body are the Home of God

This idea of God giving us a place in our soul and body which is also a home for God makes the idea of transformation and renewal easier to comprehend. It is feminine spiritual energy that allows the bringing together in cooperative relationship the opposites we encounter within. The critical voice of masculine energy often pushes us to struggle and allows our inner opposites to compete with each other. The feminine allows us to stop contending. We are able to change and grow.

While it seems like the primary movers of Perceval's transformation are masculine symbols, the Fisher King, the Grail King, the Old Hermit priest, Arthur, his knightly mentor, there are other deeply important transformers in the story that are strictly feminine. These are Blancheflor, his primary anima figure which he internalizes, and the young woman who holds the head of her dead fiancé knight in her lap while questioning Perceval about his first-night encounter in the castle of the Grail King. Of most significance in the story is the Old Witch Hag who confronts him with his sins in the presence of the Knights of the Round Table.

While it was his mother who held him back and tried to keep him in the forests of the unconscious so he might avoid the deadly fate of his father and seven brothers, it is her memory that spurs him forward in his adventures. He is trying to live the hero myth to prove to her his manhood. In reality it is the feminine of the story that forces him to become reflective, that asks him questions, that prods his conscience and reveals both true and false moral guilt so that he can eventually differentiate between the two.

It is the feminine that pulls him forward to meet the male ancestors. The Fisher King and the Grail King are his uncles, which Jung taught are symbols in medieval times of a young man's spiritual mentors. Perceval is brought to the world of his family and *ancestors relationally by the feminine spirit,* and once in the Grail castle, the masculine spirit shows him his ancestral roots and solidifies his sense of Self.

Lastly, the Grail is itself a feminine vessel capable of receiving and giving. Jungian analyst and Episcopal priest John A. Sanford, in trying to define the nature of the soul, has these insights to share in his book, *The Kingdom Within*:

> The more one tries to define soul, the more elusive it becomes. The soul is subjective. She experiences. She suffers and rejoices. The soul reflects. She both gives birth and takes in psychic life. Fantasy, image, imagination, and a religious concern for values and meaning, these are the provinces of soul.
>
> Soul longs to be loved, and longs to love; soul brings the food of life to us, but also herself hungers. Indeed the soul hungers for God. It is the soul who knows God is there even when she cannot find him. The soul knows that God is her home, and it is her faith that leads us to God. It is through the soul's faith alone that God finally reaches us.
>
> I have called the soul "she" — sexist language this, soul's final outrage against a contemporary world that is against such things. But soul herself resists being thought of in masculine terms, or, worse yet, known by neuter designations. Yes, soul is She. Soul is Yin. Spirit may be masculine or neuter, but soul, like Mother Nature, to which she is akin, will forever remain unalterably feminine in her essence no matter what our objections. She is in man or in woman, our deepest essence as soul, a feminine reality.

(Sanford, John A. *The Kingdom Within: The Inner Meaning of Jesus' Sayings*. J.B. Lippencott, NY. 1970, p.121)

The Nature of the Soul Contains the Awareness of the Spiritual Ancestors

A large part of the missing pieces of understanding in Western culture regarding the nature of the soul is our encounter with our biological and spiritual ancestors. I personally do not intuit truth for myself regarding past lives as a means to understand this connection. I know for many people this idea is helpful. But for myself, I find help in the Jungian concept of the collective unconscious, in particular that aspect of the collective unconscious held in custody by the ancestors.

In Western Christianity this reality is called historically the Communion of Saints. While some liturgical attention is given to this concept on All Soul's Day, the Burial Office and in the Daily Morning and Evening Prayer Services, very little emphasis is left regarding the reality of the wisdom, companionship, and guidance the ancestors and one's spiritual ancestors provide for us. In my thinking, much of what has become trendy in Western culture regarding the companionship of angels and other entities, spiritual guides, and other names, may also be attributed to our spiritual ancestors.

In my book *A Moment of Great Power: Sacramental Prayer and Generational Healing* I teach about the connection with our family tree, those who have gone before us. This aspect of reality is often overlooked by traditional Christian teaching. In this book I give an in-depth scholastic teaching of what our connection to our ancestors may be, and why it is important to know their histories, their spiritual stories, and to pray to and for them as part of an effectively authentic spirituality.

Who are our spiritual ancestors? For many people their family tree may include persons known to have a deeply authentic and vibrant spiritual life. Just as talents and abilities are often genetically inherited, at least potentially, I believe we may also inherit spiritual gifts and sensitivities from our family ancestors and from those who influence our spiritual development.

For reasons too complicated to list here, Western Christianity, especially the various Protestant sects, have tended to minimize if not exclude the reality of spiritual inheritance from our families, races, and places of origin. However, Western Christianity, especially Protestantism, is about the only religious system in the world that tends to do so. Even in atheistic China among non-Buddhist and non-Christian families, the adoration and appreciation of one's ancestors is still an important part of the dominant world view.

Our spiritual ancestors can help us by providing not just examples but actual spiritual support in our journeys. For instance, I was raised by an agnostic father and a believing, but emotionally ill mother. Our family rarely prayed and then only a formal prayer said by my mother at major celebratory meals such as Easter dinner when we often had visitors. I never witnessed nor was talked to about prayer by my parents. My mother taught my brother and myself the following formal, dismal prayer which she made us recite as small children each night.

Now I lay me down to sleep, pray the Lord my soul to keep. If I should die before I wake, pray the Lord my soul to take. God bless Mommy, Daddy, brother, etc. (additional names, often prompted by mother) Amen.

I did not experience a sense of connection with God reciting this formula prayer, but I did feel a type of goodness as a result of praying for the wellbeing of the people mentioned.

However, when I was ten years old my father was transferred by his company from San Francisco to New York City. We lived in Connecticut about an hour's drive from New York City, and a bit further to Freeport, Long Island where both sets of grandparents lived. I got to know them well for the first time.

While my Hungarian grandparents were not communicative about their inner lives, my father's paternal grandmother, my great-grandmother Mária was a vibrant, spiritually alive and dynamically happy woman in her late eighties. She spoke with a strong Hungarian accent and her hands were gnarled from a lifetime of hard physical work. Yet she exuded a joy that was contagious and I felt very close to her spirit. I never had conversations with her, but they were not necessary. I could "catch" her spirit just being around her sitting on the floor near the chair where she sat at family gatherings.

Mária had come to New York City as a young girl of nineteen with her husband, István, and their three small boys. Within two years her husband and the youngest boy died, requiring the oldest, my grandfather Stephen, to quit elementary school and begin working full time, caring for his mother and his younger brother Albert. Mária worked the next seventy years as the super, the custodian of their apartment house building in the midst of Manhattan's Little Hungary.

My father's mother, Elizabeth (the affectionate Hungarian nickname Sissy was given to her and used by the family) was a simple Hungarian woman of Roman Catholic faith. Yet to my knowledge, she did not attend church services as an adult. This loving woman once took my brother and me on a hot summer's afternoon to a very mysterious monastery on Long Island, where the long, dark hallways contained lighted Stations of the Cross. She would have us join her in devotion at each station and it was clear this spiritual discipline was nurturing to her and delighted her soul.

When I moved to Hungary sixty years later, I visited the church where Grandmother Sissy's mother, my maternal great grandmother also named Mária, was baptized in 1886 in the city of Székesfehérvár. The church had records of her parents' names, occupations (her dad was a postal worker) and the address of the street where she lived.

A Hungarian friend who had helped me set up an appointment with the parish priest who provided the family information, took me to the church on a Sunday evening. We both stood in the inside entrance area of the church, and watched through the glassed-in sanctuary the five or six people worshipping with the parish priest. As the communion service ended, both my friend and I heard the sound of a large multitude of people singing and were confounded because the five people in the pews were not singing at all. This experience of hearing beautiful singing voices from invisible persons lasted about ten minutes. We were astounded. I felt a deep connection with my great-grandmother who was part of this congregation with her family more than a hundred years earlier.

After meeting with the priest and thanking him for his time and help, we walked to the street where she lived. The old houses were gone and replaced by two commercial buildings. As we stood there gazing, again we experienced something supernatural and similar to what we had experienced in the church earlier in the evening. We both heard clearly the sounds of children laughing and playing and women talking with each other in Hungarian. This phenomenon lasted more than fifteen minutes. Again, a deep sense of spiritual connection was affirmed with this dear woman whom I never met but who passed on to my grandmother Sissy the joy of her faith and spirituality.

Meditating and yes, praying with and to our spiritual ancestors is another intrinsic aspect of our soul's ability and nature. I encourage people to use their imaginations to converse in inner dialogues with their favorite family members, their favorite authors and persons of history whose stories have given them hope. We are surrounded by the invisible spiritual reality of people who love us and with whom we can feel a deep connection and communion. There is no need for occult activities such as séances to experience this closeness. The presence of loving persons who encompass us is a gift from God which our souls can discern and enjoy. The conscious awareness of our loving ancestors and mentors can bring a stronger self-identity and help facilitate healing of the traumas that cause us to feel displaced, abandoned or alone.

Intense and Directive Longing Is another Essential Quality of the Human Soul

The previous story reminds me of another aspect of the life and nature of the human soul in regards to longing. I think there are many ways we experience longing that are intrinsic to who we are. Some of the longing is a pull to accomplish a task, to visit a place, or have a conversation with a special person. Other longings may take the form of an awareness of what can be, a desire for fulfillment, a longing for a specific feeling of assurance and acceptance.

These longings can take the form of a desire for pilgrimage to the place of one's beginnings, such as childhood neighborhood or an ancestral country. It has been my experience as a priest to witness many older people as they approach the death transition to yearn to return to the place of their birth.

Longing often has a deeper pull to the soul, a desire to return to one's original mind, primitive cognizance, or a previously felt innocence when God's presence was most felt, experienced and appreciated; in other words, the place of spiritual union.

One of my favorite writers, Sir Laurens van der Post, in his insightful novel *A Mantis Carol* based on a true story, wrote about the yearning of the South African Kalahari Desert Bushmen and their instinctive desire to return to the place of their birth in the desert as an outer sacrament of their lifelong yearning and hunger for God.

In the early 1950s, van der Post was in the United States for a speaking tour. He encountered a particular woman who approached him at Pendle Hill, a Quaker retreat center in

Pennsylvania, and asked him for personal counseling. She had been visited by a lifelong, repetitive dream of a praying mantis. After hearing van der Post speak about the mantis being the incarnation of God in Bushman mythology, she secured an entire evening with him to talk and bring some pieces of her spiritual journey together and heal her soul.

This woman was raised in a luxurious mansion in an Upper East Side Manhattan family. Her father has rescued a Bushman from a carnival show in Bermuda, and later, an American circus. Her father, a savvy and compassionate attorney, was able to legally free the Bushman from the abusive circus racket and basically took him in as a member of the family. He served as a butler and a type of male nanny to the children of the house as well.

The repetitive dream of a mantis spurred the woman to seek out van der Post with urgency as she was deeply emotionally troubled and in such distress that no psychologist in New York could help her. Understanding the symbolism of the mantis in her dream helped her connect with memories from childhood that needed to be healed, especially her long forgotten relationship with the Bushman. He was the primary source of God's demonstrable, unconditional love to her as a child, and at midlife, she needed to make this connection again to become whole.

The old Bushman, whose name was Hans, knew that he could never return to the place of his birth and that he could only return to it in spirit. The woman told van der Post that the night Hans died, he was lying in bed, and she, as a young woman held his hand and gave him her presence.

There was a special dance he would do when he was younger for the children of the house. It was really two dances, one, where he would stomp his feet, and wave his hands and arms close to the ground, bent over with joy. The other dance, the hand motions were in the opposite direction, stretched above his head as fiercely and determined to touch some invisible entity in the sky. The first dance, van der Post explained to her, is called "The dance of the little hunger," The second, "The dance of the great hunger," and both are never danced in a collective group but danced by the individual.

The dance of the little hunger signifies what a child hungers for, the milk of the mother's breast, the food of the earth. But the dance of the great hunger is the dance of longing for the intimacy of God.

As he was approaching death as a very old, earthly-life-tired man, Hans could barely move or speak, but while she sat present with him at his deathbed, with an unexpected energy, he grasped the woman's hand and asked her to dance the great dance for him at the foot of his bed.

She was unsure of what to do, but she remembered his movements she had seen so many times long ago, and timidly at first, then with growing abandon, she stretched her arms above her head and stamped her feet on the wooden floor with majestic passion. As she lost herself in the dance, she heard a loud, deep-bellied sigh utter from Hans, and turning to look at him she realized his spirit and soul had left his body. Through her dance on his behalf and her affirmation and witness of his life and love, he was able to fulfill the great hunger for God and be released to enter the Spiritual realm with joy and fulfillment.

To be aware of our longings and find ways to ritually express them as the Bushman in New York City did through the Great Dance, is another path we can take towards the healing of our fears of abandonment and rejection.

The Soul Has the Capacity to Be a Witness to Individual Dignity

This brings me to another important capacity of the human soul that I think needs our attention. The soul has both a specific need to be affirmed in its uniqueness by a witness, and the ability to meet this need for another. I think this can happen if we are careful to listen to our intuition and the quiet voice of God giving us instructions within.

The woman of the story above was a sculptress. She had made a bronze bust of Hans and this act was a powerful witness to him of his innate uniqueness and individuality. She had obeyed her intuition by creating this bust of Hans. When she presented it to him, he danced with utmost delight. She had met his need, as van der Post writes of the great need of the soul to be recognized in its own individual dignity of life.

Laurens van der Post felt that no one could do this better for another than an artist such as this woman. Yet I think each of us can do this for another through the artist within our innate creativity.

Each of us longs to be affirmed in our individuality, our innate uniqueness, in our "individual dignity of life." Mother Teresa of Calcutta wrote that each person longs to be "fed" with love, to be "clothed" with dignity/affirmation, and "housed" to belong. I feel these are truthfully important words as to the basic needs of each human soul.

The greatest lack I observe in many religious traditions today is the pressure to conform to some type of collective "ideal" and the lack of an affirmation of individual dignity and unconditional love for one another based on our singular uniqueness. Where this affirmation and love exists there is true feeling of belonging, whether it be in a personal relationship, a group encounter, or the human race in general.

It is my belief that the human soul not only has this need for affirmation of our individual dignity but also can discern easily when this affirmation is needed by someone. But this discernment needs to be honored, listened to and acted upon every time God speaks through the soul to provide it for another.

Laurens van der Post wrote:

None of us, however assured and permanent in our systems appear to be, can ever know our own full selves unless we have some positive act of recognition by something or someone other than ourselves.... No matter how urgent our hearts, we all need at last another to make us the one we were meant to be. The mystery of our deepest self, the mystery of all things, indeed the mystery of creation itself was always between two; in an awareness that there are always both a 'thou' and an 'I.'

Many of us today are condemned to experience the 'I' and the 'thou' solitarily and darkly only within ourselves unconfirmed by the world about us. Most of us indeed have become distorted into knowing only the 'I' of ourselves and not the 'thou.' But in so far as we could experience them we did so alone because the mirror of our time was cracked, and indeed for Hans Taaibosch must have been utterly shattered, until on the day she [the woman of the story] declared that the clay still warm between her fingers was fulfilled, and at last he was able to look and see the kind of reflection of his own living worth which I had mentioned.

(Van der Post, Laurens. *A Mantis Carol*. Island Press, Washington DC, Covelo, CA, 1975)

I believe that each of us, in the light and darkness our own feminine and masculine soul, the dark living matter of the stone Grail within, can discover when God is calling us to affirm another person of their individual greatness and mirror to them what they cannot see for themselves objectively.

This is what I think the apostle Paul may have also been thinking in his profound writing, First Corinthians Chapter Thirteen, "though I see through [in] a glass [mirror] darkly, yet then [the time of illumination] I will see face to face." Each of us can usually see the divine in the other person before we can see it within ourselves, thus the need for the "thou" to be affirmed by the other and to be affirmed by us for the other, so each of us can be truly fulfilled in perceiving our own intrinsic value.

One of the aspects of the Grail is that it can provide an abundance of all that we need and desire, not just a shallow material gain or need, but the deeper needs for unconditional love, affirmation of our dignity, and our place of belonging in the universe. The Grail overflows with this sustenance not only for our own needs but for others. Often it is in providing the sustenance and belonging for another that we discover it for ourselves as well.

There is a popular saying today, "We are blessed to be a blessing." This cannot mean some kind of sanctimonious attitude of "niceness" to be portrayed and dispensed toward others, but the deeper feeding and drinking of the Grail abundance which nourishes and sustains both the giver and the receiver. Thus, our deep need remains to stay open to honest relationships and the potential of relational fulfillment.

While most of us may not be able to paint a portrait or sculpture a likeness to affirm, each of us has the ability of soul to see the beauty in the other and to affirm it with our words not of flattery, but of honest, gentle and well-chosen words that heal, restore and create original wellbeing.

One may ask, "Why do we need affirmation of our dignity from another?" Laurens van der Post wrote above that somehow intrinsically wrapped up in the very creation of life itself by God is *this feminine relational aspect of all things*, that the "I" and "thou" of ourselves needs affirmation. Also, at a deeper level we can imagine that God created a relational universe, that in order for us to feel a sense of belonging, to experience unconditional love, to realize our greatest potential of dignity, we have been created relationally.

This is an important point because if we are created un-relationally, there is something wrong with us if we find ourselves needing affirmation and unconditional love and struggling to give this to ourselves. If we are created un-relationally, this tension we feel may be intrinsic to who we are, unable and not expected by our Creator to be fully mature in solidarity with one's self and one another.

The "thou" is our Divinity. If we are created relationally, then we are able to be affirmed in the "thou" of ourselves from another and we are able to affirm the "thou" of another which benefits both.

This morning as I write these words, I awoke with the memory of last night's dream that speaks to this capacity of the soul to affirm the other, and in doing so is self-affirmed, without ego inflation. I wish to share this dream to illustrate the importance of this work of the soul, as I trust all our dreams are messages from God through our unconscious to help us realize our potential.

The Dream

I was in a city, a university city of some kind, and down in the street of the center point of the city. There were university students on the tops of university buildings high above and all around me in every direction. I read to them in a loud voice from a beautiful, illustrated book, a short page and a half story about the individuality, the uniqueness of their own souls. I turned every direction as I read, looking up at the students above me far away on the rooftops.

I encouraged the students to write down three things that they dream of accomplishing that were very important and unique to them, and to show them to their professors to read and sign as affirmation of the importance that the students sustain their individualism. An unknown adult standing next to me on the street below asked me why I didn't use a microphone. I said because I didn't have one. I started to read again. The students above me were listening. The suggested microphone was not needed. I felt I was doing what I was supposed to do.

I understand the dream to possibly mean that myself, my

ego, what I know consciously of my own nature and being, was reading wisdom produced by another from long ago, standing in the center of the city, a mandala, facing all the directions of the wind, north, south, east and west, looking at the students, who may represent the role within me of the student of life.

The students were to write down three things they feel called uniquely to accomplish as personal goals, and to have these goals read, signed and affirmed by their teachers, the archetype of the teacher. The high elevation of the students on the top of the buildings could show that I am currently inflated, but I think, on further reflection, this interpretation is wrong. What resonated was that the valuing of the role of the student of life is being emphasized in the dream by their elevation, not ego inflation, as I and the shadow figure adult-helper in the dream were on the ground of the street.

Why was a microphone not needed? Perhaps because the symbol of a microphone can signify that there is a need for amplification and at this time there may be no need to amplify the message of unique individuation of the soul because the message is self-evident.

The students and their professors are opposites, and in the dream, the reading of the student's personal life goals and the signing by the professors shows the need for a further unity of opposites. The affirmation of the truth of uniqueness has a need to continue, perhaps in my consciousness.

There is another aspect of how we may affirm the uniqueness of each person. This is the need for us to avoid thinking statistically about ourselves and all other people.

As Marie Louise von Franz teaches in her book, *Puer Aeternus: A Psychological Study of the Adult Struggle with the Paradise of Childhood*, there exists another way to understand the nature of the soul to affirm the individuality of all persons. She writes:

To think of oneself in a statistical way is, as Dr. Jung points out, most destructive to the process of individuation, because it makes everything relative. If we begin to think statistically, we begin to think against our own uniqueness. Statistics are built upon probability. Probability is only one way of explaining reality, and as we know, there is just as much uniqueness and irregularity. This is why statistics are only half right. They give a completely falsified picture because they only give the average probability.

(Van Franz, Marie-Louise. *Puer Aeternus: A Psychological Study of the Adult Struggle with the Paradise of Childhood*. Sigo Press, 1970. Alchemical Active Imagination. Shambala Press, Boston, 1997, p. 86–87)

I will give you an example of this from my own personal experience. As an introvert, I enjoy being in a public place and people watching. I enjoy observing faces, postures and the variety and diversity of a crowd in many ways feeds my soul with the joy of creation and the mystery that is God as creator.

However, there is a dark side to this. When I find myself in a crowd of people for a long period of time, I begin to lose a sense of the individual, of the uniqueness of each person I am observing. I especially experience this "individualization fatigue" when walking in a very crowded, confined space such as an inner-city sidewalk, or congested mall. I begin to lose a sense of people as specifically unique, as if my mind cannot take in all the variables of what I am seeing and hearing and all the people fade into a kind of fog of similarity and conformity.

I find I can only tolerate a large crowd for a short amount of time because this kind of regressive depression can easily overcome my soul. I recognize that not only can I not see in the crowd the individualization of others, but I can easily lose my own sense of uniqueness in this experience as well and this causes my feelings to become depressed, and even feel a kind of despair.

I have to remove myself and remind myself of the specialness of each person, including myself. I find it hard in the crowd to believe that God is present and intimately connected to each person individually, and thus a kind of statistical thinking can arise and block out the sense of unity with all others in my own individuality.

No matter what a statistic says, it is based on averages and human behavior and rational experience goes far beyond any average sense of reality. There is always the exception right around the corner! This is true both in my life and in the lives of others. It is our soul that resists this masculine statistical thinking that can overwhelm us. Only our souls can keep us connected to the deeper truths we know are real. It is the feminine relationality that allows us to get beyond the limitations of our collective thinking and re-enter the reality of mystery, greatness and intimacy with God and others.

I am indebted to Dr. van Franz for this insight. She also points out that it is the negative mother complex in a man and the negative father complex in a woman that brings out this statistical thinking. It is the unconscious, thus negated forms of the archetypes that causes us to sink back and retreat from the mystery that all persons are valuable and intrinsically connected with one another. Perhaps the reader will also think of similar examples, such as watching the suffering of others on the news or social media articles, which can bring about a similar type of regressive despair.

The key to not being overwhelmed may be in limiting our exposure not to the suffering of others, but to the generalizations and collective analysis comprised by many of these sources of information. We can choose to stay informed in a relational, feminine, soul nurturing manner that moves us forward, not backwards in our soul development and identity with our common humanity.

Chapter Five

The Soul Contains and then Integrates Our Opposites

The Archetypes of the King and Queen

Healing happens when we realize the capacity of the soul to unite opposites within us. I do not think of this process as simply a balancing of opposites but as a proactive, relational bringing together of opposites to create a new unity, a new birth of life.

Another way we can think of these opposite energies within us are the archetypes of the King and Queen. The archetype of the King is the energy that differentiates, puts things into categorical thinking, is analytical, and provides order in the universe of our inner lives. The Queen is the archetype that balances this proactive objectivity with relational wisdom providing stability and true effectiveness to the order provided by the King. Often order may need to be superseded by a deeper need for relationship that can only happen where there is flexibility within order. Therefore, together these archetypes can rule, which to me means to provide profound leadership, direction, and a healthy self-love within our souls.

If a person is unaware of the feminine energy of the soul, the King archetype can become a Tyrant: critical, judgmental, overbearing, arbitrary, and the antithesis of true justice. Oppression, hopelessness and devaluation are the results of the Tyrant's rule. But when the King energy is balanced by an equal awareness of the Queen, there is restraint, mercy, forgiveness and new beginnings that accompany the justice of the King. The healthy soul can utilize the energy of the King to affirm one's self, to feel one's true value, to hold within the soul the God given self-affirmation of the beauty of who we are as God has created us: unique, impressive and highly creative.

If a person is unaware of the King archetype in their soul and are dominated by the Queen, she may express herself as the moody, prickly, self-absorbed witch who destroys all sense of creativity and proactive desire. If given full rein, the Queen alone can destroy all initiative and cause the soul to feel it will never grow up and individualize; one may feel that it is only through relationship with the masculine that the feminine can find meaning (a type of innermost codependency). If the relational aspects of the Queen are dominant, then a person may outwardly possess a neediness for relationship that either attracts similarly unhealthy people or drives away more conscious people.

Only a Queen archetype balanced by the King can truly nurture the soul without also smothering initiative through a negative agenda that leads to death. A Queen, ruling alongside the King metaphorically, provides the warmth and self-awareness that the masculine energy often cannot possess alone. As partners, these two archetypes provide direction, nurture, words, the needed silence, the needed extroversion and the equally needed introversion to give us clear momentum forward towards our spiritual potential.

Laurens van der Post, in his exquisite novel *The Face by the Fire* teaches how each of us has two pairs of the King and Queen, one outer (one's space-time history mother and father or substitute parents: teachers, mentors, coaches, scout leaders, employers) and the inner, God-given King and Queen. In his story, the inner archetypes sit on either side of the fire hearth on thrones of the soul (a symbol of spiritual transformation) slightly facing one another as well as facing forward to the viewer.

It is my observation that almost always the outer father and mother of persons are wounded and unable to provide a sufficient amount of the positive energy of the archetypes. Only as we begin to differentiate between the outer mother and father and the inner King and Queen, can we begin to find the nurture, guidance and love that we all seek so longingly.

Sometimes, if we are fortunate in our youth, we encounter an outer King and Queen Figure who provides what is lacking in the original mother and father of historical familiarity. It might have been the generous soul of a teacher, a boss, an interested neighbor, a coach, an aunt or uncle, or even older sibling, but always a safe and wise person who provided us with some sort of direction, affirmation and unconditional love that we needed. Thanks be to God for these persons who provided glimpses of the Divine affirmation we needed until we were strong enough to discover the archetypes of King and Queen ruling us from within.

A word about how I use the phrase written in the preceding sentence: *ruling, or to rule.* I do not think of this word to mean control, or controlling. Instead, I think of the archetypes of King and Queen ruling or as providing relational order which cares and empowers us with a fullness and strong sense of Self. Instead of an overruling, top down feeling, the archetypes bring a from-underneath, supportive feeling to the soul. Ruling means to provide a standard, a rule, a canon of truth, a supportive servant heart to the soul.

A true ruler is the epitome of Wisdom, a balance of Knowledge and deep, abiding Love. To rule implies to me what Christ taught, that those who want to lead must be the Servant of All, just as he washed his disciples' feet the night of his last meal with them. The King and Queen archetypes serve and, thus, endow those whom are served.

The King and Queen within provide the order, stability and relational communication within to govern with prudence and wisdom the other less dominate archetypes of the Teacher, the Warrior, the Handmaiden, the Weaver, the Cobbler, the Shaman, the Stonemason, the Carpenter, the Brother and Sister, the Uncle and Aunt, the Lovers both male and female, the Old

Man and the Old Woman, the Young boy and the Young Girl.

Each of these archetypes, and more unmentioned, dwell within each of us, but they must be in an attentive, active listening capacity to the King and Queen who have final responsibility for the Order and Prosperity of the Inner Kingdom. The King and Queen cooperate together exceedingly well and are a harmonious team within the soul.

The fire behind and between them is the spiritual fire of Transformation, the true powerhouse of Change able to do its work because of their cooperation. Laurens van der Post describes them in a healing dream experienced by his novel's protagonist who struggled with regressive alcoholism and artistic stunting, yet in the beginning of his end was set free by the inner work of God in his soul.

Laurens van der Post describes the dream which occurred when the alcoholic man decided to lock himself in a hotel room and do his own detoxification, bringing him near death into a healing of his deepest need, the acquisition of the unconditional love of God which has been present within his soul from his very beginning, but clouded over by the terrible tragedies of his life.

David's Dream

At this point David fell into a deep sleep illuminated through his fever like a dark tropical storm sky with a steaming rainbow. In his sleep he stood once more outside the door of Albert's [his father] study. He raised his hand to turn the handle of the door and go inside but something held him back. A curious, taut electric sound, like the noise of a great country's traffic inside the telegraph wires on a highway, was coming out of the room ... a noise suggesting constant and unending energy. He looked up and saw over the door a notice saying, "Power station: danger."

How right he was to hesitate and yet he knew that he must

enter whatever the risk. As he stood there wondering how to set about it, the old negro, slave of his other dream, appeared suddenly at his side and hung a new notice in place of the old, saying: "Throne room: Transformer."

Then he was inside the study which he had once painted so vividly. The room was as before except that now it was filled with a golden light, a dazzling fire in the grate, and two resplendent figures in the chairs. At first he thought of Mary [his mother] and Albert [his father], then my own [the author's] father and mother, and he felt intensely happy to see them so close and confidingly there.

But as he went nearer, he saw that they were two truly royal figures, male and female, two mythological persons. He stopped short in awe for he saw now that they were deeply engaged. The man was writing with an albatross quill in a large book open on his knees. The woman was holding a golden ink well in one hand and with the other blotting each line the man wrote with a most caring solicitude.

David looked at them sideways. He saw they were writing "The Progress of David the Painter." His contentment knew no bounds and he began to cry softly and quietly to himself out of a new happiness over his discovery that this ancient throne room was after all not empty, but transfigured.

He woke and the dream, such a good dream, stayed with him. He knew now that these royal persons were no illusions. What is more he realized that they'd always been there, that they'd figured over and over again in his dreams, appealing to him with the greatest and most quivering electrical urgency to stop confusing them with Albert and Mary. He was so excited at this discovery that his pulse raced at his temples and the blood flowed like Nile cataract and African waterfall in his ears.

(Van der Post, Laurens. *The Face Beside the Fire*. Chatto and Windus, London, 1985)

This fictitious description of the King and Queen archetypes exemplifies the beautiful harmony between the masculine and feminine spiritual energies within each of us. Most of us spend our lives projecting this inner reality outwardly onto our parents, our partners, or other substitutes. It is this projection we carry which either greatly disappoints or grievously represses our inner freedom.

Removing the projection is a twofold task. First, to recognize that we are projecting our royalty outward will stop the projection, and then, much needed, is an inward tending to the fire and reflective observation of the actions of the inner King and Queen.

Most of us do not abide with inner work long enough to get past the first step of removing the outward projection to move on to the gazing and receiving of love through the order and creative work of the inner archetypes. It is a rare person who has not only removed the projection, but learned to engage in loving dialogue and exchange with the inner King and Queen from whom all life and vitality and personal true affirmation flows.

As van der Post wrote:

A person [man] must go down into the gulf and walk a lonely path among the dark and terrible dangers of his [her] archaic self, they must visit their land below sea level, and they cannot come out again whole until they have found, separated and healed the ancient quarrel between the four parents [father, mother, inner King and Queen] of themselves, delivered all four from destructive bondage and fatal confusion of themselves.

I love van der Post's language above, describing our need to "go down to the gulf … and visit their land below sea level." What does this mean for us? It may be different for everyone and each of us has the invitation to find out. For myself, it means to allow myself to feel the deep insecurities that underlie so much of my waking hours. I am learning to give myself permission *to feel, and not judge*, to embrace and not flee the feelings that I find beneath my own sea level.

Carl Jung's Descent "In Going Down to the Gulf"

When Carl Jung was in his mid-thirties, he suffered a very difficult time. He and his wife Emma had become close friends of Sigmund Freud and his spouse Martha Bernays. Freud wanted Jung to be his "son," to carry on the leadership of the fledging new field of Psychoanalytical Psychology. However, on a trip across the Atlantic together by ship to receive honorary degrees from Clark University's Psychology department in 1909, while both men shared and helped each other with their dreams, Jung discovered something very distasteful about Freud. Jung felt that Freud was more interested in supporting his "theories" than in meaningful personal growth. Jung had given Freud feedback about a particular dream, and Freud's response was immature, haughty, arrogant and egocentric. Eventually over the next two years the friendship was broken by Freud. This crushed Jung immensely.

This wound opened up other injuries within Jung, and his response was to create the time and energy in his busy professional life schedule to practice creative play daily, similar to what occupied him as a little boy. He spent time every afternoon using stones and sticks to create imaginary villages in the mud on the shore of Lake Zurich behind his house. He came to a place in his spirit where he realized he needed to take a "plunge" into the abyss of his unconscious, knowing full well as a psychiatrist that he could cause his own psychotic breakdown. With great courage he jumped down into his own sea bottom, and there found solid ground on which to stand.

He spent three conscious years there wrestling with not only his personal demons, but embracing the frightening, collective archetypal visions he had of the upcoming scourge of Europe that erupted in World War Two. He came out of this time of intense, conscious introspection stronger, and with a clearer focus for his life's work. It would be many years before he would eventually heal his early childhood traumas that caused him such difficulties as an adult, but he did heal.

For the reader who knows something of Jung's life and work, it may be helpful to know that in 1997 his family allowed the truth to be publicly known about Jung's sexual abuse perpetrated by a close friend of his father, a Jesuit priest. This abuse was probably the cause of Jung's difficulty with embracing his own feminine energies which he projected out onto women in his adulthood. Deirdre Bair was given permission by his heirs to tell this aspect of Jung's story in her authorized biography (Blair, Deirdre. *Jung: A Biography*. Little Brown and Company, Boston, 2003).

Just as Jung experienced healing as he worked with his unconscious through dream work and childhood play, I work with people in spiritual direction and ask them to record their dreams. One of the reasons I do this is because I've found that the dream is the best vehicle to bring up material from the unconscious. It brings to our awareness things that have been denied, oppressed, forgotten consciously, in order for us to survive. Dreams bring this material to our consciousness with a timing and rate of speed that we can handle and appropriate.

Very often people are frightened to record their dreams because as they do, they realize they are encountering realities within, not just figments of the imagination they can dismiss. Recording and working with dreams engages us at this deep place that van der Post suggests we enter, and that Jung certainly found and worked through. I encourage people not to get stuck in the fear of the unknown, but pursue scholastic and academic knowledge about the archetypes and learn to interpret their dreams according to their own nationality, race, gender, religious heritage and personal circumstances.

The archetypes that appear in our dreams are very real images of how we can understand and relate cognitively to our spiritual selves. Just as Christians find the images of Jesus in the New Testament to be, these images portray very real spiritual realities, which, when we can consciously relate to them, become sources of great power.

Jung's courage is a deep inspiration for me to continue my own inner work. When I visited his grave in the village cemetery in Küsnacht, Switzerland, I spoke to him of my gratefulness of his example of extraordinary bravery of heart and mind. He was a very broken man who entered his own inner darkness and came out the other side into light without a mentor. His wife and friends stood by him as he worked through these deep issues that often completely defeat persons of lessor courage or strength. I appreciate his example very much.

The King and Queen Archetypes Also Represent God and Show Us Our Need for Renewal of How we Perceive God

There is another aspect of the King and Queen that I would like to suggest we think about. These archetypes are often used to describe a person's concept of God/Goddess, and perhaps, rightly so. Yet in many mythologies around the world, including our Grail Myth, there is another dynamic involved with these archetypes which may be helpful for our spiritual maturity.

In many mythologies the King who reigns must be sacrificed periodically in a literal sense, or when a period of developmental mythology has come to completion and there is no more that can be done to improve upon a situation. In these cases, the King must die either of old age, or expediently, by being killed, in order for a new King to emerge, bringing in a new prosperity and rule.

In the case of the Fisher King there are two kings present, the wounded Fisher King and the behind the scenes and off to the side Grail Castle King. The Fisher King is healed of his wound when Perceval asks the right question of the Grail procession. He welcomes and mentors Perceval for three days and then dies. Why? In order for a new King to come. It is as if the Fisher King and his fateful story has served a certain purpose, which has expired or is no longer needed. A new King must take his place as the Kingdom has now been restored, no longer destitute, and a different type of rule is needed. In our story Perceval himself becomes the new Fisher King and Guardian of the Grail. In his old age, Perceval retires to the forested mountains to live alone continuing to guard the Grail until this feminine treasure is needed by humankind again. I suspect the second, hidden, Grail Castle King is an archetype personifying God who needn't or cannot die, as this Grail King symbolizes the eternal realm.

Of course, this story line follows the basic Dying and Rising God mythology of Middle Eastern sources and beyond that influenced Western Christianity. We see this mythology enacted in history in a peculiar way in the story of Christ. We will look at this aspect of the Dying and Rising God within Christianity in a later chapter. But what are we to do with the archetype? It seems like we spend an enormous amount of spiritual energy just discovering the archetype and its ability to bring order and prosperity, only now to let it die?

I would suggest the answer to this question is a qualified, yes. One of the most beautiful statements ever spoken to me by my mentor John A. Sanford was this: In mythology, as in dream work, *there is no permanent death*. There is the cycle of birth, expanding life, final battle, dismemberment and death, the burial of the hero/heroine followed always by *resurrection*. I might add, in Christ, there is permanent, available *resurrection* as the natural cycle has been transcended and surpassed by God, God's self.

Within the larger context of the archetype of the King and Queen is a component of the Rising and Dying God, so that the current Royal couple take a back seat per se, or die, to make room for a new King and Queen allowing for new vitality, ongoing renewal of the Kingdom, Order, Creativity and New Birth. In many European folk tales the story begins with a King and Queen, a prince or a princess, or sometimes the Queen has died, and the King is left alone to rule and raise his children. But in almost all cases, when the hero or heroine accomplishes their heroic journey and the required tests and tasks, they then sit down and become the new King or the New Queen joined by their new spouse, while the Kingdom continuity persists with rebirth.

Often, if the old King and Queen do not die in the story they take a back seat. They no longer are center stage in the story. The hero or heroine and their new spouse become the new royal rulers. In dreams the images of our parents can represent the old King and Queen, the image of our children the new royal pair representing a new way we are experiencing interior order, rule, guidance and a new relationship with God.

When we use the archetype of the King and Queen, we use them to illustrate our experience and knowledge of God/ Goddess. The coming of the new King and Queen represents a letting go of the old feelings, conceptions, memories and knowledge of the old God/Goddess and an embracing on our part of the new inner reality.

This process of letting go of the archetypes in order to find them again renewed is required of each of us to grow into our full potential as created in the image of this God who is continually re-revealed.

There is another element to this release of the old so that the new can come in our artistic endeavors. Marie Louis von Franz writes in her insightful book *Puer Aeternus* that the artist will create something new and bold that catches the world's attention and is very successful. However, if the artist tries to duplicate the same creation, something is lost in energy and the multiple copies of the original work do not have the color and spirit of the first. It is important in our numinous experiences of creativity, whether in writing, filmmaking, painting, clay, or music, to not try to repeat out of greed to simply reproduce the original art. This is a regressive and uncalled for attempt.

This is why movies based on books often do not carry the same spirit as the original stories; sequels to successful movies often fall flat. One exception in my experience was the skillful moviemaking of George Lucas in his Star Wars Trilogy. Each sequel could have stood alone, each was differentiated enough from the preceding film both in character and in plot to sustain a new creativity of their own.

But in most cases, it is important for the creative person who finds success to continue to create originality and move forward, which requires great trust in the unknown of the process of creation. If they do this, they will find new depths of creative art awaiting their discoveries, and most of what they create going onward will carry the spark of divine awakening within it.

In addition to von Franz' work mentioned above, I recommend Rollo May's *The Courage to Create* as an insightful digestion of the creative act and its cycles, especially Chapter Three, "Creativity and the Unconscious."

Archetypes of Jesus and Mary Magdalene May Be Helpful, as Additional King and Queen Images in the Soul

Another model I have found helpful in my own inner healing work is that a pairing of the King and Queen Archetypes involves both the archetypes of the Teacher and the Lover in the relationship between Jesus and Mary Magdalene. I have found it helpful to think of the inner union of opposites of energies using these figures from the gospel stories, both the Canonical and the New Testament Apocryphal versions. The non-canonical New Testament gospels of Andrew, Mary, Thomas, Mary Magdalene, Peter and several others teach of the closely intimate relationship between this strong, innovative, financial supporter of Jesus and his disciples in Mary Magdalene, and Jesus' own comfort level with his sexuality, his body and life of intimacy. This self-awareness of Jesus is portrayed throughout the gospel stories in his direct, honest and relational ministry to and with women.

I believe that Mary Magdalene and Jesus most likely were a rabbinical married couple, who probably gave birth to one or more children. This has nothing to do with *The Da Vinci Code* or such fiction but is based on common sense relating to what we know as the normal rabbinical custom of marriage and childrearing in ancient Palestine.

Also, the gnostic gospels mentioned above provide several narratives which were widely accepted and used in Christianity throughout the early church for over two hundred years. It is clear from current scholarship that Mary Magdalene was the foremost apostle and leader of the original group of apostles. Stories abound of her close relationship to Jesus as she was attested by the gospels to be the most familiar with Jesus' teachings about the inner life.

I enjoy using these images of the masculine and feminine as lovers within in addition to the reality of the archetypes of the King and Queen because I was raised in a widely dysfunctional household, not a place of familiar peace. Usually chaos was the order of things. Therefore, I find it difficult to relate to the idea of a royal family. In my thinking, the King and Queen and their offspring are God-like. With Jesus and Mary Magdalene, I find an earthy, relational reality in my imagination that works very well when using the energy within from the union of these opposites.

Many years ago, I changed my cognizant consciousness

about the Holy Spirit from a nebulous "Spirit" to the Eastern Orthodox emphasis of "Feminine" gender for the Holy Spirit. As a Protestant Anglican, and the child of a mentally ill and abusive mother, I have had trouble relating to Jesus' mother, Mary, as the Mother of God and the archetype of the feminine spirit she can represent to others. While relating to the Holy Spirit as feminine in essence, I have had no concern at all affirming Mary the Mother of God for others, but for me, it did not work.

In the past decade, after reading the scholarship about Mary Magdalene, I have found the archetype of the Lovers for Jesus and Mary Magdalene within my soul to be very effective and helpful. Perhaps it is my romantic, introverted nature at work. In any case, I find the archetypes of the Lovers in these two historical persons help me in my prayer life, my journaling, and the use of Active Imagination writing for soul work.

What I find helpful is to think of Jesus and Mary Magdalene (in their respective roles as teachers) encouraging one another, sharing information and ideas gleaned from their learning and scholarship. I can imagine them processing what they are learning through their prayer lives together, perhaps their personal journaling and any counseling work that both of them may have done. I can envision them continuing to do these activities in the heavenly, spiritual dimension. When I think of the two of them in this manner, I touch on something very real and primal in my intuition and spiritual core.

How One Might Use the Archetypes of Lover to Deepen Faith

I like to think of Jesus and Mary Magdalene as an intimate husband and wife couple comfortable in their bodies, knowing the soul and body are one. I envision both of them giving and receiving pleasure in their mutual sexual life as deeply committed and happy lovers. I know for some people this may seem far-fetched, but I find this imagery very helpful.

Sometimes I use the imagery found in the Song of Solomon in the Old Testament. It is a collection of five Jewish marriage poems used liturgically long ago in wedding ceremonies. The language of the lovers going down to meet one another in a blossoming garden, the aloe oils, the fragrances, the passion and the deep trust of the lovers makes sense for me as I experientially know the character of Jesus and Mary Magdalene as portrayed in the early gospels. Meditating on these images helps me connect with my own feminine within, a task which has always been difficult to do. Words are then found to describe feelings felt, and I experience a relaxation of tension in my body and a sense of grounded-ness.

When I pray through Jesus to God as my Creator, I find the unity of Jesus and Mary Magdalene within me giving a warmth and human joy in prayer that I have not experienced on a regular basis before. There is the quality of an equal confirmation of the masculine and feminine spiritual energies that help me feel a deeper connection between my mind and my body. The emphasis is not just the lovers and the sexuality that comes with that imagery, but with the deeper sense of both masculine and feminine perspectives bringing truth to one another from different viewpoints, as both Mary Magdalene and Jesus were portrayed as extraordinary teachers in the early church stories.

The sexual energy of the archetypes of the Lovers within is also affirming and healing. Like most Westerners and people raised in Protestant Christianity, there has been very little help from Western spirituality to help with the soul-body split that I have experienced most of my adult and teenage life. Part of this split has been due to the shame-based morality that pervaded my upbringing.

However, the split occurred also because of the heavy emphasis on the mind and the soul, and a terrifying lack of balance between the soul and body. This deep disconnection created health issues and confusion around what is and is not sexually acceptable thought and behavior. I was taught that the soul was most important and the body was certainly secondary, if not an outright obstacle to the growth of the soul. I now know that it was also partially St. Paul's Greek philosophical Stoicism that pervaded his New Testament letters that has so influenced this split in the version of Christianity in which I was raised.

In working with the archetypes of the Lovers within, I have found a greater release and inner freedom that removed the false guilt of shame regarding my body. As my health improved and my soul relaxed and enjoyed more of a sense of the original connection of soul and body, a holistic spirituality has been recreated within me that feels instinctively and intuitively much closer to the original intent of God as I experience God.

In my case this was a reversal of insulin-dependent diabetes and the accompanying obesity. I am currently in my late sixties, the healthiest of my adult life. For more of this personal story, see my book *Hungary: Finding a Place to Call Home: Part One.*

The Lovers are not only about sexuality of course, for they also speak of the joy and comfort of a relaxed intimacy. I encourage the reader to do some serious study of Tantric Spirituality. It is my belief that this Eastern spiritual practice may touch on the reality that Jesus and Mary Magdalene may have experienced together as oriental, first-century lovers and marriage partners. The story in John's gospel Chapter Eleven of Mary kneeling at Jesus' feet in her home with her brother Lazarus and sister Martha, and the caressing of Jesus' feet with her hair in the Gospel of Luke Chapter Seven are good examples of Tantric sexuality between lovers and marriage partners.

At least one of the early church gospel stories talks about the intimate kissing between Jesus and Mary, and of course, true spiritual sexual intimacy would have occurred in complete privacy which no one could have observed in order to write about it! The practicality of Tantric lovemaking is such that the lovers would never have disclosed to their disciples details of their experience, but only taught the concepts and perhaps some instruction of techniques regarding the delicate sensuality of mutual Tantric sexuality.

Mary Magdalene and Jesus Embodying the Archetype of the Teacher

I cannot imagine Jesus and Mary talking about their intimate sexual life with their disciples. Such dialogue would have occurred between the two of them exclusively, that is just common sense.

However, I can imagine each of them in their masculine and feminine perspectives teaching the early Christian followers the basic love, respect, and honoring of sexuality as a beautiful gift from God to them in Creation. In their historical, cultural context, I can imagine Jesus answering sexual questions from his male followers and Mary, doing the same for women seeking greater understanding. The more progressive parts of my imagination can also see Jesus and Mary reversing roles, with each of them answering questions from the opposite sex as well!

I envision that Jesus and Mary Magdalene's teachings might be general in nature, but direct and honest in helping people with practical questions and the desire to be more whole within themselves and in their intimate relationships.

Perhaps the earliest Christians did not suffer from such a soul/body split as modern persons. The spirit of their teaching (helping and healing was part of all the gospel stories) flowing from the character of Jesus and Mary influenced the early church with profundity. There is much for us today to learn from them. The archetypes of the Lovers, using the symbolism and images of Mary Magdalene and Jesus can help us touch on the deeper spiritual realities that lie within our very souls and the cells of our bodies that communicate between one another, as modern-day neurologists have confirmed with their research.

I am very aware that these ideas may seem radical to many readers but I encourage us to have open minds and hearts and to listen to the archetypes of the Lovers within each of us to teach, guide and provide affirmation for our spiritual journeys, both alone and with our intimate partners. Such self-awareness can bring the reality of the body/soul unity into conscious experience which enriches out lives with outstanding health and strength.

I also encourage the reader to research modern biblical studies scholarship about Mary Magdalene and Jesus and come to their own conclusions as to whether or not to use this rich imagery to help in deepening the awareness of God within. I encourage the work of Elaine Pagels, Cynthia Bourgeault, Margaret Starbird, Timothy Freke, Peter Gandy, Dan Burnstein, Arnie J. De Keijzer, Phillip Jenkins, Karen King, and Jean-Yves Leloup, among others, to learn of this lost tradition and how it was suppressed by the institutional church in the third century through to the fifth century.

The Soul Can Integrate the Opposites of Being and Having

There is another important opposite that I believe can be unified in the soul to bring us healing that is portrayed in the symbolism of the Grail story. This is the pair of opposites of Being and Having. Another way to describe these two opposites is the Essence of Life and the Things of Life.

In the Grail story, the quest, the search for the Grail can be described as the search for meaning and Being, while the daily obstacles and challenges Perceval encounters can represent the Having aspects of our outer life. We must live in both spheres; that which is the inner yearning and the outer realities of daily living.

Perceval begins his quest with a completely outer projection of his unconscious desire for meaning in his young life. He wanted to be a knight without even having any idea what this meant. Status, power, competitiveness and prestige were his primary values. He was focused on Having, to the neglect of Being. Only after a lifetime of making horrible mistakes that brought ruin and great sorrow to many other people did he realize his need to change. Fortunately, he was given the grace to see the error of his ways and was transformed by his suffering to become a symbol of wholesome Being as the new Fisher King and Guardian of the Holy Grail.

Laurens van der Post, in his *A Mantis Carol* story, addressed this question of how to live with the tension of these opposites of Being and Having. All of us struggle with this tension, striving to possess a quality of soul and at the same time needing certain things for our lives to be manageable.

In van der Post's dialogue with the woman who came to him with the repetitious dream about a Praying Mantis, the lady exclaimed aloud, "What of Hans [her Bushman house servant in childhood] then? How could he endure life in a place like this [Manhattan, New York City], shut in skyscrapers, apartment rooms in which you can't even open a window because of air-conditioning, elevators, the lot, except while on vacation in the country? Not only did he not die but he thrived on it all. How and why could he do it and the others not?"

Laurens van der Post then reminded her of the duality in the ancient story of Esau and Jacob, the former being *the archetypes of the Hunter gatherer* in Esau and that of *the Husbandman* in Jacob, the in-house, mother's favorite, who tricked his brother out of whatever inheritance and material needs he may have required for his nomadic lifestyle.

Laurens van der Post spoke to her words from one of the wisest of men he had ever know, an old Afrikaner hunter, who described to van der Post the difference between African and European humankind.

"African man, he had said, is; European man has."

He continues his teaching story with the woman:

There I confessed we entered a level of that spirit so deep and subtle that I could only guess at the explanation. I believed profoundly that this great divide in our spirit was brought about as a means for making man a division; that the Esau and Jacob separation was brought about so that two essential elements of the human spirit they personified could be reunited at the end of their roads of separate development in a greater way than before. Union of like and like was conformity and not strength but weakness; union of diversity and of opposites was the only real unity and source of strength.

He felt that the human heart was born a hunter, and our spirit forever nomad, and would remain at war with the husbandman in us until all the hunter personified was given its rightful place again in our reckoning. Hans proved that the hunter could bring as great a compassion as was needed, to reconcile these opposites.

(Van der Post, Laurens. *A Mantis Carol*. Island Press, Washington DC, Covelo, CA, 1975, p.103)

I wish to use this story to not just talk about the obvious tension of opposites of the needs of the inner life versus the outer life, but at the deeper issue of a fear of lack that most people experience regardless of their outer material or financial situation. Both in my own life struggles and listening to the stories of many others in my role as a teacher and a priest, this conflict is something almost every conscious person struggles with and seeks resolution for.

The archetype of the Hunter in the case of the Bushman of the Kalahari Desert held that the only material things needed were the hunting implements, bow, arrow and his knife for butchering. These could be held in one hand. The second material needs of the Hunter were the extremely few religious and magic utensils required for ritual, both corporate within the nomadic group and individual, tucked away at one's side in a small leather pouch.

One might say for Western persons, these few material needs of the modern, nomadic young Hunter might be the backpack, the laptop, and whatever spiritual books one found most helpful such as the *Tibetan Book of the Dead*, the Bible, *The Portable Jung* or perhaps *The Art of Motorcycle Maintenance*! One must choose their own examples.

The more material needs of the Husbandman in the case of the Jacob among us might be a remodeled, efficient kitchen, a garage with a shop for repairs and hobbies, an extended yard with privacy and space as well as a sense of domain.

Or as in the case of many young people I know, today, yearn for the material needs of stable, meaningful work, whether self-employment or as an employee. Many also want the opportunity to own a flat or a house that can build equity and a configuration of friendships to provide social structure and protection in a rapidly changing and often chaotic world.

How do we reconcile these opposites? Most self-help books touch on this subject in a variety of ways, but I would suggest there may be just a few approaches that are common within their advice.

Most suggestions begin with a soul-searching encouragement for us to define what meaningful work is in our particular time and context. This usually means putting the needs of the Husbandman ahead of the needs of the Hunter. This is a very helpful beginning because meaningful vocation may reach not only into our Husbandman needs, but also some of the Hunter needs. Indeed, often these needs are combined in the search for meaningful work.

An important initial individuation task for each of us is to resist either parental or peer pressure to conform to expectations that do not fit one's inner identity regarding vocation. Travel is one means of meeting the needs of the Hunter archetype as new experiences certainly add to our self-awareness and sense of self. Traveling and meeting new people and cultures helps us define who we may think we are, and what we want to become.

Many interesting European young people I know have chosen to put off career and family building to spend years traveling and learning about different cultures, and in turn, learning much about themselves that will be helpful later in life.

But when is enough, enough? Whether it be exciting travels, new experiences, or enough material goods to create a comforting and comfortable sense of place that works for us?

I would venture to suggest that the story of Hans may provide a possible suggestion as to which path may help us find peace sooner than later. That would be the focus on the simplicity of the Hunter first, and then incorporating the needs of the Husbandman, cultivator, farmer, building of place, second.

Why in this order?

I suggest this for several reasons. It has been my observation that young people who focus on material gain to get a foothold on the things that they feel are needed, the car, the living space, the work environment needed to produce the income for these necessities, generally end up in midlife with some regrets at not having spent enough time, energy and resources in the realm of the hunter first.

This may be because the inner needs of spirit when met earlier in life may provide enough guidance as to "what may be enough" when it comes to the time of acquisition of things. It may be more of an inner-directing-outer movement which seems to work the best.

My work as a priest has shown me that the opposite approach does not work very well. Like Jacob, whose name means conniver (trickster or con man) and whose early life was riddled with conflict, fear and dread, many people arrive at midlife with huge questions regarding their intrinsic value. Some people who are honest with themselves find a deep sense of regret that they didn't put the needs of the spiritual life first, learning to trust in the Provider of life for the needs of the nomadic hunt. Many people find they have to learn all over again at a later stage in life either through a gut-wrenching emotional loss, a financial collapse, a health crisis, or a relational train wreck. They discover they have to take the time and energy to start over and discover who they are and how they want to live the rest of their lives.

This is not an either/or proposition, it is not black and white. The youthful Hunter who constantly is making vocational changes looking for greener pasture, caught up in the excitement of travel and new adventures often finds themself in a place of regret that they did not settle down as Husbandman earlier. There is nothing sadder it seems that an old hippie who is still caught up in the eternal youth archetype now in later life finding themselves dependent on the financial and emotional generosity of family members or friends to survive.

Likewise, the domesticated Jacob one often finds life sterile, void of creativity and zest due to an unbalanced focus on security. We can address both needs simultaneously but this takes great consciousness.

I believe the key to this journey is the concept in the Grail story whereby Perceval was not required to have an answer to the primeval question of "For whom does the Grail serve?" but was mandated simply to ask the question. Perhaps we can move forward in reconciling the opposites of Being and Having by continually asking the question ourselves, "What is my purpose at this moment in time? Whom am I serving, ego or the deeper Self?" When we develop the habit of asking this question frequently, we learn to hold fast to that which is needed outwardly and can let go of the striving for outward resolution when it is appropriate. We can learn to trust this process as a way of life.

Christ had these words for us, "Do not be anxious for tomorrow. Your Father knows you have need of all these things. Put first the Kingdom [asking the question of the Grail] and all will be added to you."

I have found in my life that what was needed outwardly was provided. I was required to trust and let go of what I thought was needed, and to accept what came to me with trust that it was more than enough. As a young man I struggled with these issues greatly; raising a family and providing a home for them. But in retrospect I did not trust enough and was often filled with a sense of angst and dread because I felt I was not measuring up to some undefined measure of success, and of not having achieved the necessary goal.

As an older man I wish now that I had worked far less when I was younger and had more energy to be present with my family while the children were small. I also wish I had made more time and energy for my own solitude and self-nurture. I know now that the striving I carried within was unnecessary, a burden I did not need to carry. We had more than enough at all times, especially the moments when it felt that our needs were not being met. I know now that the most necessary needs were met then in ways I could not see at the time but in retrospect, can see clearly.

Chapter Six

Balancing the Need for Stability of Outer and Inner Needs Is Essential for Our Healing

So what is the answer concerning outer and inner balance? I would suggest that somehow we stay aware of these opposites and not come down with both feet in one department or another with a sense of permanence. Perhaps there is a way for our souls to keep us open to the possibilities of the unknowns of the Hunter journey, and at the same time, *allow an intuitive dance to guide us* to make the stable place that we need for the necessities we find ourselves wanting.

This is one reason I encourage young people to not commit to marriage and creating a family with the responsibilities of raising children until they have had a decade or two under their belts as a Hunter "out in the desert." The wisdom one can bring from that journey can empower the partnering and parenting of the nesting to help create a non-static environment that contains both the stability of the Husbandman and the excitement of the Hunter archetype.

The Grail story has two beautiful things to say about this dilemma. First, Perceval only had to ask the question "For whom does the Grail serve?" This is the inner awareness question of the Hunter asking the Universal question regarding purpose and destiny. The King was healed, the whole kingdom was restored and the outer was born anew after the proper Hunter-question was asked, *the inner hunger dance*, was danced by Perceval, "For whom does the Grail serve?"

Second, the Grail provides nourishment from its vast resources and heals the intuitive wound of the Fisher King. This is followed by the larger healing and renewed prosperity of the kingdom. *Inward to outward* seems to be the best motion and movement of this dance.

Being aware of both the Hunter and the domestic simultaneously within us may be the key to overall progress and not coming down on one side or the other. The Hunter question is asked first, followed by the domestic question. We ask first, "Whom do we serve? Then we can confidently ask, "What is it that we need?"

This teaching is found in this New Testament story of Jesus. When antagonists tried to trap him in publically saying something against the ruling class by asking him the deceptive, either/or question, is it lawful (meaning allowed by Jewish civic and religious duty) to pay the Roman taxes, he responded by saying, "Hand me a coin." They gave him a Roman coin. He held it up in front of them and asked them, "Whose inscription is on this?" They answered, "Caesar's."

Jesus, knowing their intent to entrap him, replied and turning the coin around showing the inscription on each side proclaimed, "Give unto Caesar what is Caesar's, and to God, what is God's." This is another way to talk about meeting the needs of the inner Hunter and the outer Husbandman. Differentiation, using our conscious intuition is a path forward through balance to meet both needs. The soul is more than capable of providing this intuitive knowledge if we are willing and quiet enough to listen to our inner voice. It is not an either/or dilemma, it is a both/and opportunity.

In this statement Jesus provides us a methodology for dealing with this predicament and tension of opposites. He suggests keeping the archetypal needs separate, and not mixing the two of them together. Not mixing, but listening to them with differentiation.

What do I mean by this? Let me give a few examples.

The Mixing of Archetypes, Catastrophic Wounding of the Soul

One of the greatest tragedies of modern life is the mixing of archetypes that represent inner and outer needs of the human spirit and soul. For illustration, unconscious people project their lack of inner freedom outwardly onto society and demand that others conform to their ideas of a cultural norm.

In my own country of the United States, fundamentalist Christians, unaware of their own inner turmoil and insecurities, are now acting desperately to feel some control in the unconscious aspects of their lives. Many are trying to force their religious dictates on the rest of society creating untold oppression, cruelty and extreme hypocrisy. This is a mixing of the outer and inner archetypes, or one could say, a mixing of the Hunter focused on spiritual freedom and the Husbandman focused on material gain and stability in outer life.

Keeping the archetypal needs separate within the soul creates room for growth, health and movement forward to new creativity and solutions. We cannot control what the wider population is doing but we can try to control whatever mixing we may be doing unconsciously within our own souls. But the question remains how does the soul do this redemptive work of integrating without mixing the opposites of life as we experience them? I will take a look at this phenomenon in the next section.

How does the soul integrate the opposites?

Before we begin to look at *how* the soul processes this integration of opposites providing us a way to live and utilize the creative tension between them, let's look at some of the more common opposites we experience and then try to apply what we have learned to understanding how we can experience vitality from their integration.

Here is a partial list of opposites that I encounter within myself and have observed that people struggle with in my counseling work. I will later discuss the ones that seem most prevalent and in need of reconciliation and balance.

A List of Opposites that the Soul Can Balance because of Its Feminine Vessel Qualities

Body and Mind

Left- and Right-Brain Intelligence

Extrovert and Introvert

Judgment and Process, Making Decisions Quickly or More Slowly

Intuition and Sensing (getting information from within by intuition or outwardly through the Five Senses)

Thinking and Feeling. Analytical Objectivity and Inner Valuing Feeling

Feminine and Masculine Characteristics

Being Competitive or Relational

Spending or Saving Energy, Money, Time

Controlling and Letting Go

Trust and Fear

Faith and Doubt

Wealth and Fear of Poverty

Ego Inflation and Low Self Image

Sexual Interaction and Abstinence from Sexual Activity

Stoicism and Self-Nurturing

Honesty and Denial (denial is believing and living a lie)

Wordiness and Conversational Silence

Immersion in Relational Activities and Solitude

Feeling Connected with Others and Disconnecting

Independent Thinking and Collective Thinking

Independent Action and Codependent Action

Work and Leisure

Known and Unknown

Sacred and Profane

Creation and Destruction

Beginning and End
Mother and Daughter
Father and Son
Parent and Child
The Role of Spender and that of Earner
Joy and Despair

What are we to do with these opposites? I would suggest first that we continue the list with our own words for opposites we encounter both in our outer and inner life. Then maybe we can each pick a few and work with them reflectively, as language is very personal and the opposites described above may not fit what the reader feels. *Therefore, individuating the language is a first step.*

Next, in order to understand for ourselves how our souls integrate opposites we can pick one or two examples from our personal list that we feel are currently being integrated and are no longer a source of anxiety for us. Then we can look back and ask ourselves how did these opposites first make themselves known to us, what problems did we experience because of them, and finally, how did the conflict get resolved and what energy was provided for us that helped us grow and become more the person we feel called to be?

The Grail story does not give us specifics about how the soul integrates opposites but I want to make a few suggestions from the story that hopefully will be helpful.

The nature of the mythological Grail itself may give us a few clues. One of the older German versions of the Grail says that the Grail is a spherical stone with all-seeing eyes able to give and receive sustenance in all directions. Other versions change the shape but keep the substance of stone, changing it to the vessel-container bowl.

Stone signifies that which is basic, natural, authentic and original. In thinking about the nature of the soul we might trust that it is naturally versatile and able to give and receive sustenance both without and within, from all directions, and with all positive influences. Being stone means it is matter (from Latin *materia*, from which something is made) and intrinsic to our nature, not something we have to create. Stone as symbol is basic to what is. The spherical or cup shape both retain the relationship nature of the circle; equal distances between sides perhaps signifying balance, integrity, awareness and equality; a lack of one-sidedness.

Another aspect of the Grail as spherical stone is that duality is not the nature of the soul. Many religious persons talk as if our lives are a continual battle of two equal forces of Light and Darkness, Good and Evil. I personally do not find this to be true. Yes, there is a very real dark evil in the spiritual realm, but no, I do not experience it as a duality. It is more like a child who has his head down flailing his arms at the air, not realizing that the fight is over and his victorious opponent has walked away unscathed.

The Grail does not do battle. It is profuse with abundant grace, sustenance, utterly inexhaustible, fully flowing over with mystery and knowledge in all directions for all time without ending. It is eternal.

Likewise, the soul. Yes, the soul can be hurt, but healing is not only possible, it is predictable and inevitable. In many ways one could say the soul is invincible. The only thing that can slow down its growth and maturity is the believing of *lies*. Thus, the darkness pushes hard on that angle, asserting itself hard to convince and persuade with lies and deception. But when truth comes forth in momentum, the lies evaporate and their total powerlessness is exposed. Evil is always on the defense unaware that the battle was over before it even began. More about this in a future chapter.

Other versions of the story state that the nature of the Grail, while continuing in its vessel form, is created from wood or clay, again, natural materials. Only later stories describe the Grail as a jewel encrusted, perhaps, human worked, metal with a numinous glow that emanates the abundance of its divine character. Thus, earlier versions retain the idea of naturalness being intrinsic to the Grail and, thus, in my opinion, the soul has this circular nature which can give and receive that which nourishes it. I like to think of this primeval nourishment as complete, unadulterated Love.

As we think of how our souls can integrate the opposites we feel within, *I would suggest that we let go of the notion that this integration is something that we do.* Instead it may be helpful to see that this ability of the bringing together of opposites is a gift from God in our creation. It is in our very nature to be able to do this.

I do not use the word *grace* because most people think of grace as a gift from outside ourselves. Instead, we can think of the ability to integrate the opposites as a given within, as opposed to a gift from without. For some others, the use of the word *grace* may fit.

Perhaps our conscious act is simply to be aware of this reality and affirm it as opposed to thinking we must act in a certain way. From this awareness there may be a need for us to take some action revealed by our intuition, some change of behavior or thought. However, at our core, we need not strive, but rest and reside in the ability to reconcile that which is our true nature.

I would also suggest that the reconciling is both a balancing motion and a dance. We can think of the sphere again, a movement of intuition that brings that which is above, to the below, that which is to the right, to the left, that which is outer, to inner, and that which is at steep angles to lesser degrees.

Perhaps the integration is not just a meeting together at a central point, *as it is an energy that keeps things in a balanced orbital movement*, bringing into the forefront and view that which is needed at any particular moment and keeping that which needs to reside in the distance within reach, so that each aspect of the opposites is present and available to be utilized when needed by our consciousness.

How Psychological Projection May Cause a Mixing of Opposites of Outer and Inner Issues

C. G. Jung partially described psychological projection as the following:

> Just as we tend to assume that the world is as we see it, we naïvely suppose that people are as we imagine them to be.... All the contents of our unconscious are constantly being projected into our surroundings, and it is only by recognizing certain properties of the objects as projections or images that we are able to distinguish them from the real properties of the objects.... We always see our own un-avowed mistakes in our opponent.
>
> Excellent examples of this are to be found in all personal quarrels. Unless we are possessed of an unusual degree of self-awareness we shall never see through our projections but must always succumb to them, because the mind in its natural state presupposes the existence of such projections. It is the natural and given thing for unconscious contents to be projected.
> (Jung, C. G. *General Aspects of Dream Psychology*, C. G. Jung Collected Works 8, p. 507)

Projection happens when we are unaware of aspects of our unconscious and we project them outwardly to other people, situations and circumstances. The first key in removing projection is to realize that we are doing it. This in itself can help.

I would venture to say that all outward projection is an inner issue for us. If we are constantly in turmoil because of constant injustice that we see in the world, we may be listening to an inner unjust critical voice. The key here is to find out what we are tormented by within, confront and correct it, and create justice for ourselves with the reality of God's unconditional love and forgiveness. We can recommit ourselves to self-affirmation where it is needed. This does not mean we become desensitized to the injustices we know exist in the outer world; quite the contrary. Determining inward justice for ourselves allows us to see the outward injustice for what it is and find a means to do something about it without losing our equilibrium.

The key also may be awareness and a sense of fluidity regarding outer and inner conflicts. If divine motion is required of the opposites, perhaps our role is to restrict judgment and to trust the inner dance and do our best not to interrupt the fusion and energy of the outer and inner conflicts we are experiencing. We can trust our intuition to tell us when the energy is ready for us to use in thought and deed.

One of the hardest things for me is to trust my own intuition and instinct as these skills were shamed early in life by parents, Little League coaches, and school and Sunday school teachers. To be my own parent and teacher within is one of the greatest challenges I face. What has helped me in experiencing the dance of opposites has been to first heal my shame. I do this by writing my personal history, remembering all the incidents of shame that I can recall, then speaking to my child within and proclaiming protection, freedom and affirmation of the child by my mature, adult self. This exercise helps me to relax in spirit and sink my soul down into my body. In that place of rest, I feel the letting go of the struggle to perform and to appease others. Most of all I let go of my self-expectations that are so destructive to my inner being.

I have had many experiences of shaming in my work as a parish priest, sometimes by authoritative, bully-type bishops, sometimes by colleagues and people who attended my churches.

Often people who have had positions of power in their business lives but have never dealt with their personal unhappiness, use churches and other nonprofit organizations as places to assert themselves in order to attempt to feel more powerful than they really are. These parishioners may have worked in positions of social prominence, primary school teachers, middle management bankers, middle ranked military retirees, and sometimes medical doctors. Until I learned to recognize and deflect their unhappiness, I often felt shamed by their criticism, or condescending attitudes.

I've learned that my angry response to such people is useless in dealing with unconscious people and each time I have allowed myself to act out my feelings of anger in this way I have regretted it later. Regarding current politics where fascism is rampant around the globe especially in my native country of the United States, I can work myself into a frenzy of anxiety, toxic hatred and animosity that poisons my entire outlook.

I am learning now to see the bullying and abuse of current politics as an outer issue that pushes my buttons, which is another way to describe my inner realities. I have learned to speak to my inner child and remind him that I will always take care of him, that he is safe within my soul. This attention to the inner self allows the differentiation needed between outer and inner and the peace of God which has always existed and is now able to be experienced. I can continue to stay informed of political realities without creating undue anxiety. I do not mix the outer information about world politics with my inner tendency towards self-incrimination.

I remonstrate that the focus I use to nurture the frightened child within does not take great effort, but instead takes a type of addition by subtraction. I move forward in inner peace, addition, then by subtraction, reflect within and find the rest that is already there in my soul because of God's innate presence and love.

There Is a Conscious Type of Mixing of Opposites that Brings Life and Not Death to the Soul

Another symbol of the Grail is its bowl shape, indicative of the soul's ability to be stirred not to confuse, but to integrate that which may seem contrary. Our independent nature often is afraid of the chaos of stirring. Yet I suspect our very nature given in Creation is very comfortable with the integration of opposites. However, our ego like a fishbowl stirred, is fearful of such integration until the stirring is allowed to settle like sand disturbed in a fishbowl, and we can see our inner gold again with clarity and certainty. From this clarity we can take the appropriate action. For more information about the imagery and symbolism of the bowl, I refer the reader to Sue Bender's book *Everyday Sacred*.

Rainer Maria Rilke wrote of this comfort with mixing reality and the longing of the human soul to trust. He spoke of the great freedom and love that comes with such trust. In one of his first poems in the series, *Book of Hours: Love Poems to God*, he writes about the presupposed opposites of the present moment and the future, creative possibilities that intuitive people know and experience.

I believe in all that has never yet been spoken,
I want to free what waits within me
So that what no one has dared to wish for
May for once spring clear without my contriving.

If this is arrogant, God forgive me,
But this is what I need to say.
May what I do flow from me like a river,
No forcing and no holding back,
The way it is with children.

Then in these swelling and ebbing currents,
These deepening tides moving out, returning,
I will sing you as no one ever has,

Streaming through widening channels into the open sea.

(Macy, Joanna and Barrows, Anita. *Rilke's Book of Hours: Love Poems to God*. Riverhead Books, NY, 1996)

Rilke was raised by a mentally ill, religious-zealot mother, and a weak, strict, and immature father. His older sister died soon after he was born and his parents raised him as a girl to replace the dead sister. He was dressed, groomed and treated as a little girl until, at age thirteen his father decided Rainer was too effeminate and sent him to the most macho military academy in Prague.

Once there he was bullied unmercifully by the other boys. When beaten by the other students, he would lay in a ball on the floor repeating incessantly the Our Father or Hail Mary prayers aloud. He spent most of his time in the infirmary during his stay in the academy until after nearly two years, his father relented and he was brought home. He studied at home with tutors then went on to university to excel in social relationships and in writing, publishing his first poetry at age seventeen.

He was a highly intelligent, sensitive, and immature young man, who did what he could to make his way as the first Czech to earn his full livelihood as a poet. He became attached to a much older woman, a Russian countess, with the permission of her platonic husband of senior years. Her name was Lou Andreas-Salomé. With her, he traveled to Russia and was deeply influenced by Russian Orthodoxy. His poetry matured as his soul did likewise and yet his work was rarely known outside of Europe until the late twentieth century.

In much of his intimate poetry related to his inner life, Rilke used the imagery of vegetative growth to describe spiritual progress and his abiding love of nature. The above poem shows his yearning for authentic living coming from his strong desire to live his life fully. A famous book translated from the German into English and published by Norton and Company is *Letters to a Young Poet*. In it he stressed the importance of staying open and living with the tension of the opposites, finding in them questions that one must ask in order to participate fully in divine life, knowing the answers may come, if at all, only late in life.

His writing reminds me of much of the Grail myth, especially his insistence that we ask the unanswerable questions and wait patiently, just as Perceval had to ask the right question, not knowing if there would be an answer, and through the asking, brought the freedom and healing that was needed. I highly recommend *Letters to a Young Poet* to all young people as a guideline how to be patient with all that has not yet been revealed to them about meaning and life purpose.

In *the swelling and ebbing currents* in the poem quoted above, we find similar imagery to the dance of opposites within the soul and the soul's ability to not only withstand the tension created, but thrive in it, arriving at the freedom of *the open sea* within the soul.

The need for waiting is a feminine quality and necessity. As Irene Claremont de Castillejo wrote in her famous book, *Knowing Woman: A Feminine Psychology*:

It was Mrs. Jung who drew the dreamer's attention to the importance of the waiting room. They had often talked together of waiting as an essential positive quality of the feminine. The masculine side which is busy with active achievement but I believe that every woman if she looks deep enough will find that the essential core of her is waiting.
(de Castillejo, Irene Claremont. *Knowing Woman: A Feminine Psychology*. Shambala, Boston. 1990, p. 178)

I would add that the feminine in men must adhere to the same task of waiting patiently as well, as Rilke instructed the young poet.

How much do we control what happens within the soul regarding the movement of these swelling and ebbing currents that move us forward? I am not a fatalist, nor do I believe in reincarnation simply because as a system of justice I think it is incredibly unjust, and I don't view life that way.

Christianity, and in fact, almost all major world religions place much emphasis upon the will as a determining factor in spiritual growth. When I was a young man, I held to this tenet strenuously, but now as an older person I am much looser.

While I see people often making very poor choices I feel anger and pain that they do not make wiser ones. Yet of course I also know personally the fear of facing the unknown, and the courage it takes to overcome it.

One idea that has materialized for me with strength is the concept, again based on my experience, that not only is there an indefinable power moving us towards wholeness (which I will address later in the book) but I believe buried deeply beneath the despair we often feel is a guiding Presence, of Something, or more importantly and subtly, a *Someone*.

Laurens van der Post describes this indelible presence in *The Face by the Fire* as:

A dream within a dream, a face by the fire in the midst of us, which guides us in our sleep, a love-to-be of a face-to-come like thread of Ariadne's gold wound between the trees of the labyrinthine wood. The gleam of virgin gold had never failed. Through great creeper-entwined trunks of trees, in dark air troubled with bats' wing and serpents' hiss there was always flame of fire on slimy, protozoic waters.

Rilke wrote of the same reality again in his *Book of Hours*:

When gold is in the mountain and we've ravaged the depths until we've given up digging,

It [gold] will be brought forth into Day by the River that mines the Silences of stone.

We can ask, "What is this gold, this thread of gold that the mystics speak lying within the human soul?"

My mentor John A. Sanford often repeated his belief that our "gold" lay within our shadow. By gold, Jack meant that which is truly our best attribute, our treasure. In the final pages of *The Faces by the Fire*, van der Post speaks of the thread of gold being the essence of human divinity in complete accord and unity with God. He named this essence within us eternal, unconditional, triumphant *Love*.

Similarly, St. Paul wrote in his letter to the Corinthian Greek church long ago that Love was the one reality that endured forever and was most valued. I think Paul might agree that Love is not valued because of what it gives to us but what Love makes of us and through us, when we hold Love up as the highest endeavor and value, that which ultimately gives us true meaning and purpose. I believe it is the reality of Love that is our gold, buried deep within the hard rock of our own life mystery, which is brought up by the continual movement of God's Spirit, the Internal River of Life.

Many years ago, I had an experience that touched me to my core. I, like everyone I knew, was prone to perfectionism, self-criticism and recrimination. I struggled most days to keep my spirit "above water." I was rector of a large church which had hired me to bring in new young families, as it was an older, large, but regressing congregation. I did my best to make changes that could help younger people but each step forward, was sabotaged backwards by the status quo. A few politically powerful older members acted threatened, and some of these shrill people were those who had actually hired me to bring about the changes.

The entire three-year experience was a toxic battlefield work environment. My self-image was basically destroyed. Day after day, month after month, I would find anonymous, unsigned notes shoved under my office door complaining and attacking each and every talk I gave and each new direction I suggested to move the stuck congregation forward. I did not have the emotional maturity to withstand the daily onslaught against my integrity. After a while the feelings of failure and dread at having to face such toxicity on a daily basis deepened into a clinical depression. My medical doctor told me frankly that if I didn't get out the stress would kill me by a massive stroke or heart attack within three to six months. He made it clear he was not exaggerating.

So, I told my bishop I needed to quit. Then I told the congregation. The antagonists were delighted. The majority of the congregation eventually left the parish as the destructiveness in the ethos of the congregation was obvious and the guilt was strong for many. For me emotionally there was no feeling of relief, just a deadening dullness combined with a fear that I would never recover my sense of self. I felt that I was basically worthless as a priest, and probably, as a human being as well.

At this low point, feeling like I could not feel or hear anything positive in my spirit again, I heard a distinct thought; like a still, strong voice from within, and my intuition knew the voice was God. One could say the gold was still in the mountain and was coming up to daylight for a slight moment so I could see and hear it clearly. The thought was:

Peter, there is no judgment in God, only Love.

These words carried me through the year of clinical depression to the decision to leave parish ministry and to do what I loved best, teaching people who wanted to hear what I had to say, and to write books for others who wanted to read what I wrote. This, plus using my music to enhance the teaching, became the focus of my recovery from the deep grief I felt, helping me enter a new time of richer ministry, teaching, spiritual direction counseling and doing what I do best, innovation.

I would do intense, scholastic research on this topic of judgment: theological, psychological, sociological, and mythological and others, and discover that the words I heard were true. God does not judge us, we judge ourselves. Whatever true judgment occurs, it comes from within us through lightness and forbearance. It comes as needed to help us turn around and find who we were really were meant to be. *In place of judgment, what I discovered was the presence of an uncompromising, ever present Love.*

I am so thankful for this revelation, and each year I learn to trust this truth more. Each time I am faced with feeling like a failure, not good enough, smart enough, loving enough, the word comes back to me that there is no judgment. What remains is the invitation to accept the reality that before all things, beside all things, behind all things, above all things, and below all things is Love. Life is as simple and profound as this.

Chapter Seven

Love Is Behind All Reality

How can we trust this idea that Love is behind all things? I have only an incomplete answer. Perhaps the opposite is too hard, to choose not to trust or to believe that the universe is simply vacant of purpose, that we are the product of pure, random chance? But this goes against all that the most modern physicists and other disciplinary scientists are learning. There is purpose in the chaos of the universe. The perceptive natural scientists repeatedly are reminding us of this great truth.

But I am not a scientist, only an observer and doctor of the soul. To this certainty of Love, I come not by belief but by experience, which generates my small trust and grows it in ways I cannot quite understand.

The primary place I experience this Love is in my dreams. The third-century Greek-Christian apologist Tertullian wrote, "Dreams are the voice of God." I have discovered this is true not only for me but for the many people I have worked with in spiritual direction over the years.

The best form of inner work that I have known has been to honor and learn God's symbolic language speaking to us in the dream. This discipline has given me the most rewarding affirmation of Love I have ever experienced.

Many years ago, I was at a large conference on the East coast of the United States. John Sanford, Robert Johnson and Morton Kelsey were the speakers. Someone in the audience asked Dr. Kelsey how a person could know God's direction for their life. I have never forgotten his practical and astute answer. "One must pay attention to one's dreams, journal their reflections and spend adequate time in prayer." I have found this simple answer to be most fulfilling and accurate for myself and many others with whom I have worked in counseling and direction.

But I am often reminded of the great truth spoken by the most influential people in my life, most of whom I have known only through their written words. This is the truth that change does not come about collectively until it first happens internally and individually. C. G. Jung, in a famous BBC interview was asked during the Cold War of the late 1950s shortly before his death:

"Dr. Jung, do you think we in Western Civilization will make it?"

Jung leaned back in his chair, smiled a beautiful smile, then leaned in towards the British interviewer and said:

"If enough individuals do their inner work, yes, we will make it."

The Hungarian theologian László Boros wrote a similar statement *from another* spiritual perspective. In his book, *Being a Christian Today*:

The upheaval caused by the Gospel [of Christ] aims at the conversion of individuals, and only in second place at a transformation of the social, economic and political order. Revolution on the part of Christians comes from within, not from without, from above, not from below. It is non-violent without bloodshed. Hitherto we have certainly been too prone to regard Christianity as something conservative and preservative. But in reality, the teaching of Christ is capable at any time of suspending the privileges of family, nation, rank, education or property in favor of the commandment of love.
(Boros, Ladislaus. *Being a Christian Today*. The Seabury Press, NY, 1979. p. 9)

When I was in middle school, I made a project to read every biography and autobiography available in the school and city libraries where I lived. There were about two hundred such books. One thing I took away from this adventure was the fact that the most valuable changes in society happen because individuals acting within their own conscious, take seriously their own small sphere of influence as enough to work singularly for change. They did not wait for others to tell them what to do. They listened to their own inner guidance and tested it in action, leading to new solutions to persistent problems.

Mother Teresa of Calcutta, founder of the Sisters of Mercy organization, was often quoted as saying, "Don't wait for leaders, do it alone. Begin with one."

This action that we must take alone is the act of living out the Love that we have within the soul. This release of Love by individuals is what makes the difference and why there is always hope for the future.

Laurens van der Post wrote in *A Mantis Carol*:

The idea that there were intellectual, willful, short cuts to any real change for the better was one cause of the barbarism and violence of our time.... Individual examples determine the rate of change. This is why the crucifixion of Jesus haunts us still, we need to recover a love as complete. The crucifixion is in front of us, not behind in history, we have not yet caught up with it.

The collective thinking of our time is impersonal and demands a below average conformity to shallowness. The collective pressure we feel is dehumanizing, putting the needs of institutions above the people the institutions are to serve. By institutions I do not mean just universities, churches, and governments, but also media influences and social pressures, especially family and marital expectations.

These institutions often put forth a paralyzing generalization of all things which removes the life-giving differences of diversity and individual creativity. The collective of our time hides the terrible truth in fragmented oppression, that the leaders of such institutions that demand such blind loyalty are dispirited, broken and unloved selves underneath the veneer of their positions of power.

It is not the collective that brings about real change but the individual, because this Love at the core of all things cannot be known at the deepest level of need in a corporate fashion. A gathering of people may experience a collective euphoria in an event with great emotion and energy, but change from this experience is always enacted individually. The collective, because its focus is maintaining power, cannot get beyond the emotive event and summaries of it with their words to get to the core of the Love that all persons seek to be affirmed. Thus, the leaders cannot lead and the followers have no desire to follow.

I read the other day a post on Facebook speaking about this question. A woman with a background in educational studies asked the question, "Is it okay to be a charismatic leader? Why do we always get disappointed in the charismatic leaders, of whom all eventually disappoint, fail, or self-destruct?"

I was reminded of van der Post stating that as the turn of the twenty-first century came, he felt the day of leaders was past. They simply did not exist any longer, mostly because they were no longer needed. He said that each of us must be our own leader and that those people who chose this most difficult, lonely path, would somehow find one another and build a new type of community that would not vie for power and position, but would simply affirm and continue to move forward in a mutual individuality toward the common good.

I sense there is a great distrust in many institutions for God to work in the life of the individual and I think this distrust starts with each of us, we do not trust our inner self. This must change, because this is the only way it can happen. We need to find and use for our own healing the Love that dwells within us.

Only then can we move outwardly.

Laurens van der Post wrote in *A Mantis Carol* that individual love opens up the collective. One person begins and the universe conforms to it. Individual love opens the collective to love and submission to this great law of Nature, that Love is before, behind, above, beneath and on each side of all things.

I would suggest that individual love is like a wedge that opens the crack in the door of the collective, and slowly, without injury, but perhaps with the pain of loving confrontation and consciousness, the collective yields to the love from the individual source, just as the crucifixion was a wedge in the darkness and eventually brought a great lasting Light that has never been diminished.

Not only does individual love open a door to collective changes, it can and does arrest the cancerous spread of impersonal, conformist, collective obsessions, with no lives of their own except that which is parasitical.

It is my educated guess that our souls are so individual that allowing a collective mindset or conformity onto our inner creativity squashes the deepest place of true knowledge within us: the place of gnostic knowing. Perhaps the soul, while it can reconcile opposites, does not honor the collective conformity because the soul does not think of the collective as an opposite to our individuality, but experiences the collective as an archetypal Antagonist to true spirituality?

It has been my experience in working with people who are in earnest of spiritual growth that when they conform to a collective expectation to the exclusion of being truthful to themselves, without exception, they experience a diminishing of creativity and vitality. It simply doesn't work. I don't think it is because they are rebelling or immature. I think there is something basic to the nature of the soul that collective conformity is antithetical to spiritual growth.

Jesus taught his followers that they are known individually

and uniquely by God. Jesus taught all his supporters to address God as Abba, or intimate father. He said that even the hairs of their head are numbered, which can mean minute details about their personal bodies are fully embodied in the consciousness of God. In much mythology worldwide the hairs of the head have also been understood as the thoughts of the individual unconscious, the hairs grow without our knowing. Perhaps this was also the meaning of Jesus' words regarding God's knowledge of "the hairs of the head being numbered."

Jesus taught that all persons are extremely valuable and cherished. He taught this by embracing children whom his disciples wanted to dismiss as being unimportant for the attention of the teacher. More than once he picked up a child, placed him or her on his lap and then taught from the seated position, the posture of the teacher with authority. He then spoke saying unless his disciples become like a little child in trust and honesty, they could not enter the kingdom of God. He taught that if we as human parents have the wisdom and knowledge to give good and beautiful gifts of food, clothing, shelter and unmerited kindness to our children, how much more God gives loving goodness and kindness, God's Holy Spirit, to all of us.

The individuality of the human being was also shown in how Jesus discerned how energy passed from his body to others, or the energy of people passed into his physique. We see in the gospel story of the dense crowd pushing in on Jesus from every side, that a woman who had been hemorrhaging for years crawled through the crowd on her knees and touched not even his skin, but his garment. Jesus felt the energy in his body transfer out to heal the body of the woman. He stopped walking in the crowd and asked his disciples, "Who touched me?" They replied, "How can you ask who touched you? Everyone is pressing hard up against you, how can we answer your question when so many are touching you?"

Yet he remained still until the woman, realizing that she was recognized by the teacher, spoke up (putting her life in danger as the Mosaic Law said such a hemorrhaging woman in public should immediately be stoned to death) and said it was she herself that touched him. He raised her head to look at him squarely, beheld her in the eyes and said, "Woman go in peace you are healed of your illness."

Jesus constantly affirmed the individuality of the body and the soul in his teachings and his actions.

Perhaps this is why the collective is so alien to our souls that collective appeasement cannot happen. Maybe what is required of us is a conscious categorization of outer persona and inner authenticity as a way to manage the collective outwardly and consciously. But I suggest that the collective either cannot or should not be integrated within because of its innate destructive, minimizing spirit and quality that ignores who we really all are in our individuality and beauty. The collective always seems to diminish our uniqueness, not confirm it.

If we are involved in an institution of some kind, a marriage, a business, a church, a nonprofit or a government organization, let us seek how to use our positions and power to affirm individual creativity. Certainly, we can use our own creativity to encourage this in others.

Corporations are learning that it strengthens their profit margins to encourage and support their people to problem-solve on their own, not telling them what to do. Smart business leaders are asking people questions about what they see in their roles at work and what they want to accomplish and how they want to reach their goals. Business leadership teams are discovering the strength that deepening trust between team members brings, and then encouraging team dialogue with conflict so that everyone knows they are heard and honored. Then instead of a conforming, diminishing push for consensus, a vote can be taken, a decision made and people, who have had their opinions heard can buy into the decision and move forward. In the case of a tie the primary leader must make the pivotal vote so the decision is made.

A wonderful resource to learn how to apply this individualization focus within a business team of people is Patrick Lencioni's workbook, *Overcoming the Five Dysfunctions of a Team*.

One of the most successful leaders of a church of all time is the Korean David Yonggi Cho an Assembly of God Denominational leader in Seoul. When he realized that his apprentice pastors under his leadership were copying his style of communication, Bible teaching and pastoral care, he called them together and asked them not to follow his style but to discover their own.

Cho was not highly educated or sophisticated in a Western viewpoint, but he is very self-educated and excellent at what he does because he recognized and valued the uniqueness of each person even in the midst of the hugely conformist culture of Korean tradition. His church grew to over half a million members. I do not agree completely with Cho's, perhaps, rigid use of Scripture, but in this principle of leadership, his encouragement of individual creativity is remarkable biblically and practically effective! In many ways he himself is equally extraordinary. His pastors took him at his word, used their own intuition, common sense and experience to solve problems and create new opportunities for growth within their spheres of influence. As a result, the bottleneck created by their imitation of Cho was removed and the church congregation grew phenomenally as each pastor used their unique individual creativity.

Jungian analyst and writer Robert Johnson, while doing his therapy with Emma Jung and later, Toni Wolf in Switzerland, was told by Carl Jung that Johnson was the most extreme introvert Jung had ever met. As a warning Jung cautioned him to never join a group, as such a practice could injure his soul immeasurably. Johnson would go on to discover this was true. Each time he went against this advice, due to the external pressure he felt to be part of a larger collective grouping or from his own longing to belong, he would get sick until he removed his participation or membership.

I don't think this just because Johnson was an introvert. I think it suggests that Johnson, like all of us, needed so to affirm his individuality that joining any group was contrary to his spiritual health and the self-awareness of his own beauty. Somehow his awareness of his own gifts and unique spirit would be minimized by any collective association. Thus, he remained a loner. While he developed several very close friendships with both men and women, he never married. I wonder if this same danger to our self-awareness of our inner gold exists in collective participation as well. At the very least, we can be asking this question of ourselves.

I met with Robert Johnson many years ago at a huge conference of nearly a thousand participants. He was a soft spoken, excellent speaker who took his time, was in no hurry to say what he wanted to say to the group gathered. He was reflective, thoughtful, relaxed, humorous, and kind. One on one, he and I had a short visit between sessions and he struck me as being a much grounded, quietly self-confident, wisdom character, which indeed shows itself in his writings. He seemed to have excellent social skills and did not display visible body language of a person uncomfortable in a large group setting.

Yet I perceived while he must have had a strong ego and sense of self, he did not need to be admired or affirmed beyond a normal, healthy desire to be loved for who he was. A remarkable man, he has been a great example to me of a person who has matured to where he needed to be and wanted to become. He was not a joiner and at the same time not adverse in any way to normal social interaction. Certainly, being a speaker at a huge conference is different from joining a group organization. Yet

I felt that Johnson must have worked through his own inner difficulties and found a place of participation with others that did not infect or poison his introversion nor his self-awareness of his innate greatness realized by his lifetime of inner work.

More Ideas about Balancing Outer and Inner Realities

How are we to handle the challenge of being informed and involved with the external world; and at the same time not get infected with the negativity that prevails in the collective culture? I do not have *the* answer to this question, but have some ideas to share to see if they help or not.

I think what may be required of us is to pay close attention to what we read, listen to and watch in regards of information from outside of us, and the limits of what we can assimilate in terms of quantity and quality. My guess is that each of us has both a content and a time limit of how much we can be exposed to collective information from social and national media, opinions of friends, and ideas from reference, fiction and nonfiction books.

This limit probably in most cases fluctuates over time with our capacity increasing or decreasing depending on our hormonal cycles, adequate sleep or depravation, even the time of day or night. In addition, we need to stay aware of how information affects us. Each bit of information may be a trigger to memories and emotions associated with past experiences which can affect our energy level and our ability to not become overwhelmed.

Of course, not all information is negative, even human stories that deeply affect our emotions of compassion and joy can be overwhelming if our souls are not rested, receptive and capable at the time to assimilate the information without overload.

I do not suggest that the soul is hypersensitive or fickle. Just the reverse. The soul has its own ebb and flow, and stimulation from outside needs to be consciously monitored *so that the primary function of the psyche, to relax into the relationship between self and God,* can remain a constant. I believe the soul is extremely versatile, full of courage and sustenance, and at the same time a finite, human capacity.

The Old Testament Book of Proverbs (4:23) encourages us to care for our hearts as a gardener tends for the garden because from the heart flows our source of vitality. The original story of humanity's creation in Genesis states that the human being is to "tend the garden [of Eden]" a similar symbol of the Self and our incarnational essence.

Perhaps we need to know and realize on a daily basis that the information that our souls desire in being most conscious comes from within, not without. Perhaps this is why we struggle with a reliance on outer stimulation instead of trusting the steady flow of information coming to us from within the soul.

What information comes to us from within? I would suggest our memories, our intuition, fantasies, dreams, imagination, the thoughts of God, God's Self, and our connections to the information coming from the collective unconscious and the images of God within us.

The story of the Fisher King illustrates for us this need for individual creativity and capacity

In the beginning of the story, long before the wounding of the young King, there was a spring in the forest filled with deep, cool, crystal clear water. In the pool of the spring lived a salmon which ate only of the fruit of the Hazelnut tree which hung its branches over the water. The Hazel was the sacred tree of the Greek fertility goddess Artemis and the Roman goddess Diana. Both were considered the source of wisdom, the goddesses of wild animals and natural intuition.

The salmon, a symbol for God, and of course, for Christ to the medieval and earlier Christian Church, fed on the fruit of one of the oldest symbols of feminine spiritual wisdom, the filbert or hazelnut. This tree was believed to be quite magical.

Jacob used branches from it to deceive his father-in-law Laban in securing for himself the prized spotted calves of the goats and sheep (Genesis 30:27). Hazel was known throughout the ancient Middle East as a spiritual and enchanted symbol.

In Medieval times, the English anchorite Julian of Norwich wrote about the wisdom of God contained in the spherical shape of the hazelnut held in the palm of her hand:

And in this he showed me a little thing, the quantity of a hazel nut, lying in the palm of my hand, as it seemed. And it was as round as any ball. I looked upon it with the eye of my understanding, and thought, 'What may this be?' And it was answered generally thus, 'It is all that is made.' I marveled how it might last, for I thought it might suddenly have fallen to nothing for littleness.

And I was answered in my understanding: It lasts and ever shall, for God loves it. And so have all things their beginning by the love of God. In this little thing I saw three properties. The first is that God made it. The second that God loves it. And the third, that God keeps it.

The salmon is the same fish that the young Fisher King derives his wounding from and his name. He partakes of the broiled fish, prematurely, and perhaps without permission from the Divine, in the same manner as I would like to think Adam and Eve ate of the fruit of the Tree of the Knowledge of Good and Evil prematurely and without consulting the Divine. This untimely and unconscious partaking of experiential knowledge, this gnosis, wounded the Fisher King with the self-awareness of his own divinity, the awareness of seeing Christ within himself. He was overwhelmed, as he had no way to contain this illumination and work it into the warp and woof of his daily living.

So, each of us has eaten of the salmon, the bearer of eternal wisdom, and now we long to return to this initial experience of our Divine genesis. But at this moment of longing for this primeval capability, usually occurring in midlife, our return to the Garden of our Creation is a huge step forward because it is a conscious choice, not an unconscious blunder. It was not the act of eating the fish or the fruit that was immoral and brought about the wounding, but the fact that the decision was unconscious. The divine spiritual wisdom could not be ingested, appropriated and used within.

Another way to say this is our individual spirituality was shown to us by accidental design to give us a glimpse of who we really are, so that we could spend the second half of our life rediscovering what we have always instinctively known: that we are loved, cherished and immeasurably valuable.

When I wrote above of the capacity for the soul for inner information, I was not suggesting that our divinity is limited, but that our humanness can only take in so much spiritual light at one time without causing either an overload of feeling or an inability to distinguish light from dark. This is because all seems light and our humanity is overwhelmed and unable to differentiate.

I am not speaking of spiritual ecstasy, for that often happens to most people for short durations of time. I am speaking of being caught up in the world of spiritual information to the extent that we forget our humanness and are cut off from the holistic connection to our bodies. We can experience a split that can continue unabated unless we find a way forward to self-awareness of the inner divinity in balance with full knowledge of our humanness. Despite its euphoric feeling, the ecstatic split of soul and body is not an indication of a mature spirituality, but the opposite: a one-sidedness, which can lead into an unhealthy denial and impoverishment.

We are created with a unified body and soul, and information or illuminations that can cause a permanent split can do us great harm. It is partaking of the wisdom of the salmon prematurely, our Christ within, and not having the experienced wisdom of being able to differentiate between our ego and that which is Divine which results in an identification of the ego with the Self that is harmful. This wrongful identification of the ego with our divinity causes inflation, and if not checked, can result in egocentricity, and at worst a grotesque narcissism.

In my counseling work, I sometimes come across a person who is stuck in the world of ideas, of spirituality, and not in close connection to their body. This split is often shown by a repeated dream motif of being stuck in an elevator, or living on the top floor of a house or building. Even common flying dreams can warn against such an ego inflated split between soul and body.

Very often this split condition is due to sexual abuse by a most closely trusted family member, or by having to fulfill the role of parent to a mentally ill parent in the immediate family system. These harmful situations always result in an extreme loss of childhood experience.

The healthy child lives in his or her body, and knows intuitively its limitations and pains. But an adult with this split is not at home in the body, with all the resulting addictions and codependency that can arrive from such a state. Such a person often refuses to deal with the reality of financial issues. Many times, these people demand that others carry their shadow for them concerning their neglect and refusal to grow in this earthly realm of dealing with money responsibly.

The goal of inner work for this type of person is not to diminish their authentic spirituality, but to improve self-care and set boundaries so that the body is protected, nurtured and honored to such a degree that the soul and body become unified and balanced relationally in co-equal valuing.

The person may also need to get their "hands dirty" by taking responsibility for "dirty," perhaps unpleasant money problems.

They may need to get their physical hands dirty by cleaning the toilets or doing hard physical work such as gardening, dish washing, and general cleaning. These activities center and ground the soul in the body and bring a renewed balance.

We find this motif of the fish being the bearer of wisdom helping us differentiate between inner and outer truth in the gospel story of Jesus being asked by his disciples about paying the civic tax money.

The coin in the fish's mouth is one of the miracles of Jesus, recounted in the Gospel of Matthew 17:24–27. In this Gospel account, the collectors of the temple tax in the city of Capernaum ask Peter whether Jesus pays the tax and he replies that he does. When Peter returns to where they are staying, Jesus speaks of the matter, asking his opinion: "From whom do the kings of the earth collect duty and taxes—from their own children or from others?" Peter answers, "From others," and Jesus replies: "Then the children are exempt. But so that we may not cause offense, go to the lake [the Sea of Galilee] and throw out your line. Take the first fish you catch; open its mouth and you will find a four-drachma coin. Take it and give it to them for my tax and yours."

A coin is a symbol of our personal power and a mandala shape, a symbol of wholeness. One might say it represents that which is our completeness, Christ himself. The fish is also one of the primary symbols of the earlier earth goddesses of the Mediterranean and North African world. Fish was one of the foods eaten in the worship of the earth goddesses and the early Christian Eucharist. Many early Christian communities remembered Jesus both with bread and fish or wine and bread for the Holy Eucharist.

We have the similar motifs of the fish, of divine wisdom, and of eating and digesting to assimilate and commune with the gods. Jesus makes the distinction with his wisdom by asking Peter from whom do the Kings of the earth get their taxes, from their own children, or the children of others than their own. This is the common early church motif of the followers of Jesus being a royal people who are exempt from taxation, a continuation of the people of Israel as a royal people with God as their archetype of the King or Queen. The tax is paid from the children of others, from outside, not from within which is instinctive and innate. The outer must pay outwardly and the inward is exempt because of the inner royalty and belonging is intrinsically given. That which is outer is affirmed, and that which is inner is also affirmed. The two are not mixed. Thus, the emphasis on the miraculous provision of tax money in the mouth of the fish. The inner wisdom is exempt from outer payment. Both outer and inner integrity remain separate and spiritually intact.

There is a very early Coptic Egyptian manuscript of this passage from Mark illustrating and showing Jesus standing in a boat with a net reaching down to catch a fish below which is Christ himself. The outer Fish as Christ in the boat is fishing down into the unconscious spirit of the water and catching the inner fish which is also an image of Christ. Outer and inner are not mixed, but differentiated, and thus the inner treasure is allowed to bring forth its bounty and the outer need is also fulfilled by the valuing of the inner provision freely given.

I love this image of Jesus fishing for himself. It portrays to us the need to be very aware to use our spirituality consciously to bring to light the treasure within. We do not do this with egocentric motives or techniques, but with the intentional process of seeking inside, the intuitive "fishing" and bringing it to the surface, the light of consciousness. We do this instinctively because this treasure dwelling in us does so intrinsically. It has always been.

Chapter Eight

Trusting and Using Our Intuition for Guidance

What happens when we pay attention to our intuition before we act or speak outwardly, and how can we get a sense of what to do or not to do? What is this basic spiritual principle that helps us trust our intuition? What is it that allows outer and inner life to work in harmony and bring new vitality to us?

Most recently I had an experience like this, just as each of us have these experiences of acting upon direction from our intuition. I was walking from the gym here in Pécs, Hungary where I work out daily, to the local Mall food court where I do my writing each morning. As I approached an intersection of very old residential streets, I saw an elderly Hungarian woman and her helper, perhaps an adult daughter, trying to get the old woman's leg up on a curb from the street, in order to enter a doorway, maybe to their apartment house or doctor's office.

The Elder supported herself using a walker which was up on the sidewalk, but no matter how hard she tried, she could not get her foot up on top of the high limestone curbstone. As I approached them, I first paused, knowing my extroverted-introvert American habit of helping wherever I see a need, would not be understood by the very reserved and proud Hungarians. Instead, I walked quietly near the women, stopped and listened to my intuition. I sensed that I needed to move slowly and let the women somehow direct me as to help or not. In Hungary, one does not even greet a stranger on the street without first considering if it may be an invasion of the person's personal space. This ethos is not about fear of strangers, but respect for the solitude and privacy of others.

I waited. The helper and the elderly woman both made eye

contact with me. I gesture with my hands to indicate I could help if they wanted it. I spoke to her, "Segíthetek?" The old woman looked me straight in the face and nodded yes. I slowly moved to stand behind her. She leaned back hard against my torso with her body, and using me as leverage, was able to lift first one leg, then the other, up and over the curbstone. At that point I realized how crippled and bent over at a ninety-degree angle she was. By pushing back against me she was able to lever the front of her body enough to lift her legs.

The women quietly, with great formality and dignity, thanked me saying, "Köszönöm szépen" and I replied just as formally, "Szivensen," you are welcome. I felt a deep sense of connection with these two women. I could feel God's love within each of us, touching us all in these brief moments.

I believe the spiritual principle that allows us to trust intuition is the Feminine Spiritual reality. One may call it the Holy Spirit, or any other name. The key characteristic of this energy is relatedness, where we begin to trust and relate to ourselves, and as a result, can relate with clarity to others.

Laurens van der Post taught in his books and rare interviews that when an individual pays attention to their feminine intuition and God's love flows, the collective negativity and abusive elements of outer life are affected. The universe is not the same after such an encounter as it was before. The entire cosmos conforms to the individual act and moves a little bit collectively in the direction of Love.

In our story of the Fisher King we have this truth illustrated in different ways. A major theme of the story is the dying of the old king to make way for the coming of the new king. In our story the Fisher King dies three days after his complete healing and Perceval becomes the new king and protector of the Grail. The restoration of the kingdom, however, unlike the now dead Fisher King, continues in its vitality and renewal. This restoration has come because the Fisher King can partake of the

Grail, which is a symbol of the Feminine of Life. The kingdom's vitality was restored in the act of Perceval asking the question which healed the Fisher King. Despite the death of the Fisher King three days later, the vitality of his kingdom continued uninterrupted. Thus, the act of love affected the universe in an eternal way.

When we pay attention to our intuition, not just for moment by moment experiences such as my story of the Hungarian women above, but at a deeper level, great change happens and affects the entire collective. In ways we may never understand or know, our deepest intuitions transform collective death into universal life.

Malcolm Boyd calls these moments of collective change tipping points. Each of us participate in such tipping points when our current concept of God no longer fits our reality, and is insufficient for what we currently need. We come to the end of what has worked before, and we embrace the unknown before us, and everyone in our sphere of influence is affected by this change.

Mythology explains this phenomenon with the concept of the dying and rising God, or the death of the old king and the installation of the new. As a Christian, I experience the finality of the death, burial and resurrection of Christ in such a way that I continually look for and find a new view or perception of God. I yearn for this new expression of God to be revealed because the story of Jesus has broken forever the Natural cycle of the vegetative dying and rising God, creating for each person an eternal open door to experience God anew on a continuing basis.

This perpetual opening to possibilities is the central meaning to the resurrection of Christ. Life is no longer a cyclic, closed system of reality, but an open organic, ever evolving certainty. The Feminine principle of Life can now continue to move through death and burial to new birth within us. This continual new birth provided for all individuals affects the entire collective. This is one way that I understand evolutionary reality.

Ladislaus Boros describes this basic evolution regarding the development of the world in his book, *Being a Christian Today* (The Seabury Press, NY, 1979. p. 30).

God's promises, of which the risen Christ is the fulfilment, can already be deduced from the event of creation. On the level of experience, this event is seen as a process of becoming or evolution. We can better express the development of the world in terms of the basic law of 'becoming new' as something that is dominated by the law of 'self-improvement.'

Cosmic development 'works its way upwards' from an original state of being. It evolves Milky Ways, solar systems and planets. Right from its most basic beginnings it presses forwards towards ever more complex material systems. It searched for the 'upward path', and thus creates at first primitive and then ever more complex forms of life.

The quest takes many paths, and in its details, may appear almost devoid of direction. Yes, despite this, the development of the world, viewed as a whole, traces an ascending line.

I would put forth that Boros' idea of the upward path is the relational feminine principle at work in all creation. Carl Jung believed, based on his observations of human development in the collective unconscious, that there is an unseen force moving each individual forward into original wholeness. Jung also believed this force to be an aspect of the feminine principle. John Sanford felt strongly that both the male and female soul are feminine in nature, partly, I think, because of this *relational* movement in the universe towards completion.

I believe each forward-movement challenge we encounter allows us to experience the birth of the new God at every junction where our self-awareness perceives it, and our spirituality recognizes the need for new insight. By allowing the Feminine of Life to touch and lead us inwardly, we can partake of the deep trust in life that this deeper relationship with God and all of life is not only possible, but is a determinant and a certainty.

Irene Claremont de Castillejo writes of this feminine, forward movement in these words:

> Achieving inner clarity is I believe the prime task of both men and women. I have used the expression inner clarity before but I should like here to enlarge upon what I mean by it.
>
> I like to think of every person's being linked to God from the morning of birth to the night is their death by an invisible thread, a thread that is unique for each of us, a thread that can never be broken.
>
> Our bodies are at the lowest point of this thread which runs up through every sphere of heart and head and spiritual attainment. To be on our thread is in Jungian language to be in touch with the Self. I am saying nothing new.
>
> I am using the expression inner clarity to mean conscious awareness of being on one's thread, knowing what one knows, and having an ability quite simply and without ostentation to stand firm on one's own inner truth.
>
> (Irene Claremont de Castillejo. *Knowing Woman: A Feminine Psychology*. Shambala, Boston. 1990, pp. 136–137)

Mythologically, it was not one of the male apostles who first spoke with Jesus after his resurrection, but Mary Magdalene who encountered him fresh from his transformative experience. So the feminine in us can wait at the entrance to the tomb of the burial of the God we have known and be present to usher in and joyfully welcome the new understanding of God.

In the Grail myth, Perceval as a very old man retreats into the forested mountains to live alone in a cave as guardian of the

Grail until the time comes that the Grail's influence is needed again to heal humanity. Perhaps this elderly Perceval, now fully aware of the need for integration of the Feminine principle symbolized by the Grail quest, represents the capacity within us to wait patiently for the renewal of the God image within us. Perceval waits in solitude and is patient because he knows his calling is one of deepest Love. This is an interior waiting. Our Masculine and Feminine wait together within the transformed Perceval. Patience and openness are profoundly feminine qualities.

Rainer Maria Rilke wrote of this spiritual reality within our souls in his *Book of Hours: Love Poems to God.* Rilke speaks of his soul as a Father, and the renewed God as the Son.

> I've stayed home like an old man, who no longer understands his Son.
>
> For He must go out to a high place, where he can see out over all things.
>
> I am the Father but the Son is more, He is all the Father was and what the Father was not,
>
> He is future. He is the Sea. He is the Womb.

Writings once attributed to Bernard of Clairvaux, but now known to be written by one of his disciples, states this reality of God as the Son, and the believer as the mother or father.

"Blessed is the one who can give birth to God, as a mother or father brings forth a new son or daughter."

Each of us can have this trust as we let go and release the concept of God that we have known but is no longer sufficient. We need the new God who will be revealed to us when the revelation is most needed by our thirst, our spiritual longing. Our intuition is the revealer.

Recently I was discussing sin with a close friend, a leader in the alcoholism recovery movement. I shared with him the idea that sin is not a breaking of some commandment or moral code. Instead, I see sin as an inability, resistance or spiritual blindness to seeing God's presence in us.

As a young evangelical in college, I was taught by my Neo-Pentecostal influences that any sense of separation I would experience in my feeling arena with God was due to unconfessed sin in my life. While I know that this concept has aspects of truth, (when I sin consciously and create true moral guilt as a result, I sear my soul's sensitivity to God. This is just as if I lie to a friend or my spouse, there is an ongoing distance and fear in the relationship until things are resolved) *but most of my inability to sense God's love is a blindness*, caused by my upbringing of continued criticism and a void of unconditional love and appreciation.

I carried this sense of invisibility and being unvalued as an individual person into young adulthood. Now, as a much older man, I know experientially that I am always deeply loved, but my lack of being able to receive it blocked my self-valuing, *and this was a cruel and unnecessary false guilt.*

St. Paul wrote in his Letter to the Romans:

"I know that nothing shall separate me from the love of God that is in Christ Jesus."

I know now that nothing, not even our sin, separates us from God who is Divine Love.

When the same St. Paul wrote earlier in his teaching to the Church at Rome that "all people have sinned and come short of the glory of God," I realize the same truth. Paul is not talking about a moral code being violated, but a missing of the mark of seeing who we really are as an expression of God's *doza*, glory.

The Greek word used in the passage above for sin is *hamartia*, a word used in archery to describe not hitting the center of the target. The archer misses the center of the target as a result of lack of clarity and attention, a carelessness of purpose and devotion to the task at hand; a type of blindness.

The result of such unconsciousness is alienation, discord, confusion and a broken relationship that does not have to be. Jesus did not die on the cross to take punishment for our sin. He died to bridge the chasm between the infinite, personal God and finite human capacity to perceive reality. His death identified and connected the unknowable mystery that is God with our humanness and removed the blinding, unconscious obstacles of our finiteness. It is our feminine intuition that can illuminate this truth for us.

Chapter Nine

What Is the Ontological Purpose of Our Life Expressed in the Soul?

I hope to provide some insight into the following questions. Is there a goal, an end result that we are being moved toward and an overall purpose? Or are all things soul-wise, simply arbitrary and out of our hands? To begin I would like to quote a famous saying in the life of Jesus of Nazareth, which was included in his Sermon on the Mount in the New Testament Gospel of Matthew 5:48. This verse often leads people to confusion, to misguided attempts at self-perfection, and unrealistic self-expectations resulting in false guilt. Jesus said:

"Be therefore perfect, as your Father in heaven is perfect."

The word translated as perfect is the Greek word *teleios,* which means completion, or wholeness. Bringing that which is distant into focus in the present. We get our word telescope from *teleios.* Bringing that which is far away, up close and visible.

The verse can logically read:

"Be therefore complete, whole, as your heavenly Father [Abba, the word for father that an individual child uses with great affection and love] is complete, whole."

Another way to understand this passage is given by Aramaic biblical scholar George Lamsa:

The Aramaic word *gmera* means perfect, comprehensive, complete, thorough and finished. In this verse it does not mean perfect in character as God is perfect but perfect or complete in understanding. Jesus knew that no one could be perfect like God. A learned man is called *gmera biolpana,* which means he is acquainted with every branch of learning. Gmera bnamosa means one who is well versed in the law.

Also, when a young man reaches the age of maturity he is known as gmera which means that he has become a man of understanding.

(Lamsa, George. *Gospel Light: An Indispensable Guide to the Teachings of Jesus and the Customs of His Time.* Harper and Row, NY, 1936, p. 43)

C. G. Jung and Jungian analyst John A. Sanford taught that because of their observations from listening to people's dreams and walking with them on their healing path, there is an unseen advocate who was constantly leading to individual wholeness. For myself, I experience this inner guidance towards wholeness by the symbolic language of my dreams to be most loving, honest, patient, and affirming. There is a loving personal quality to this inner advocate.

Regardless of the strength or weakness of my self-image at any particular moment, within my unconscious is a loving force that encourages and guides me towards the heightened awareness that I am loved and created for great goodness, creativity and purpose. This may be what George Lamsa means by completion in understanding.

I think of Jesus' words in the passage above as not so much an admonition or directive *as it is a statement of what is.* Whether we have a need for recapturing something of our being that was lost or affirming an aspect of Self that was denied or oppressed, I believe it is God who continually moves us in the direction of becoming who we have always been, created in completeness with nothing missing!

The twentieth-century German Jesuit theologian and philosopher Josef Pieper wrote in *The Concept of Sin*, this notion in more traditional Western theological language:

The phrase "by nature" basically meant; by virtue of having been created, by virtue of one's being a creature....

Everything, therefore, that a (human being) can do as a self-aware, consciously deciding essence is based on, and necessarily already presupposed by, what one is by nature.

And here "nature" means not just the earliest and first genetic endowment (nature in the sense of "by birth") but also the permanent norm.... Accordingly that which human beings "should" become, that is the good – not something arbitrarily spun out and invented, not something unrelated to humanity's innate essence or to the nature of things one must deal with.

The good, on the contrary, is that final end toward which all one's natural drive aims to find articulation and fulfillment. Yet for that very reason evil is not something that should be thought of as somehow separate from that same pregiven ontic condition. *To sin is nothing else but to hang back from the good that belongs to one by nature* [emphasis mine].
(Pieper, Josef. *The Concept of Sin*. St Augustine's Press, South Bend, Indiana, 2001)

Pieper taught that human nature is created noble and because of this self-awareness moves us towards that which we already are. This is another way of describing what Jung taught – that the Self, the image of God within us, moves us towards our ontological wholeness.

I do not find formulated answers to complex questions helpful. Thus, statements such as from the Catechism of John Calvin "Our purpose is to love and enjoy God forever," are prepositional, images of a deeper, symbolic process of reality within my soul. I cannot nail down my soul's purpose to any particular phrase or language. The mystery that I feel within cannot be adequately expressed in words. However, the idea that there is a persistent movement within that is moving us towards comprehensiveness makes a great deal of sense.

I am a visual learner and story narrative is what speaks

to me at my core. This is why Jesus' saying about wholeness taking place in the countryside is so believable. I can visualize with my imagination his teaching event within the context of the Palestinian countryside surrounded by open-minded, eager truth-seekers, with the noise of children running about, and possibly the bleating of sheep and goats chomping on the grass nearby. He concluded his long Sermon on the Mount with this beautiful statement of what is our fullness within the wholeness of God.

Within the mythology of this aspect of Jesus' story, the words written by the gospel writer speak to the reality of how I feel, intuit and receive love. I can definitely hear intuitively the freedom and joy of his words, "be whole" in understanding, as a statement of fact, not a goal to strive for.

I hear the power of this truth within the context of the entire "teaching of loving God and one's neighbor as oneself." The oral teaching of Christ summarized, be whole as God is whole, gives me the inner assurance that not only is this *not* a directive, *not another task for me to try to achieve*, but a statement of where the inner movement of God is taking me. We grow forward to who we already are but as yet cannot perceive. From this new place of knowing our true identity, the loving of God and serving our neighbor flows as a conscious outworking of this truth.

Rainer Maria Rilke, one of the most broken and psychologically challenged individuals in the world of European poetry, wrote of this certainty in his *Book of Hours: Love Poems to God*:

"You [God] dark net threading through us."

Like a Navaho dreamcatcher, we have within our souls a Divine net affecting our being, catching and moving forward all that will accumulate in detail; this wholeness, like pieces of a puzzle finally fitting together, which is our spiritual and bodily inheritance.

In another poem from the *Book of Hours* Rilke wrote:

"It [one's gold, inner treasure] will be brought forth into day

149

by the river that mines the silences of stone.... [E]ven when we don't desire it, God is ripening."

Our gold, our true inner mysterious Self, will be brought forth (into daylight) continually by the action of God's feminine (water) river energy of Spirit at work in us. One day it will be fully revealed to us for what it is, our true treasure, precious, shining, soft and hard to the touch and most beauteous.

In her book *Tramp for the Lord*, Corrie ten Boom, the great Dutch lover of souls and survivor of Ravensbrück concentration camp, carried with her at all times a piece of hand stitched tapestry cloth. On the back was a dizzying array of threads, running helter-skelter every which way in confusion and disarray. Turned over, the topside portrayed the elaborate, intricately beautiful design of handcrafted artistry, which could not be fathomed from the underside of the cloth. Again we find another symbol that speaks to the hidden, silent movement of God within our souls towards intrinsic wellbeing.

She often would pull this tapestry out of her purse when explaining to another person her response to the question of why the difficulties of life happen that make no sense. She taught that the chaos of the underside of the cloth was only revealed when turned right-side up; the beautiful design making sense of the chaos, a meaning perhaps only revealed in the next life.

C. G. Jung wrote many insightful words about the purpose and meaning of the human soul in his personal Active Imagination Journal known as *The Red Book*. One aphorism that stands out is how the opportunity that we are faced with is the challenge of identifying the present shape in which the essential spiritual life force continues to exist, and how it is currently expressing itself. John Sanford taught that whenever religious institutions and cultural norms fail to meet the spiritual needs of people, God, in God's love for all, always finds an avenue of expressing spiritual reality somewhere outside conventional expectations.

It is my belief that much of the power of the attraction of

the New Age Movement energy of the past fifty years has been due to this reality. As the more progressive, highly educated, patriarchal religious institutions in Western Culture declined in their ability to speak to the individual soul needs of people in the decades following World War Two, writers, teachers and other sages found a hungry audience among the seekers from those aging, cultural icons.

Sanford wrote in his book *The Kingdom Within*, just as an artesian well may dry up due to neglect in one location, often another will spring up in its place in another setting. As the mainline churches, of which I am a part, became more focused on outer issues to the exclusion and diminution of the individual needs of the human soul, people looked elsewhere for affirmation of deeper truth and clarity.

While some people left these institutions and some joined different religious organizations, my observation is that most of the more astute people who left simply stayed away and found spiritual nourishment from other, non-church sources. While Eastern religions and practices filled some of the void, my work as a healer among people who are outside religious institutions reveals that many who stay away from institutional religion are finding spiritual encouragement in self-help books, seminars, and the personal disciplines of meditation, yoga, and private pilgrimage.

Just as the monastic communities became sources of spiritual nourishment and encouragement for common people during the Dark Ages (a period of extreme corruption in the institutional churches) so today the New Age movements have met a very real need.

In my current resident country of choice, Hungary, thirty-nine percent of the population identify themselves as Roman Catholic, five percent Protestant, and the rest with no religious affiliation at all. In my experience much of the current culture was not only influenced by oppressive communism, but that the traditional religious institutions have remained today fairly stagnant and perceive themselves as bearers of societal norms which they certainly are no longer. Relevance to the individual needs of the soul has been dogmatically overlooked as this past authority continues to be used as a pressure to motivate people to conform to a religious cultural norm of bygone decades.

When I visit Hungarian churches the vast majority of them are practically empty. I believe this is where the American churches will be in another twenty years, unless they begin to address the needs of the individual soul.

Most of the young, highly educated Hungarians I love and have as friends are atheist or anti-religious, yet deeply, individually, very spiritual people. They possess an uncanny self-awareness of the sacred in relationships, Nature, the environment, sacred space, sacred time and a vast reverence and knowledge of world history with a global awareness and self-motivation to create a fulfilled life.

These young people enjoy more feminine spiritual values as celebration, traditional festivities such as sausage making, housewarming and Name Day parties. These gatherings have an almost royal feel to them with friendly banter, camaraderie, serious listening amidst meaningful conversations and much nonverbal, physical and eye contact, and other affirmative behaviors. Despite the lack of religious influence by the historical Catholicism and Protestantism of Hungary, these non-religious young people have an astute innate spirituality that I find refreshing, inviting and open to great possibilities for advancement.

Perceptive individuals are continually asking themselves the questions of spiritual purpose, and seeking where they can find spiritual reality and nourishment existing and expressing itself. This is the task of all regardless of religious orientation, institutional participation or not. Each of us can identify what brings life and vitality to us, and it is our task and loving opportunity to discover what energizes our souls and what our commitment will be to use it and continue towards experiencing our wholeness.

My personal opinion is that much of religious life is one-sided, and tends to project its shadow outwardly onto people and organizations that resemble that which is being rejected. For instance, in the Episcopal Church, there has been a fifty-year one-sidedness of emphasis on rational thought in such a way that the non-rational aspects of intelligence have been almost completely ignored.

One might define these terms of rational as left-brained and non-rational as right-brained. More specifically, rational thinking can be understood as analytical, and non-rational as intuitive and instinctive intelligence. My experience in the church has been that rational thinking has been insistently called "academic," and intuitive, intelligent knowledge has been neglected.

It is interesting that the Episcopal Church denomination to which I belong was heavily influenced by the Neo Pentecostal Movement (Charismatic) of the sixties and seventies. However, within ten years such groups which emphasized the non-rational intellect and emotive expression of spirituality were so marginalized by the denominational leadership that many split off to form Anglican worship within a Fundamentalist mindset of scripture.

In my opinion the conflict was not so much differences in theology but an antagonism towards integrating rational and intuitive intellectual spiritualties, thus pushing out by default persons who experienced a more individualized, intuitive spiritual orientation. An institutional us-versus-them mentally by both parties split off what could have been a vital aspect of renewal because of an out of balance insistence on rational thought alone. Frankly, it seemed to boil down to power issues, not ultimately theological ones. Many of the people I know who left the denomination felt unheard, dismissed and unloved.

Why these conflicts?

The soul is primarily a feminine vessel or container of feminine proportions. This reality is contrary to the top-down, masculine, categorical manner in which most corporate religious institutions function. The soul as a vessel can assimilate and take into herself and transform the tension of opposites in a way that masculine energy and rational thinking alone cannot. The feminine within the soul can withstand suffering as a means to open the soul, embrace and transform its suffering into a positive energy for growth.

Most masculine approaches to suffering, especially in Western culture, regard such an embracing as counterintuitive and instead see the need for a combative overcoming of suffering. This continues and escalates the problem of opposites and hinders the soul from its ability to transform suffering by healing the tension between opposites.

While I am aware that many of my peers may believe that the battles have been due to issues of social injustice, and I certainly agree this is part of the struggle, I also feel this deeper perspective is needed to more fully explain some of my denomination's conflicts over the past decades that have caused a loss of influence and membership.

The masculine energy approach, perhaps symbolized by the piercing rays of the sun, is one-sided and stuck in the proactive approach to things, in contrast to the reflective, receptive, mysterious and transformative light symbolized by the moon. I believe the lunar quality is more effective and compatible to the nature of the human soul. As the Genesis story revealed, it was a coming together of opposites, earthly material and heavenly Spirit infusion that created the first mythological human soul in Judeo-Christian mythology.

Josef Pieper writes in his book *The Philosophical Act* that even religious prayer can be debased to a utilitarian, masculine-valued, pre-emptive task or duty that fails in its essence as prayer:

> In a totalitarian world of work every form and manner of transcendence is bound to wither: for where the religious spirit is not tolerated, where there is no room for poetry or art. When love and death are robbed of all significant effect and reduced to the level of a utilitarian banality, nurturing, supportive humanistic philosophy cannot prosper.
>
> But worse, even, than the silencing or simply extinction of these experiences of transcendence is their transformation, their degradation into sham and spurious forms; and pseudo-realizations of these fundamental acts most certainly exist, giving the appearance of piercing the dome of everyday life. It is possible to pray in such a way that one does not transcend the world, in such a way that the divine is degraded to a functional part of the workaday world. Religion can be debased into magic. *Then is no longer devotion to the divine, but an attempt to master it* [emphasis mine].
>
> (Pieper, Josef. *Leisure: The Basis of Culture; The Philosophical Act*. Ignatius Press, San Francisco, 2009)

Even in the deeply personal and seemingly reflective act of prayer, an overtly masculine energy can destroy the very essence of worship and devotion. We need the reflective balance of the feminine spirit to keep us grounded in a saving sense of wonder and devotion to that which is holy in God, others and ourselves.

What Is the Truly Devotional Life?

Josef Pieper goes on to say what the truly devotional life is:

> To philosophize is the purest form of speculari [to look at, a lookout post], of theorein [contemplation, speculation] it

155

means to look at reality purely receptively, in such a way that things are the measure and the soul is exclusively receptive.

The human (soul) spirit, or to have (soul) spirit, means to exist in the midst of the whole of reality and before the whole of being, the whole of the universe, both visible and invisible, meaning both physical and metaphysical. Spirit and soul do not exist in "a" world, or even in "its" world, but in "the world, "the" world in the sense of all of creation.

I understand this to mean that our spirits (souls) are spiritual but they have the responsibility and opportunity to reflect and understand up until the point of complete mystery, and including this mystery, to reflect reality as it is, not as a projection of what we want it to be or not to be. Our souls are spirit, and thus are objectively able to observe and enjoy all of reality, and not be satisfied with something less than reality, such as the utilitarian one-sidedness that a dominant masculine approach to life demands of us.

I make a distinction between some modern spiritual teachers in stating that I believe, based on my experience, that we are created spiritual and finite beings. I believe we are created (and it stands to intuition and reason that while we are truly spiritual in nature and essence) in the same essence as the Creator. However, we are not in fact, the Creator. In our sense of being, we are separate and distinct from the Creator as Creatures.

By saying we are finite I do not mean to say we are limited or that we cannot do infinite good or attain infinite possibilities as creatures. But by our finite-ness in being, we are indwelled by God, but we are not God, God's Self. In the words of the Psalmist and Jesus himself who quotes the Psalmist, "we are gods." Also, we find in the theology of the Eastern Orthodox tradition that we can become "Deified," but, I repeat, we are not God, God's Self. Thus, our being, as creatures created by the Creator, sustains us, moves us forward to become experientially who we already are creatively. All of our life meaning flows from being Co-creators with our Creator.

We sustain hope as creatures in the yet unknown, unreached, the un-finalized. If we were to say that God and human beings are one and the same, then we have most likely reduced God to our own known and experienced perception of reality. If we have projected God as Spirit within us and indwelling us out onto God as Creator, we have minimized who God is beyond our current comprehension.

Our capacity as human beings is to be fully human, meaning creations of the Creator. Our devotion is not demanded of us but springs from us by invitation from the very sense of wonder that our hope brings up from within us. For me, wonder and devotion, or worship is at the core of meaning of my life.

It is not my duty to worship. *It is my natural response to behold* the beauty of the Creator and all of the Creator's Creation! Worship is a natural outflow from the hope within of continuing to learn, to grow, to manifest this divinity with and to take my place in the broader scheme of things.

As St. Paul wrote in his pastoral Letter to the Roman Church long ago, "For all creation waits for the manifestation [opening showing] of the sons [daughters] of God."

Pieper also taught that our souls and spirits are reciprocal to reality, and nothing less than honest observation and devotion to the reality in the divine will satisfy who we are. Our souls are not nourished by focusing on the egocentric projections of what the ego wants reality to be. Instead, our souls are created in such a fashion that only that which is real, both in the material and spiritual worlds, in relationship to the soul, can satisfy and give the peace we seek.

This is why the symbol of the Holy Grail is helpful to us as an icon of the soul. A vessel is a container that is able to hold within itself the tension of the opposites of masculine and feminine, human and divine, and bring forth a new, creative synthesis of life itself. This synthesis is the result of communion with the reality of life, both inner and outer.

In the Grail myth the cup is not empty but overflowing with vibrant feminine energy that is portrayed as diffused, perhaps, reflective and inviting light. The Grail does not emit a penetrating and unapproachable light. It is an outpouring, healing and lunar light. Each person in the banqueting hall receives from the Grail the desires of the heart in abundance whether it be spiritual food, grace, and courage, whatever is needed. There is no lack, no one-sided presumptuous opinion within the Grail. The cup listens to the heart and brings forth that which fully satisfies. All who receive from its abundance are healed.

Chapter Ten

It Is the Fool Who Saves Us

In the Grail myth all are satisfied at the first banquet which Perceval observes with the exception of the Fisher King. His wound cannot be healed by the Grail alone, but by the transformative outworking of grace in the life of the long-anticipated Fool, who will publically ask of the universe the Great Question, "For whom does the Grail serve?" The question is one of attitude and the intuitive direction of listening with an open and non-defensive heart.

It is interesting that Pieper in his work *The Philosophical Act* notes that both Plato in his *Phaedo* and *The Symposium* writings, uses the character of Apollodorus as the messenger of truth to be spoken. Apollodorus is a fictional young man, overzealous, uncritical, and, yes, a holy fool, who gives a speech to the businessmen of Greece who are only interested in making money and the material realm.

Apollodorus tells them he is sorry for them because "You think you are doing something when you are really doing nothing. You may think I am bad off, but I not only believe you are bad off, I know it!"

It is the fool within us who is our redeemer to our deepest truths. Just as it was only the jester who could speak the truth to the medieval king or queen without being punished with death, so the fool within us can speak to our egos in such a way that we have to listen and use the opportunity to choose life-giving truth.

Robert Johnson, in *The Fisher King and the Handless Maiden* points out a very important fact from the Grail story. Perceval is only required to ask the question that arises from his intuition when encountering the Grail Procession, "Whom does the Grail

Serve?" or in my words, "What is this all about, what is the purpose of our life?"

This is an open-ended, both/and, feminine approach to Mystery and can be asked by anyone without fear of rejection or judgment. Perceval is not required to have an answer to the question put forth, which would shift the incident over to a more masculine, either/or predicament.

So the questions regarding our souls' purpose, meaning, and relationships are feminine in nature. They are open-ended, not closed system questions. This is very helpful to me and is one of the genuine qualities of the myth that speaks deeply to this question of human nature.

We will look at this problem and how it is solved later in following chapters. In using the Grail as a symbol of the nature of the human soul, suffice it to say, the soul is a feminine vessel, symbolized by a bowl, a stone or wooden or golden cup encrusted with precious jewels, many images, all which contain the same mystery bringing forth generative vitality and healing to every need that one could have. It is my belief, that only feminine energy or principle can take the opposites within us, synthesize them, and bring forth a new creation from them. Masculine energy is needed to differentiate, categorize, compete, and clarify our life for us, but cannot integrate without causing more disharmony. A true balance based on the nature of reality is the key to freedom.

As John Sanford so wisely commented, "The unity of opposites is a mystery that can only be resolved by God." *We cannot force internal unity.* We can only be enlightened to perceive it, and then receive the grace to trust it one step of revelation at a time. This requires trust in the holy fool within us.

On one hand, the symbols that convey intuitive knowledge have been taught and encouraged by the institutional Church: the sacramental acts of Baptism, Confirmation, Ordination, Unction, Penance, Eucharist, and others. But *how* these sacramental acts teach our souls to learn and grow through the intuitive digestion of these symbols has been mostly lacking.

My observation after sixty years of participation in institutional Christianity is that assumptions are made by many leaders that the symbols speak to us, which of course they do. But dialogue and discussion about *the power of action taken from the interaction of our intuition with the symbols* has received inadequate teaching. I believe this silence is a result of an unconscious fear of loss of perceived authority.

Intuitive knowledge is not encouraged. I would suggest this may be because institutions are afraid of the individual creative nature of such an open dialogue. Institutions, often by their very nature and purpose, are antithetical to spiritual creativity. I also think this institutional fear of the unknown effect of the feminine spiritual principle is part of the reason for the oppression of women in the Church. True feminine spirituality cannot be controlled.

I will give an example. A few years ago I was asked to teach a seminar on sacramental healing prayer at an Episcopal cathedral. The host for the event was the cathedral staff-in-resident, Doctor of Divinity theologian, who was considered a highly regarded spiritual director. During the seminar I stressed the importance of trusting the guidance of the Holy Spirit through one's intuition in praying for others in need of emotional and physical healing. I gave examples from the New Testament gospel stories and the Book of Acts of the Apostles to illustrate the reality that God can direct us in our prayers when we are seeking it and open to this guidance. Examples were given from church history as well as my own experience of healing occurring which followed listening to and acting upon intuition in prayer.

In a written evaluation of the seminar, from which there was much positive feedback from the participants, the theologian shared his outrage that examples were used from my experience and those from church history to encourage the group to trust their intuition prayerfully when praying with others in need. This church leader wrote, "I would never tell my people to trust their intuition. What a horrible thing to encourage!" I was a bit shocked at this response and decided not to respond.

I assumed that either this person's experience with their own intuition has resulted in personal pain or that they somehow were brainwashed to believe that only an analytical, left-brain, rational approach to prayer was proper. Certainly, this person felt the non-rational aspect of our intelligence was not to be trusted. In any case, this attitude of distrust is not unusual in many places in the Christian Church today. Hopefully, the future will find the Church in a healthier and more effective place of trust in the human intuition infused by God's Spirit and become a place of profound healing as it was in its earliest days of conception.

I feel it is important that one can personally digest and assimilate at an intimate level how and why sacramental symbolic words, gestures, and rituals speak to us. This means personal empowerment, something which sometimes hierarchical institutions dread and try to avoid. In my mind there is no mystery as to why so many Western Christian churches have been in steady decline as more people take individual responsibility for their spiritual lives. So much of what we call soul is ego, that which we are conscious of about ourselves. Depth Psychology has shown us that so much of who we are, our very souls, also includes the unconscious self. Hopefully, one finds a faith community where the entire person is understood and affirmed.

In my view, the main reason for the emergent strength of the fundamentalist and evangelical sects of Western Christianity which grew during this same time period of decline in the mainline American churches, was the evangelical emphasis on personal soul work, the honoring of individual experience of the holy fool within the soul.

Phrases such as "give your life to Jesus" and asking Christ "into one's heart as Lord and Savior" are not clichés when held within the sphere of honoring the individual experience. In fact, the very prepositional phrases, such as "do you turn to Jesus Christ and accept him as your Savior?" came from the historic Catholic churches and their baptismal creeds and prayers of the first five hundred years of the church. There is nothing new about the phrases that Christian Fundamentalism identifies with or their honoring the individual's particular experiences of God.

The difference between the groups that have grown and those who are diminishing has been the devotion of individual soul work and encouragement for people to find, as Jung wrote, "where the Life is expressing itself." The holy fool speaks on behalf of the experience of the soul in the individual and is protected against the onslaught of the collective depressant of creativity.

At the time of this writing, for the past twenty years, the rise of the Fundamentalist Christian institutions has waned, until now, the decline is rapid. I feel the reasons may be similar as to why the mainline churches waned in the United States beginning in the 1960s. As the Fundamentalist Christian churches began to ignore the individual soul and push for more collective conformity, whether for political, financial or power purposes, they began to decline. As they continued to thwart honoring the individual's meaning of soul to discern for itself spiritual values, the decline in spiritual vitality of these institutions accelerated.

It is my assertion that only *the individual soul* can serve as a vessel of spiritual transformation. One-sidedness is an individual problem. Such error by emphasis can only be healed by singular personal attention to its causes and a willingness to risk all, *perhaps appearing foolishly* to find balance between one's outer and inner life.

It is the holy fool within us who can consciously access the ability to listen to the Holy Spirit intuitively. My hope is that the individual seeker will find their personal experience of the sacred and holy affirmed, and with that affirmation, greater self-understanding and God-Wonderment transpiring. It is also my hope that people everywhere continue to honor the individual soul needs of all people and abandon the push for collective conformity and blinding power.

The Human Soul Is a Student of Life

Our souls are students of life taking in lessons from our outer circumstances and integrating them with inner values, perceptions and truths that were placed within us by God. Sue Bender, in her book *Everyday Sacred*, points out that one of these aspects of being a student is that our souls have the ability to know that *irregularity is a gift*, a place for Mystery. Perhaps irregularity is another way of speaking about the holy fool within us who saves. My work with the dreams of seekers shows that the symbol of a student in the dream is a figure of the great role of being a student of life.

What does it mean to be a student of life? A student of Life is not just an observer, but a participant of curious endeavor, seeking and desiring not just the information about things, but asking the important questions of Who, What, When How and Why. A student acknowledges their ignorance and prays for a thirst for awareness of things and summons courage to step into the unknowns of life, *the irregularities*, as they draw them forward. They may feel they cannot but help to seek out possibilities as to the foremost questions of life within and without.

My observation in spiritual direction with many people is that the more rigid we are, the less in touch with our intrinsic soul we become. Flexibility does not mean being valueless or pure relativity, but instead flexibility is a sustainment of the ability to stay open. Being flexible can mean desiring to learn new ways of being. Thus, suppleness is a major aspect of how our souls are meant to function.

Outer circumstances do not mold the soul. They open our inner eyes to the beauty, the trust, and the wonder we have been created to behold. Our inner attitudes are what mold the soul for receptivity or rejection of the unknown. This flexibility allows the soul to carry the outer circumstances of our life with deeper ampule ability and grace.

Everyone has difficult outer circumstances and these are relative to one's experience and life situations. But how we respond to events in our outer lives is our choice, either retreat into rigid fear and tremble, or choose to stay vulnerable and curious, trusting to face life with faith.

Laurens van der Post, writer, statesman, and former prisoner of war during the Second World War in Java, wrote beautifully about this innate ability of the soul to face the darkest circumstances with trust. He tells his own story in the book, *A Walk with a White Bushman*.

Laurens van der Post himself was scheduled to be executed in the early morning by his Japanese captors. He was shaken to the core as any rational person would be. Yet with just a few hours before the dreaded moment, he looked out of his prison cell to the full moon overhead and was filled with an indescribable joy and serenity.

It was not just an acceptance of his fate. He was a young man in his mid-twenties at the time. It was a gift from God that he experienced deep within his soul that life was indeed richer and beyond death. He was illuminated with the truth that love was behind all the circumstances of life that could be thrown at one.

He had written his last letters to his family members and was able to carry this inner peace to the execution wall where the firing squad then fired blanks from the several rifles. He did not go into extreme shock or a psychotic collapse as other prisoners had when the sound of the gunshots dissipated. His inner soul had moved beyond space and time into the very depths of love for which we are created and this love had removed all fear in him, and replaced it with an abiding stillness.

The writer of the First Letter of John in the New Testament has these beautiful words of this same reality that is ours for the taking.

"There is no fear in love, but perfect love casts out fear; for fear has to do with punishment, and whoever fears has not reached completion in love. We love because God first loves us" (I John 4:18–19).

This true story of van der Post is an extreme example, but it shows the latitude and greatness of the human soul to integrate outer circumstances with inner reality, not with denial, but the opposite, the embracing of greatest truth.

I find the following story from the New Testament Gospel of Luke illustrates through the teachings of Jesus this same emphasis about the ability of the soul to prioritize an inner attitude versus the focus on outer circumstances or achievements.

The story says that Jesus sent out his first large group of followers to do what he had been teaching them, heal the sick and mentally ill, teach about the inner reality of God's love and presence available to all defined as a reign or the kingdom of God. After their adventure, Jesus gathered the group to process their experiences.

The seventy returned with joy, saying, 'Lord, in your name even the demons submit to us!' He said to them,

I watched Satan fall from heaven like a flash of lightning. See, I have given you authority to tread on snakes and scorpions, and over all the power of the enemy; and nothing will hurt you. Nevertheless, do not rejoice at this, that the spirits submit to you, but rejoice that your names are written in heaven. (Luke 10:1–24)

This last sentence, for the disciples not to get excited about the spiritual authority they possessed and witnessed against evil afflicting the mentally ill, but to be happy that their names were written in heaven, states that their names, the essence of their being, is contained and sustained by the spiritual dimension, not just in the outer world of circumstantial living. This reality is what Jesus taught his followers to honor.

Like van der Post, the disciples were to remain focused on the inner reality of their souls' relationship with God, and this centeredness is where the real joy of living could be found. Thus, they could not be shaken from this center by either ego inflating or destructive circumstances of life. This perspective requires of us unyielding trust.

In the gospel writer's story, Jesus himself practiced this centeredness. His disciples had been successful in carrying out his mission, but Jesus focused on his personal gratitude to God for the growth of his followers as it was spiritual revelation that helped them be open, like children, to these wonderful truths of the inner life.

Chapter Eleven

The Soul Helps Us Face the Death of a Vision as Well as Our Physical Death

Another purpose of the soul is to help us learn how to face not only our life, but our death. Western culture has continued to avoid the subject of death. Yet within each individual, is the need to listen to the soul which teaches that death is a mystery for which we need to prepare ourselves in the same spiritual of submission and humility as we once learned to prepare ourselves for life.

(Joseph L. Henderson's writing in Jung's *Man and His Symbols*)

How does the soul prepare us for death? Perhaps there are a variety of ways. One may be that our soul, possibly by midlife, has helped us see that continuing on the hero's quest of conquering and upward achievement takes a turn-around in the direction of a deeper appreciation of the meaning of one's life. Some of us arrive at this turning point gradually and some of us with a sudden, perhaps, rude awakening through tragedy, or even the achievement of a lifetime goal, only to find that personal satisfaction is not fulfilled. We discover we must find another avenue for inner peace.

Jesus taught about the need for many people to find this inner about-face via an awakening in their outer life requiring an abrupt shift of attitude in a short sequence of time. When questioned about the validity of John the Baptist's ministry of preparing the hearts of people to be receptive to God, Jesus corroborated John's work, but went beyond it saying:

"Since the time of John the Baptist until now, people take the

Kingdom of God by violence."

In the Mystery cult of Dionysus, many people came to spiritual awareness by experiencing an ecstatic "thunder rite," where they undertook a conversion experience that included a shock to their system and their world view: how they perceive and experience meaning and purpose. One might call such an encounter with the sacredness of one's soul life, a rude awakening.

But my observation as a priest is that most people find this inner awareness gradually, as it normally takes a tragic event, loss or an overwhelming encounter with primal fear to cause such a needed, abrupt awakening. Most people, in my experience mostly women, enter this new awareness as a steady process, and do not require such a shock to their possible egocentricity.

Other ways the soul prepares us for death is to communicate to us through intuition, dreams and synchronicities that we are intimately loved, guided and upheld by an unseen Presence. Just as a child who is properly loved and nurtured by affectionate parents, so we can relearn how we are cared for, guided, and carried by God in the second half or last third of our lives to the time of eternal transition in the death of this material body.

We are accompanied by the loving Presence through the threshold of our dying to the other side of a new and vibrant life. Just as van der Post experienced a deep abiding comfort that carried him as a young man through the horror of an execution by firing squad in the jungles of Java, so each of us can and will be carried through whatever we face in our futures to the new life beyond.

It has been my privilege as a parish priest to be present with many people as they have worked through the difficulties of terminal illness into the death process, and the secession of the soul from the physical body. It has been these experiences that have emboldened my trust in the Beyond and in the ever-present Love of our Creator. I have hope that I will be able to face my own death when it comes with anticipation and an open heart and mind.

A Story of Transcendent Contentment: A Beautiful Soul that was Prepared to Live and to Die

In Lubbock, Texas, I had an elderly parishioner who was confined to a Medicaid Care Facility. It was crowded, smelly and very noisy. She shared a room with a woman who was completely out of her mind. The roommate kept her television on high volume from early morning to late at night. When I would visit my member, I would turn the television off and exclaim, "How can you stand this awful incessant yapping all day and night long?" She would smile and say, "I have other things to listen to," pointing to her heart in her chest and to the side of her head and ears.

My parishioner was confined at all times to her bed because of extremely brittle bones. Just turning on her side in bed would break bones and increase her constant pain. I have no idea how she endured such suffering. Yet she always greeted me with an authentic warm smile as if she was hosting my visit in her Texan parlor over iced tea and sandwiches. She was not acting. It was truly amazing. She maintained her attitude of positive joy in the midst of a horrible situation.

This woman was an art teacher, as was her deceased husband. She had three of his paintings on the wall where she could see them. She did not use her television at all. She would read books, try to sketch on a notepad, and simply lay on her back with a contented look on her face. She did not act needy, nor overly enthusiastic and dependent on my visits. I was told by the facility staff that I was her only visitor.

I learned that when she was very young, she lived in Canyon, Texas, just north of Lubbock. Her husband was a professor of art at what is called West Texas State University in Canyon when Georgia O'Keefe was his student. This woman and Ms. O'Keefe were the same age and would take drives to Palo Dora Canyon where they would set up their easels and paint the desert scenes. I would sit for two or more hours listening carefully to her fascinating stories about her adventures with this famous American artist.

I was not with my parishioner when she died. She was very old, and when I learned of her death from the care facility staff they told me she died in her sleep. I performed her burial service alone. There were no people who attended the simply gravesite service. This woman and her husband had no children, and all of her Texas relatives had been gone for twenty years or more. I did the service as if there were hundreds there, indeed, the communion of saints was very present as well as angels of God on that windy, cold spring morning at the cemetery.

I learned much about contentment and the deep trust witnessed in the life of this dear woman. She told me that often her husband would visit her and join her on the bed in the care facility, usually at night. They would talk and have long conversations, and he would reassure her he would be there for her when her time came to pass to the next life.

Her soul was alive and well. She had learned how to find God's presence in the small things of her life. She knew she was deeply loved and that the difficulties of life were just there, yet she did not let the hard things define her. They did not diminish her joy or hope of an ongoing fullness of life.

How Our Souls Prepare Us for Death

Of course, as a priest, I have also borne witness to tragic, unexpected and sudden deaths from accidents, rapid illness and even murder. Yet in each instance, the person doing the dying has received what I can only call a grace, a loving strength to pass through the difficulties of last breaths, of pain, of shock and trauma, to a definitive peace and quiet tranquility. Most often the persons needing preparation for death were not the dying, but their family members.

However, I can remember being a young father at age twenty-one lying in bed and thinking about death, especially a fear of the physical pain of dying. For many weeks I wrestled alone at night when I should have been sleeping. I carry in my memory the actual filming of executions in documentaries on television carried out by the Nazis, the Hungarian communists, the American and South Viet Nam army, and other cruelties. These mental images haunted me much of my young life.

One night, while trying to fall to sleep, I prayed and asked God for help with this fear of pain at death and fear of the unknown. Within an hour I felt a lifting, a light in the dark room that I could not see but could feel. I felt that God was present with me and would be present no matter how awful a death I might encounter one day. I experienced a removal of the fear. It was replaced by a presence of comfort that has carried with me to this day about these issues.

I am not a person who looks forward to death and dying as an escape from the difficulties of life. But I know and hope that when my time comes, whether it be tonight, by a sudden health issue or an accident, or much later after a long lingering death by illness, I will be ready and present in the moment without undue fear.

My wife is thirteen years younger than me. Sometimes I think about how hard it will be to leave her at my death. We are soul mates. We feel that we have known each other in spirit somehow since each of us were young children. There is such a sense of oneness, a unity of spirit that defies words to describe.

When I think of my death most likely proceeding hers by many years, I feel a deep, abiding, sweet feeling of sadness and longing. We have talked a bit about this reality we may face one day. I have the sense that when that day comes we will have the grace and lightness of being to give thanks for our life together, and to anticipate this future union after my physical death. We know our goodbye will be temporary, and in many ways, unnecessary. We are one in spirit and soul. We feel very fortunate.

The Soul's Preparation for Death by Bringing Inner Unity

The soul also prepares us for death by helping us bring about a unity of our consciousness with the unconscious contents of our mind. When this happens and integration occurs, as C. G. Jung wrote, "there comes the transcendent function of the psyche [Greek word for soul], the full realization of the potential of one's individual Self."

In my words, as we begin the last stages of life and look at death without denial, we have the opportunity to integrate our conscious awareness with our unconscious thoughts that have been there since birth, or before, and through this union we experience our divinity, our ontological oneness with God. This unity allows our full potential as human beings to be expressed both inwardly and outwardly.

I don't think that there is a fear of death for most people who begin to take stock of their spiritual awareness. Instead, I have observed that often at midlife, creative people who have always used their creativity only to earn and spend more money begin to find less utilitarian, transient reasons for self-expression. Creativity frequently becomes an expression of their spiritual relationship with God and others.

This integration of the conscious mind with the unconscious contents is often symbolized in mythology and dreams as the lone journey or pilgrimage. Often the hero of the journey dies or must enter the underworld, as in Goethe's *Faust*. This is not a permanent death. Such a mythological death is always followed by an ascent, a rising, new resurrection into a pioneering vista of living.

This transition requires us to move into a different pattern of life as the first half of our life is often conformed to societal and familial expectations. The second half of our life can be nonconformist, a movement from captivity to a more complete and greater stage of authentic being.

Wonderful Musings from Frederick Buechner Regarding the Questions about Death and Afterlife

One of my favorite writers and thinkers is Frederick Buechner, novelist, theologian, and one-time mentee of Agnes Sanford, mother of John A. Sanford. I highly recommend to all readers to invest in his autobiographical writings. In one of them, *The Eyes of the Heart*, Buechner uses active imagination dialogue with his deceased grandmother and mother, to intuitively write out the ideas he has come to trust regarding death and the reality of afterlife.

In describing an imaginary conversation with his grandmother, a primary figure of love in his childhood, Buechner provides with remarkable clarity some ideas about what death and the next life may be like. In the active imagination journaling, Buechner asks his beloved grandmother, what the departure from this life is like. She replies with exquisite beauty:

I always thought that "passed away" was a silly way of putting it. Like calling the water closet a powder room—or calling it a water closet for that matter—and I am here to tell you that it is also very misleading. It is the world that passes away.

I could feel the world gradually slowing down more and more until one night, after that charming nurse whose name I regret to say I've forgotten turned out the light and was getting ready to go home, I realized it was finally slow enough for me to get off, and that is what I proceeded to do. It was rather like getting off a streetcar before it has come to a stop—a little jolt when my foot first struck the pavement, and then the world clanged its bell and went rattling off down the tracks without me.

For me there really wasn't any sadness. I felt nothing so much as astonishment.

(Buechner, Frederick. *The Eyes of the Heart: A Memoir of the Lost and Found.* HarperSanFrancisco. New York, 1999, pp. 12–13)

Buechner goes on to talk about the three reasons he wrote his mother in a letter why he believed something happens to us after we die. In my own paraphrase, he wrote that first, if he (Buechner) were God, because he loved people, he would give everybody unlimited time to become the best they could be. Second, he wrote that he had "a hunch it was true, I intuited it," he wrote. Third, "because Jesus said so."

I love how he wrote that his soul simply gives him a "hunch" that life continued after death, and that he values his intuition the way he does. I highly recommend all of Buechner's books as his perceptive and honest theology is not just based on academic study but because he is one of the very few living authors today who has and continues to practice at age ninety-three, his inner soul work.

The Soul Integrates with the Self: The Genesis Creation Story

I see this progression from the first half of life to the next as a movement of the soul forward to a place where we have always been, created in the beginning to be at one with God and with Self. Another mythological analogy is the Garden of Eden in the biblical story of Genesis.

The first human beings were created to be in harmony with Nature and with their natural instincts, intuition and insights. Friendship with God was an ongoing reality. But with the Fall, when humanity chose unconsciously to become conscious by the action of eating the forbidden fruit, the mythological first man and woman were cast out of the Garden to pursue their pilgrimage and lone journey.

It is my belief and conviction that the reason the story says a flaming, rotating sword was placed by God and the heavenly court at the entrance to the Garden was to show the way back, like a lighthouse beacon, so that human beings could return to the Garden, to Paradise.

But for us it would have to be a conscious, fully aware and mature spirituality that could partake of the abundance, sustenance and virility of the Garden where union with God would be found. Our naïve, original innocence and potential wholeness, followed by our expulsion into the first half of life containing true moral guilt and trials by fire, will hopefully commence with our conscious return to the fulfilled entirety for which we were created.

The Symbolism of the Lighthouse

I have lived near the Pacific and Atlantic Oceans for much of my life, first on the San Francisco Peninsula and in Rockport, Massachusetts, then during college in Humboldt County, Northern California, followed by many years on the Oregon central coast. Today, I live very close to the Pacific in Ocean Beach, San Diego, California. Lighthouses have always been prominent in paintings, photography and thus the decor of my home environment.

I believe the symbol of the lighthouse can be a masculine beacon symbol of both the life-giving phallus and light. Simultaneously, the lighthouse draws the soul forward by a feminine quality of reflected, and thus, magnified light, and a looking back and beyond the obvious past, to a return to the salt water of our instinctive beginnings in the mythological Garden, our Mother the Sea. The rotating aspect of the lighthouse can also be symbolic of the world tree or navel upon which the universe turns its axis in all directions.

It is a feminine quality to look back and to remember our origins. It was Lot's wife who looked back remembering home in the Genesis story. She was killed for remembering, which is a patriarchal rendition of the story. She was not necessarily looking back for the purposes usually acclaimed to her: that she was longing for the deprecating life as before. She was looking back because she was leaving the home that she had worked hard to create, preserve and had known.

The Bible story of her punishment by being turned into a pillar of salt is horrible. If the masculine energy of Western Culture could include the feminine quality of looking back, reflecting and remembering, the continued slaughter of wars, political turmoil and agitation just might cease. We were once mythologically removed from the Garden so we might not eat of the fruit of eternal life in our unconscious state. We were removed so our longing within might cause us to remember who we are as creations of God, and that we might desire to return by conscious awareness to our state of a loving relationship with our Creator.

Chapter Twelve

Our Choices at Mid Life

Our attitude seems to be the determining factor in our spiritual growth. We have an ability to choose to enter these internal mysteries when they present themselves. This requires a profound courage.

Dr. Jung was in his mid-thirties when he realized he needed to take a conscious plunge to the depths of his unconscious. He was a psychiatrist and knew the psychic risk he was taking of a psychotic breakdown. Yet he chose to submit to the mysteries of his unconscious and showed great courage in doing so.

For three years he set large chucks of time aside daily to playful activities he remembered doing as a solitary child. He played on his hands and knees in the sand and soil of the backyard at his home in Küsnacht on the shore of Lake Zurich. He would make an appointment in his busy life of working at the hospital, writing and seeing individual clients for therapy, to get down on the ground near the lake. He would build miniature cities and villages with sticks, rocks, sand and mud from the lake water's edge. This play gave him access to his child within and loosened his unconscious so he could begin to hear its messages with greater clarity.

Jung faithfully recorded his dreams and his active imagination encounters in his journals and did the artwork and inner dialogue required to understand what the contents of his unconscious was saying. At times the visions and dreams were so terrifying he thought he would have a psychotic breakdown and be permanently shattered. Yet his faith in the Presence of God's guidance in his dreams gave him the courage to keep moving forward.

As mentioned earlier, it would be four decades after his

death before his family would allow a biographer to write and publicize the unknown fact that Jung was sexually molested as a young child by a Jesuit priest who visited the family home regularly, a close friend of his Swiss Reformed pastor father. My work in counseling with sexual abuse victims tells me the depths of the courage Jung must have had to get through for such an encounter with his unconscious without the help of a mentor or therapist.

It has been my counseling experience that sexual abuse survivors experience shaming, whether it is conscious or unconscious to them. In some ways, due to cultural expectations about strength, self-defense and virility of the male, men often have a harder time coming to accept that they were abused. Men, even more so than most women who suffered abuse, can have a very difficult time climbing out of the abyss of shame, hopelessness and extremely low self-esteem.

I cannot imagine how difficult Jung's inner work must have been. While he never spoke or wrote about the abuse in his public life, his family knew. The only way they could have known was if he had told them, or requested that another confidant disclose the information to them.

My guess is that in his late forties or fifties, when his writings showed he had worked through much of his inner conflicts regarding alienation from his feminine energy, he told his wife and perhaps a colleague such as Toni Wolf about his past. In most cases I have worked with regarding men abused as small children, they have deeply buried the memory of such trauma in order to survive psychologically and often cannot even remember the abuse incidents until they have done a year or more of intense inner work.

Jung's ability to heal shows another purpose of the soul. Our souls have the unusual capacity to take the challenges and hurts of life *and transform them into strengths, attributes, and qualities* that normally are completely destructive.

How is the soul capable of this transformation of such pain? I like to reflect on the image of the soul symbolized by the lunar light, the nighttime moon. The reflected, feminine light of the moon craters, crevices, are symbols of receptivity, opposite to the ever-expanding gases shooting off from the proactive, masculine sun. The moon is quiet, and reflects bright light bringing illumination without destructive explosiveness.

Similarly, the Holy Grail with its concave, circular interior, is a feminine symbol of great reflectivity.

I believe our souls, like the lunar landscape and the Grail, are created with this feminine capacity to transform suffering and create great beauty alongside sorrow or replace the pain in time altogether.

The Soul Transforms Suffering when We Are Honest with Ourselves

The soul, as an organ of suffering, can assimilate, take into itself, the experiences of life and transform them into positive wisdom in a way that the rational mind alone simply cannot ensure.

For example, one of my life heroes who exhibited great courage in the last third of his life was the renowned clinical psychologist B. F. Skinner of Harvard University. Raised in a rigid, Presbyterian but non-spiritual family as the only son, Skinner was unusually sensitive and profoundly intellectual. As a child, teenager and into his university years, Skinner experienced many numinous God-experiences for which he had a deep respect. He spent much time in Nature, which nurtured his profound intuition and self-awareness.

Unfortunately, he was surrounded by family members and school teachers who shamed his interest in spirituality. These authorities exhibited great embarrassment when Skinner asked of them religious questions or tried to share his numinous experiences with these people in order to understand his ecstasy. He was very much alone.

After a final attempt to find safety in discussing what he experienced subjectively with a very outwardly devout college professor, Skinner decided his inner world must either be unimportant or simply his imagination gone wild. He made a conscious decision to embrace Bernard Shaw and Alfred Lord Whitehead's more material world view of reality and build his scientific career on the presuppositions of modern, secular, closed system, post-Christian Logical Positivism.

As an older man he suffered deeply when his work, once highly acclaimed in the world of Behavior Modification Clinical Psychology, was surpassed by a more holistic paradigm and his views fell into polite disfavor. But the turning point for him, the place of violent confrontation and all the pain accompanied with this, was the conversion of the younger of his two daughters to Christianity. He was a loving father and cared about both girls deeply, and he simply couldn't understand why she would turn to traditional religion as a world view. His older daughter followed him in his work as a behavioral scientist, but the younger, did not.

He beautifully told of this pain in his third and last volume in his autobiography. He wrote that he came through the suffering of disconnect with his daughter and the hurt of rejection by his colleagues regarding his complete deterministic prepositional scientific world view, by realizing he had tried all his life to create a Calvinistic philosophy and epistemology of science. According to Skinner, the Presbyterian religious determinism with its emphasis on predestination carried over into his scientific work. He realized it was not a complete world view, and did not allow for grace to enter into the individual life. His world view was too determined.

The Three volumes that make up Skinner's three volume autobiography are *Part I: Particulars of my Life, Part II: Shaping of a Behaviorist,* and *Part III: A Matter of Consequences.* I found this autobiographic work to be some of the most honest and transparent writing I have ever encountered in American literature and highly recommend it.

It is my hypothesis that it may have been due to his inability to process his numinous God experiences at formative moments in his life that unconsciously drove him to create what he called in his own words as an astute researcher, a scientific Calvinism.

An example of his deeply spiritual awareness as a child and teenager is apparent in a story he shares in his autobiography. He was heading home after a summer day of swimming in the river not far from his house. He lost a penknife, a very special boyhood possession, on his romps in the wild of the Pennsylvania countryside. Instinctively, he prayed and asked God to help him backtrack to find the treasured knife. To his surprise and great numinous joy, he found it directly, looking where his inner voice guided him in the high weeds and brambles several yards away on the side of the dusty road.

He ran home and shared this experience of a direct answer to prayer with his father who turned away in embarrassment and scolded him saying that such things were nonsense and the family never discussed such things. Skinner was at first confused, then shamed, by his father's reaction. This type of experience was repeated several times when he was in middle and high school, and into his first years at university. He learned to not value these personal spiritual experiences because those in authority felt they were childish wish projections and not to be taken with any rational seriousness.

Skinner, because of his profound personal honesty and ability to reflect deeply, was able to return to the Garden a whole personality. I have strong respect for his integrity. He was sad about certain aspects of his life, but his sadness was transformed into a beautiful acceptance, and example of highly refined consciousness in his late years. Skinner's commitment to truth led him to such honest self-reflection.

The Soul Uses Both What It Has and that Which Is Lacking to Bring Healing

What is the current nature of the human soul in Western culture? How can we understand who we are, what we possess and what we lack, so that we might live in all the fullness God intended for us in Creation?

C. G. Jung, in his book, *Man and His Symbols*, has some helpful ideas about how we can understand the current condition of modern Western humanity. He wrote:

[Modern Humanity's] contact with Nature has gone, and with it has gone the profound emotional energy that the symbolic connection supplied. This enormous loss is compensated for by the symbols of our dreams. They bring up our original nature ... its instincts and peculiar thinking ... unfortunately they express their contents in the language of nature, which is strange and incomprehensible to us.

Jung pointed out that the human soul by its very nature has a tremendous energy that is released naturally through communication with us by symbols. Today this communication is given to us directly by the symbolic language of our dreams. This includes information, guidance and knowledge from our instinctive, sophisticated animal nature, and with it, a strange, but direct and powerful (non-rational, yet highly intelligent) communication to our conscious mind.

This observation came to Jung after listening to and analyzing thousands of dreams of patients, clients, and his own inner experience. This knowledge brought healing to hundreds of hurting people. My own experience in dream work confirms the reality of this innate, natural symbolic language, which when understood through the scholastic study of international symbols, makes a great deal of sense. This language from our dreams is uncanny in how it speaks healing to the conscious mind, and helps us connect our intuitive and analytical intelligence together in harmony and balance.

In the opening chapter of my book *Dreams: A Spiritual Guide to Healing and Wholeness,* I tell the story of how dream work brought a rapid and permanent healing of Lupus to a middle-aged woman who had suffered from the debilitating disease for over forty years. Here is a summary of her story.

Joan, a parishioner in my church had asked for an appointment immediately following the death of her father. I assumed she wanted to talk about it.

However, the conversation turned to issues in the family that centered on abuse and rejection by the mother. Susan had suffered all of her life from Lupus since her early teen years. She was wearing white cotton gloves on this hot August day. When I asked her about the gloves, she took them off gingerly, and showed me the awful, deep lesions the disease had opened on her palms. She explained that everywhere her skin creased on her body, behind the knees, her crotch, underarms, between her toes, under her breasts, the skin was cracked and bleeding. Daily, her husband anointed her with medication to minimize the pain. I was shocked, as such a physical condition from Lupus was new information to me.

In regards to the relationship with her mother, I asked Susan to write down whatever dreams she could remember and to come back when she was comfortable to talk about them, hoping the dreams would reveal any emotional pain she was carrying at the unconscious level.

Three weeks later she returned with some dreams written down to discuss. I noticed her hands were uncovered, no gloves. When I asked her why, she happily held up her hands to show me complete healing of the deep fissures that had been there only a short time before. She explained that one day, about a week prior to our second session, her husband was anointing her, and he realized the lesions were gone. It seems as if it were overnight that the healing occurred.

Twenty years later Joan wrote and told me the healing of the Lupus was permanent and that she was convinced it was doing the dream work. I give God thanks for such a reality of the connection between the natural inner work of the dream and the healing of her body and soul.

Jung continues in his *Man and his Symbols*:

Modern man [humanity] is in fact a curious mixture of characteristics acquired over the long ages of his mental development. This mix-up being is the human being and its symbols that we have to deal with and must scrutinize his/ her mental products very carefully indeed. Skepticism and scientific conviction exist in his/her side by side with old fashioned prejudices, outdated habits of thought and feeling, obstinate misinterpretations, and blind ignorance.

Jung believed that gaps in one's childhood memory may be symptoms of the loss of the primitive psyche/soul with which we were born. He wrote that the main task of dreams was to bring back a type or "recollection" of the pre-historic, as well as the infantile world, including the most primitive instincts. I would add that included in this recollection which dreams bring us is an innate instinct within each of us to desire closeness with our Creator.

While I think that a lapse of memory is not solely a loss of the primitive soul, I feel that Jung has a very good observation. Perhaps even when we were in the womb, we have a kind of innate consciousness of being completely taken care of by the mother's body. We were kept warm, comforted, and protected. We were fed and did not suffer lack. We could experience sound, touch, vibrations, music, voices, both tender and harsh, all within the confines of the maternal womb of protection.

(The reason I know that a loss of memory is not just due to

a loss of consciousness of the primitive soul is that my work with sexual abuse victims shows that disassociation is one of the ways young abused children survive. This disassociation shows itself with memory loss or absence of memory of certain ages in childhood when the abuse occurred.)

Wayne Dyer, in his marvelous video, *The Shift*, (see bibliography for the YouTube reference) encourages the listener to remember that we were once in the womb completely safe and cared for. He challenges us to believe and trust that this God-given, loving, maternal environment continues to be available for us as adults, living in the everyday world. I have found this admonition helpful in my own life in times of great conflict, adversity and challenge.

By shifting my thinking to remembering this time in the womb being extended now into the reality of my waking life, I find an inner ability to rest, sink back, relax, and at times, to feel almost an ability to metaphysically "float" as I once did in the womb. It is as if there is a distinct memory in the very cells of my body of this time within my mother's body. I don't think this is just my imagination, because it takes no effort for me to experience this sense of inner safety. *In fact, I experience it as an opposite of effort.* I shift into this familiarity of deep union with Self by refusing to use effort, a type of inner letting go and resting in a reality that does not need to be created, only to be inwardly perceived, and "sunk down into."

The writer of the interesting Letter to the Hebrews in the New Testament wrote of a similar experience and reality in the spiritual world. The writer encouraged the reader and listener to "enter into the [Sabbath] rest that God has already provided for the people of God" (Hebrews 4:9–11).

Robert Johnson wrote in *The Fisher King and the Handless Maiden* that there is a negative, regressive mother archetype and a progressive, positive mother archetype, or perhaps two sides or opposites of the Great Mother who gives life and destroys life.

The sinking down into an inner rest that God has created for us which Wayne Dyer refers to as our early infancy experience, is not participating in the regressive, negative mother, but a trusting in the forward movement and all-encompassing nurture towards life itself of the positive mother archetype. While an immature man or woman could use this idea of "rest" to avoid the challenges of life and remain infantile in attitudes and subsequent behavior, we also can use this inner rest to feel the companionship of God/Goddess intimately connected to us by Love, moving us forward, getting us unstuck, without fear of the unknown.

The Chinese pastor Watchman Nee was a prolific teacher in pre-communist China. His spoken teaching was written down by dictation by two English stenographers and made into excellent books on the inner life.

In the book titled *Sit, Walk, Stand* he taught that the Apostle Paul, a proactive action person if there ever was one, wrote to the newly developing Christian house church in the Greek city of Ephesus. Paul wrote that the correct inner posture of the soul was to see one already in a resting position of "being seated in the heavenly places in Christ Jesus." Then he discusses how we, from within, could move forward to "walk" the spiritual path from a mental state of first sitting down in Christ. Lastly, he wrote, when confronting insurmountable obstacles, especially encountering archetypal Evil, we are "to Stand," in a *defensive stance of standing*, while first sitting and walking ... *to stand still in the rest that God has already provided* for the soul regardless of the intensity of the evil onslaught.

This is what I believe van der Post experienced looking out of his prison cell at the brilliant full moon the night before his execution. He described a deep sense of inner peace and tranquility of soul, just a few hours before being led out to the firing squad.

Many people have written and spoken of similar experiences when their souls were filled with unimaginable peace in the midst of what we would think of as an extreme panic-attack situation. As a priest, I have witnessed so many instances of great courage being present with people as they face the ultimate unknown of death. I have felt this psychic rest in the very air of the hospital room, or in one case, the atmosphere of the wet highway and a tragic automobile accident, being present with the dying driver as he breathed his last. The "rest" the womblike tranquility, the spiritual energy falls on the place of death with an uncanny persistence, and can be physically felt by others present.

So, even in lessor stressful situations of life we can experience this "recollection" of the infant soul through the symbolism of our dreams, to heighten our awareness of this reality of the closeness of God's all prevailing love and presence.

One of my favorite spoken words of Jung was shortly before his death during an interview with the BBC, a television interview one can find on YouTube easily.

The interviewer asked C. G. Jung a final question:

Dr. Jung, do you believe in God?

To which Jung gave a beatific smile that lit up his entire face and replied directly and happily:

No, no. I don't believe in God, I KNOW God.

This is the essence of living a life facing reality and working through one's difficulties to the end place of deep abiding rest. There is no need to struggle or even think in the realm of cognitive believing, but a deep, experiential KNOWING, like an infant within the womb of the mother, intuitively knowing the truth of all-encompassing contentment, joy and anticipation of Life itself.

Dreams Help Us Know God through a Symbolic Language

Jung wrote in his book *Man and his Symbols*, that for human beings, "meaning and purposefulness are not the prerogative of the mind [only]." He felt that meaning and purpose are found throughout our nature, both the rational and non-rational aspects of intelligence. He said that we should not separate organic, or natural/organic/biological growth from psychic growth (of the soul). He believed, as I also do now after decades of working with natural dreams of my own as well as those dreams of hundreds of counselees, "as a plant produces its flower, so the soul creates its symbols. So by means of dreams [*and I would add, plus all kinds of intuitions, impulses and other spontaneous experiences we all have*] instinctive forces influence the activity of consciousness."

In my words, dreams are a natural phenomenon occurring in everyone providing the symbols within that help the conscious mind (rationality) to understand organically our meaning in life and purpose.

I have found this statement above to be quite true in my work as a counselor and priest.

Also, I have discovered that people possess a genetic or spiritual inheritance from their family of origin, in addition to what Jung named the collective unconscious, the collected memory of all knowledge gained by humanity over the ages until now. This inheritance, generational or cultural collection, contains presuppositions with traditions of thought and feeling which may have a mixture of rational and non-rational aspects to it. It is with this idea of an inherited, collection of thought and feeling that I wish to move to the next subject regarding the human soul, the nature of evil in the world and in ourselves.

Section III

The Nature of Evil, and How We Understand and Overcome Its Influence

Chapter Thirteen

Where Does Evil Originate?

As a priest of large, suburban and university-city churches, I have seen this curious mixture of goodness and evil intent throughout my counseling experience. Sometimes it has been beyond exasperating how the primitive and irrational aspects of human nature co-exist in some of the most highly educated and sophisticated people I have ever encountered. I cannot account for this as many of the people I am thinking of were not taught such prejudices by their family. Often the primitive aspects of this mixture seem to come from farther back in the past in the cultural history than the current family of origin, almost like an infection that somehow skipped one or more generations.

B. F. Skinner might say that all of this prejudice is environmental conditioning, but I am not sure. In either case, I think Jung's concept is true, that there exists in human nature a "disconnect" with our natural selves and this disconnect expresses itself in bizarre and inexplicable ways.

As a priest, I have a hard time believing that the ignorance and stubborn refusal of current readily available knowledge is a God-given natural state. Yet somehow, I see it as a distortion of our Divinity due to the large amount of unconsciousness in individuals.

John Sanford disagreed with Jung in that he did not believe evil came from God and the Self, which is the psychological archetype of God in the human soul. He wrote:

"I don't see evil as an integral part of God. I see it as something allowed for the higher purposes of God, and in that respect I differ from Jung."

Sanford spoke in an interview many years ago about how he disagreed with Jung in the following online interview discourse:

Jung's epistemology of the knowledge of God would be that the knowledge of God is mediated to consciousness through the Self, the self as the archetype of God, and that's the way that one knows the nature of God, and he would tend to nullify theological speculation, and his argument would be that the Self contained both good and evil.

Now in the first place, I don't agree with his premise that the only way to the knowledge of God is through the archetype of the Self, the archetype of order and completeness within the psyche. He has a sort of encapsulated epistemology, and I don't agree with that.

Nor do I agree with his premise that the Self is a compendium of good and evil. He confused the words light and dark with good and evil. In the image of totality that the Self represents, there is light, and there is dark, but dark, you see, is not intrinsically evil. It is, indeed, the complement of light. One wouldn't know there was light if there wasn't also dark. But it is not tantamount to evil.

Now this is where Kunkel comes in, because Kunkel said that evil does not come, genuine evil does not come from the Self. It comes from the ego, and to the extent that the ego is in an egocentric state, it partakes of the nature of evil. He has an emphasis on the importance of the ego, itself.

In Jungian psychology you sometimes get the feeling that the main function of the ego is to observe the Self, and that it is not an active agent of its own. So I would see that to the extent that human beings are egocentric, the ego partakes of the nature of evil. And that's not a Jungian position. That's Kunkel's position. And I have written about that, and some people occasionally read what I write, and some of them like it, but by and large it is not a position that is very widely read in Jungian circles.

(https://www.youtube.com/watch?v=zkK8ll0JamQ)

Again, using Jungian language to try to find a rationale for the nature of evil, I would quote this passage from Jung's autobiography, *Memories, Dreams and Reflections*.

In speaking of the archetypes (including the Self, and Evil Archetypes) Jung wrote:

[T]he phenomenon of archetypal configurations – which are psychic events par excellence – may be founded upon a psychoid base, that is, *upon an only partially psychic and possibly altogether different form of being* [emphasis mine].

Jung, because of his insistence on a scientific rationale, would not say what the true nature of the archetypes is, including evil, only that:

"We have good reason to suppose that behind this veil there exists the uncomprehended absolute object which affects and influences us."

Is evil a spiritual reality or is it a psychological phenomenon? While Sanford says that it is activated in the egocentric ego, and Jung says it has an objective, possibly different form of being from the human soul, I believe, based on my personal experience, evil has an invasive quality to it that effects people in such a way that *I view its essence as autonomously objective and spiritual,* which expresses itself through the human psychological and behavioral realm.

Sanford, states in *The Kingdom Within* that it is the dark side of God that allows very difficult circumstances (suffering beyond our knowledge to understand why), that we can only get through by developing an immense inner bearing. He believes that this is the dark aspect of God and is not to be confused with absolute evil. He writes:

The dark side of God is intent on destroying everything that is not fit to exist and on forcing the growth of the highest

195

moral and psychological virtues. *Evil, on the other hand, seeks to destroy that which is good, whole, and sound. Unless this distinction is clearly drawn in our minds we will fall into confusion about the matter of evil and Jesus' view of it* [emphasis mine].

(Sanford, John A. *The Kingdom Within: The Inner Meaning of Jesus' Sayings.* J.B. Lippencott, NY. 1970, p. 103)

Another great Christian thinker from another era was Irenaeus, the Bishop of Lyons in the second century. He too did not believe that evil emanated from God. Nor did Irenaeus deny the reality of evil, indeed, much of his writing was in combating many of the Gnostic sects that arose in Christianity at the time. Some of the Gnostic Christian teachers of that time equated all suffering and darkness in life and the dark side of God not as imperfections or mysteries of a creation not yet completed, but viewed these deficiencies as evil itself, much like many modern Christian fundamentalists today.

Irenaeus did not want to banish God to the sunny side of the world, as László Boros insightly writes in his essay "Irenaeus and Patience" in *Open Spirit*. By regulating all unknowns, mysteries and sufferings to evil, one is forced back into an untenable dualism which removes all hope. This dualism, as stated above, puts evil back in the realm of emanating from God, thus God is both good and evil.

Irenaeus was a pupil of Polycarp who was himself a disciple of the original apostle John. Irenaeus taught that God was constantly moving not only the Christian, but the entire world and universe in the direction of perfection, which would be realized as heaven, a state of completion. Irenaeus believed that our vulnerability to suffering, mistakes, and pain could be understood as part of our salvation or healing. Not that God gives the suffering, but that it is one of the tools *God can use to transform us* into the perfection God intends for all humankind.

Seen in this way, our deepest regrets in life can be viewed as elements of our transformation and inner growth.

Boros writes of Irenaeus:

Behind this thought, as behind Irenaeus' whole conception of being, stands the image of a God who is great, good and master over all evil: Just as God is always the same, so also humankind, when found in God, shall always go on towards God. Neither does God at any time cease to confer benefits upon or to enrich humanity.... For the receptacle of his goodness, and the instrument of his glorification, is the human being who is grateful to God that made them.... God has promised that God will give very much to those always bringing forth fruit.... "Well done," God says, "good and faithful servant.... enter into the joy of the Lord." The Lord God's self thus promises very much.

(Boros, László. *Open Spirit: Irenaeus and Patience.* Paulist Press, NYC, NY. 1980, pp. 43–44)

Thus Sanford, Boros, Irenaeus, the teachings of Jesus Christ and many others do not give an answer to why evil exists, however, they all regard it as something under God's control and love. These thinking believers felt that somehow, beyond our current ability to comprehend, the aspects of suffering in our lives are a part of God working out the perfection of the human being, and is not part of a duality, but a tool that moves us towards our wholeness.

Regardless of how we define the nature of evil we have to contend with its presence if we are to heal ourselves and be of help to others. I use the psychological language of archetypes when I am speaking to someone who is not of a spiritual persuasion and I use the language of the New Testament and other sacred texts from the world's great religions when speaking to a spiritually orientated person or audience. It matters not to me one way or the other, it is a pastoral judgment. My pastoral focus is to deal with it and heal its destructive effects on the people I encounter.

How is prayer involved in confronting evil?

In dealing with evil, I believe we must bring prayer to the forefront of our discussion and actions. John A. Sanford, in the dialogue above, stated that prayer is not a psychological endeavor, but a spiritual practice. Jesus in his teaching makes it clear that we are to use spiritual tools in dealing with spiritual realities.

In the Third Chapter of the Gospel of John and Jesus' conversation with the doubting but spiritually-hungry Pharisee leader Nicodemus (later, to be a leader in the early Christian Church in Jerusalem), Jesus taught that spiritual rebirth is necessary for a person to understand intuitively the spiritual kingdom of God. He taught that spiritual birth is a spiritual issue and natural birth is a natural one. "That which is of the spirit is spirit, and that which is of the flesh, is flesh," was Jesus' response to Nicodemus' question regarding the possibility of spiritual rebirth. It is a spiritual rebirth for a spiritual purpose, something which a religious leader of the Jewish tradition would know a great deal about from their long, religious heritage of national and individual mystical rebirth.

I think this means that evil has a spiritual element to it, as well as a psychic component. Thus, it is important that we use the spiritual influence of prayer to bear upon it. If bringing prayer to bear on spiritual or archetypal evil is an effective tool, how are we to do this?

Resisting Evil in Prayer Is Not Succumbing to an Impotent Dualistic View of Reality

It is important that we remember that true prayer does not get drawn into an immature dualism, as if the prayer itself, even as it is difficult and feels agonizing, as the before mentioned prayer of Jesus in the Garden of Gethsemane; the prayer is not a dualistic endeavor and battle between two equal spiritual forces. Prayer can be difficult because it requires honest reflection and discernment as when and how to pray, and this may not be an easy task to discover.

From a place of quiet confidence, we can first pray and ask God if it is now our time and place to pray against the forces of evil, and to ask how to go about this. It is important not to make assumptions about the presence of evil, especially in the life of an individual. We cannot know its source, its cause, only the effects exhibited through the person's words and actions.

We can begin by asking God for wisdom regarding how to pray. A key principle in this type of prayer is to ask for guidance in how to pray against the darkness in a person's soul, and additional petitions asking God to fill the person with illumination, conviction and grace in Spirit in order to change.

I will illustrate this in a personal example from my parish work. I had in my parish in a southern part of the United States, a distinguished and stately gentleman, with dignified, snow-white hair, and a very composed behavior. He invited me, as his new priest, to accompany him by plane to fly to Austin, and to meet the governor at the time, George Bush Jr. It turned out that Bush had made other plans that day and we were not able to see him, but I was introduced to many of the leading state representatives and senator friends of my parishioner.

As we were exiting the Texas Capitol building, my parishioner spoke to me in a voice that had a feeling to it that I can only describe as extremely primitive, almost demonic in sound and quality. Out of context with the rest of our conversation, his lowered, hushed and strange voice said, "Peter, you know things have really gone downhill when you realize that a person cannot simply call someone 'a damned nigger' anymore." As I turned to see his face as he spoke, what I felt I saw was that a horrid darkness descended on him. He waited for my response.

I felt he was asking me to love the sinister, destructive side of his shadow that he would not own, the part of him that needed to be removed, not integrated. His presence at that moment was profoundly ominous, and I can only use one word to describe how it felt intuitively, and that is evil.

I was shocked. This man was a leading citizen in my city. He was demurred in every way, the perfect gentleman. But he exposed not just his dark shadow, but something more disturbing which I could feel in my spirit. He communicated a deep, long-standing inferiority-based racism of his ancestors. I felt that a despicable slave owner was speaking to me directly through his white hair and gentlemanly-looking blue eyes. The experience shook me to the core.

Sure enough, after leading my first Sunday services in this parish, this man came to my office the very next morning to tell me that he had spent seven years manipulating the leadership of the church to create a stoic, formal worship service just to his liking. He told me in no uncertain terms that if I made any changes to the deadly formal liturgy that he has forced on the congregation, he would begin to remove his financial backing of the church one third at a time, over three years, until there was none. He reminded me that he was the largest contributor to the church budgeting, giving sixty thousand dollars per year.

I tried to remain calm and replied that his giving was between himself and God, but I was called to bring new life and young families to a dying parish of elderly people, and it was my job to make changes to the liturgy that was spiritually cold, remote and out of touch with the needs of younger people.

He quietly stood up, held out his hand to shake mine, and with a false, polite smile, said that he would immediately talk to the church administrator and reduce his pledge by one third, and continue to do so until he had removed all financial commitment to the congregation. He said that he would tell others in the church that it was his displeasure with me as the new priest, as to why he would eliminate his financial support. He smiled, wished me a good day, and left, bowing slightly.

What Is the Root Cause of Such Ugliness of Spirit?

Where does such a mixture of genial behavior and ruthless, primitive ugliness come from? I believe that human beings are created in the likeness of a loving, creative God/Goddess, but if this is so, how do I explain the evil behavior of so much of the human race? The cruelty, the bigotry, the ugliness and selfishness of so many oppressive people?

One response to this question may be the reality of how unconscious most people are regarding their inner soul life. When we have repressed and alienated our own God given qualities, and separated our consciousness from the unconscious, shadow aspects of the unconscious show themselves in destructive and pathological behaviors.

At the same time, like Jung, Dr. Morton Kelsey and John A. Sanford, I know that there are evil and extremely archetypal forces loose in the realm of the soul that can not only infiltrate unconscious people, but dominate them in ways that empower them to commit atrocities against others. The biblical name for these overpowering, consuming archetypes in human nature is demonic activity. The modern Psychological world states this extreme form of evil reality is clinically known as Possession Syndrome.

This world view and biblical language came to Jewish theology from the influence of ancient Persia and the Mesopotamian Valley culture. Earlier Jewish thought identified the cause of evil with Yahweh, the God of Israel. This concept and belief of God contended that both good and evil came from God, thus evil was a punishment on unrighteous people, and goodness/ prosperity was bestowed on the righteous, clean and good. This is how their shame-based culture worked.

Jung was intimately aware through his counseling work

and his dedication to stay informed of what was happening in European cultural shifts, of the evil of Nazi Germany, and the Fascism that spread throughout Europe by Franco in Spain, Mussolini in Italy and in the Japanese military complex in the East. He named this evil for what it was. When he used the term archetypal evil this was not some kind of watering down, or psychological whitewashing of what was happening. He was using psychological language to describe the same reality of evil which spiritual language called the demonic.

As a human being and as a priest, I have had to find for myself a workable understanding of evil. In seminary, our studies in Theology focused primarily on Thomas Aquinas' theory of evil being the negation of good. Basically, this is saying that all things are good, and evil is when the good is diminished. Aquinas' thinking was based on Aristotle, among others, who was emphasizing the particulars over and against Plato's emphasis on universals. This theology is a logical, rational outworking of Aristotle's philosophical system which downplays the non-rational aspects of reality.

When I say that evil is an archetype, I am not saying that evil is not simply a name or a philosophical concept. The archetypes, as Jung taught are:

Pieces of life itself, images and forces intimately connected to the living individuals by the bridge of the emotions. This is why it is impossible to give an arbitrary [universal] interpretation of any archetype. The archetype must be explained in the context of the whole life situation of the individual [person] dreamer.

I do not find evil to be an abstract concept, or some kind of nebulous "force" that descends and ascends upon human beings at will. My experience in working with souls is that evil is specific, and direct in its influence upon individuals. How we manage this impact must be individually based.

Collective Evil Exists as Well as in Individuals

There is also a collective evil that Fritz Kunkel identified as a "group soul" where collections of individuals get caught up in a very real "spirit" or realm of evil feelings, thinking and actions. While on one hand, my experience is that most individuals participate in collective evil due to their own lack of individual consciousness, I have witnessed in very negative, destructive group settings the oppressive, "so thick one could cut it with a knife" feeling in the air which I identified as evil. I refer the reader to Sanford's book to learn about Kunkel's idea of group soul (Sanford, John A. *Fritz Kunkel: Selected Writings.* Paulist Press, NY, 1984). Having done much counseling over the decades with former military officers and soldiers involved in combat and war encounters, I have felt firsthand the darkness, terrors, and the real and false guilt feelings that many veterans experience. Also, having started my priesthood in California, I have counseled people who were heavily involved in destructive aspects of the occult, especially black witchcraft, which sole intent is to use spiritual power to harm and destroy. In addition, I have encountered such bigotry and closed-mindedness due to either enculturation or participation in cultic group activity, that the darkness that reeks from such persons is extremely prolific, and can only be described as demonic or an alliance of some kind with archetypal evil.

To give a few examples of this phenomenon, many years ago when beginning a new congregation from its concept in California, I met with a sibling of a member of the fledging church who asked to help lead the evolving youth group. This man was in his early thirties, gainfully employed, intelligent and had been coming to worship services on a regular basis. I met him for coffee in a public restaurant and asked him to tell me his story and why he wanted to work with the teenagers. This conversation was not in a confessional setting. It was simply an open conversation in a coffee house.

He told me quickly that he was unhappy. He had retired earlier than he wanted from being a Navy Seal operative. As he told me more of his story, I could see his face darken and his mood take on an almost sinister demeanor. Then he leaned forward and said something with a voice of intensity that I will never forget. He said, "I really miss the missions, you know, when we assassinated people. Fr. Peter, there is nothing that compares in excitement and happiness in my experience, better than any sex, than to slit the throat of an unaware person from behind, and slowly feel their blood drip down over your hands, as they died slowly in your arms, just fantastic!"

Needless to say, I was both shocked, angered and repelled by his comment. But it was even more than his words that repulsed me, it was the feeling he conveyed of dark, demonic evil in his delight in killing another person in a most horrible way. I quickly brought the conversation to an end telling him that what he had just told me was not told in the confines of the confessional and that I would suggest that he get therapy. I informed him that I would not allow him to be around our young people.

I told him that if he wanted my help to change his attitude about his past, I would be a priest for him. However, from what he conveyed, there was no indication of remorse, or sense of real guilt. In fact, it was quite the opposite, a pride in what he had done and, yes, a sickening, sadistic sense of joy in killing. His story struck me as evil as any Nazi doctor experimenter I had read about in the Holocaust history.

The young man was offended by my response, repeating that he had not shared what he did with any sense of remorse but of great pride and sadness that he could no longer legally do such killing. He left my congregation and then eventually departed from our geographical area.

Another example of an encounter with archetypal evil involved a clergy person of my acquaintance. Once in conversation, this person told me about their delight and joy in molesting boys in his parish and that this was a loving act and right in the sight of God. I know this sounds unbelievable but the facts are known in the church that there are priests who think and act like this.

Having spent years counseling and networking with my bishops, medical doctors and psychologists, I am very aware of the horrible destruction that takes place in the soul and body of a child when sexually abused, especially by a member of the clergy. In the case of this priest, I cut off the conversation, said nothing, and immediately contacted my bishop who then dealt with the situation effectively.

Yet there are other, less dramatic instances of archetypal evil which happen in groups and individuals which probably have more to do with gross unconsciousness than outright selfishness. This is how I explain the intense, self-righteousness of some religious persons I have encountered. I have witnessed this deeply depraved, ignorant and destructive self-confidence in Fundamentalist Protestants and the well-publicized racist and homophobic evangelicals. But, also, I have had conversations with fundamentalist Roman Catholics and Anglicans who insist, in the most anti-loving and hateful manner, that only their brand of religious tradition is correct and truly Christian.

I have experienced members of my own Episcopal parishes so threatened by needed change and profoundly stuck in false beliefs in what they considered holy behavior that hatred seeped out through their eyes without a shred of deflection or humility. Frankly, I have grown to be weary of deeply religious and zealous persons, preferring to spend my time with more mature, open and reasonable types often found outside religious institutions.

For some reason, the religiously distorted persons come

across to me as the most spiritually evil. I don't know if this is because I am a priest and hope that religious people would be better than they are, or if the psychological and emotional sicknesses some people have, when tied to a religious agenda, take on a deeper, more sinister and truly evil sense about them. I have no answer to this question.

One final example, again from a religious group, unfortunately. I was hired as the priest at an Episcopal parish, where the former priest was really theologically a Christian fundamentalist wrapped in the false garbs of an educated liturgical priest. He was the graduate of a Baptist seminary, attended one semester of a few classes of Anglican studies and was a professional actor. He was a charismatic personality and attracted a large following, almost cultic in nature, including the well wishes of our bishop at the time, another former Baptist who transitioned to the Episcopal Church years prior.

Unknown to me, the parish was controlled politically and economically by a group of very angry, immature fundamentalists who had no knowledge of church history. I should not have taken the job. The bishop foolishly told me that my Jungian background would be appreciated and help the people in this church find a more holistic outlook.

Within days of starting work in this parish I was being told by the "leaders" of this congregation that I was not a "born again Christian" and animosity began and escalated until I decided to resign ten months later under duress. Life was too short to put up with such nonsense. I was part of the California Jesus Movement as a college student, and lived in a fundamentalist cultic commune. I was very much part of the "born again" world and chose to leave it as a young adult because of the mentally unwell aspects of such a restrictive world view. So, I knew what I was up against and was happy to leave to do work elsewhere, perhaps, with a more astute bishop.

However, after talking with the assistant to the bishop and

my primary parish leader known as the senior warden, I led a final monthly business meeting with the elected members of the church board. About forty additional members of the fundamentalist camp had organized to take over the meeting. They wanted the church to remove me because they convinced themselves I was a "heretic," a non-believer and that I was destroying "their church."

I will never forget the feeling in the room as this group of fanatics attacked my integrity. Some of the speakers spoke with such hatred and venomous energy it felt like the room was infiltrated by large, poisonous snakes in attack mode. The spiritual energy that these people brought to the church meeting can only be described as extreme ignorance, or, perhaps, archetypal evil.

The result of their behavior was a mass exodus of the rest of the parish members. They had witnessed the unleashed hatred and bigotry of their fellow members and they wanted nothing to do with it.

It is my belief that whenever a group disconnects and identifies a common "enemy," and they dehumanize and demean others with their words and attitude, this collective evil can take over and prevail over any kind of decency, order, or rational discourse. The only way to deal with such an encounter that I know of is to disengage and leave. If one cannot leave, being silent and still may be the best course of action.

An example of being silent in the gospel stories is that of Jesus before Pilate on the night before his execution. He stood silent both before the Sanhedrin and Pilate, "as a mute lamb before the slaughter" as the writer of the Gospel of John portrayed this drama. He was being confronted by the high priest and, later, the Roman ruler of Palestine, Pontus Pilate, with untrue accusations they did not provide for themselves, but were received from the collective lie of the masses stirred up to inflammatory accusations not based in fact by Jesus' enemies.

His accusers were amazed that he did not speak up and defend himself. He stayed centered and grounded in his being, faced the consequences with great courage, dignity and poise. Often collective evil cannot be dealt with by a counter aggression, only a composed silence.

Chapter Fourteen

The Nature of Sin and the Proliferation of Evil Lies in the Acts of Unconscious Living

The reader may remember that John A. Sanford taught insightfully that we are affirmed by Jesus in the gospels to be whole as God is whole (complete). Wholeness implies a lack of polarity or even mixture. The ancient Hebrew shamed-based culture stated that any kind of mixture was unholy and defiled such as: human-made combined with natural fiber for clothing, water for washing mixed with water for other purposes, food cooked in appropriate containers so different items are not cooked and mixed together. Intermarrying between Jew and non-Jew was outlawed for the same reason, because mixture meant a loss of identity, thus, a loss of meaning and authentic spirituality.

For us today, psychologically and spiritually speaking, wholeness requires differentiation, without the polarity of black and white thinking due to an unconscious lack of self-awareness. When the ego acts as if it is the whole (wholeness defined by all being made conscious and submitted by the ego to the Greater Self) we end up with the evil of egocentricity, narcissism, and sociopathy. Also, when we are unconscious of our shadow, we project it onto others and easily make them our scapegoats. This projection of our shadow is another form of an unhealthy polarity.

Reflecting on the Grail myth, Emma Jung and Marie Louise van Franz in their book, *The Grail Legend*, write the following regarding a need for us to differentiate, and avoid polarized thinking and action. At the end of the Grail myth the authors write:

It is clear that Perceval does not succeed in redeeming the

hidden humanity, the Anthropos. He chooses holiness instead of humanity, evil as the opposite of good, is constellated anew. At the end of our myth, Perceval, instead of taking the Grail back to King Arthur's Round Table, and sitting himself in the Judas Chair, thus providing the availability of the graces of the Grail to minister to the Public needs of the world, Perceval goes into hiding with the Grail, he retreats into the world of the spiritual, alone, and the world is at a greater loss of hope, than existed at the beginning of our story.

I have always wondered why the story of Arthur's Table of Camelot did not reach further down through history to penetrate the Now. I would suggest that this retreat into seclusion by the possessor of the Grail seems to appear upright and good. In reality this retreat into the spiritual realm without integration with the world, is a great disaster, and invitation for evil to continue its lies, immortality and deception onto humankind.

(Jung, Emma and von Franz, Marie Louise. *The Grail Legend.* Princeton University Press, Princeton, NJ. 1998)

Balance between two opposites is very different than mixture. Mixture implies an unconscious confusion, an unsuccessful attempt at integration without clarity, which is anything but integration. Balance requires astute self-awareness and differentiation, after which a conscious choice of when to appropriate an opposite and when to leave an opposite position alone. How can this principle be applied to our discussion about the nature of evil and the soul?

Insight into the Nature of Evil
John Sanford wrote in his book, *Evil: The Shadow Side of Reality*:

As long as people observe morally scrupulous lives only

because of outer sanctions, but with no knowledge about themselves, their morality is on a collective level. A higher morality can come about only through individual self-knowledge. Moreover the higher moral values people hold are effective only within the range of consciousness.

When we are unaware of our inclinations to darkness or evil, in that area of unawareness our moral codes and sense of value are ineffective, for where conditions of ignorance prevail, the Shadow remains an autonomous figure who is unrelated to the rest of the personality. For this reason, a true morality must necessarily go hand in hand with personal knowledge of one's Shadow.

Each solution to the problem of the Shadow is an individual one, and each person must, in the last analysis, find his or her own appropriate way of living creatively with the dark side.

(Sanford, John A. *Evil: The Shadow Side of Reality*. Crossroad, NY, 1989, p. 66)

It is important that we all have a strong and healthy persona which we use to express a certain part of ourselves to relate to other people. The problem arises when we identify too strongly with our persona or mask and we actually believe that we are the persona. If this happens, we lose touch with our shadow side and we end up with a fake, dangerous, shallow personality and lack of authentic character.

Often people try to hand us a persona to carry for them. As a parish priest, people would try to force to me carry a persona of the constantly, loving, gentle, patient priest of their imaginations of what they thought a priest should be. Sometimes both men and women who had no solid relationship with their fathers or other authority figures in their life would project this image onto me, asking me to make decisions and take on a parental role for them. Thus, they could avoid taking responsibilities for their own lives.

Of course, I had to have a persona as a priest but I was careful not to accept the projections from others of a "holy man," or someone with a higher standard of love. I know my own heart. I would use my writing in my private journal to write out and process my true feelings about people, especially people whom I disliked, or whose personalities I found sickening and repulsive.

The converse was also sometimes true. A person with authority issues could project their hurt, anger and sense of injustice onto me as the parish priest. It was a constant challenge to deal with these projections and not unconsciously carry this shadow aspect of my parishioners for them.

Simultaneously, I would write out whatever self-awareness I had regarding my own projections, whether projections of romantic attraction, or the opposite, extreme feelings of disgust or hatred towards people in my pastoral care. I had a role to fill and I would do it to the best of my ability, but I never believed that I was a holy man, somehow above the common grounding of all humanity. This journaling would help me deal with the projections and not assimilate them into myself unconsciously. This self-reflective writing would provide the safe place for me to own my own Shadow and not project it outwardly where it could do great harm to others.

Jesus was very aware of both the persona and the Shadow in himself and in others. If a person does not like the idea of Jesus having a Shadow (that which might be unconscious) one could use the term "the dark side" of Jesus instead of Shadow.

He often rebuked the Pharisees and other religious rulers of his day for their hypocrisy which resulted in their acceptance of their persona and the projections of others as true to their full self-identity. He said they were similar in character to whitewashed tombs on the outside, but were full of dead men's bones and every kind of corruption within. Outwardly they would appear to others to be honest good people, but inside, they were full of hypocrisy and moral law breaking.

To the man who wanted to follow him and who called Jesus good, Jesus replied, "Why do you call me good?" He made the fellow own his projection thus enabling the man to clarify his thinking and his spoken words. Jesus would not carry the man's projected goodness for him but allow him to carry his own shadow.

Sanford points out that Jesus was quite tolerant and easy going about most human frailties. He hung out with prostitutes and the reviled tax collecting Jews who worked for the Roman government in their oppression against the people of Palestine. But Jesus toughly confronted those persons, such as the religious leaders, primarily the more progressive Pharisees, who identified with their persona. He challenged them with strong language and actions knowing that not to do so could endanger their souls.

Jesus was fully aware of his Shadow, and used the energy of it consciously to bring about actions that brought life, not destruction. For example, his angry bursts of action overturning the tables of the money changers in the temple in Jerusalem was a very conscious act of acknowledging his anger and using it to do what was needed. He used the energy in his Shadow to confront the evil he perceived of the temple moneychangers, who turned the forgiveness of God available through the prescribed rituals of cleaning and giving in the temple cult into a selfish, greedy, self-serving deception of theft and power abuse.

Another example of Jesus honoring his Shadow is found in the Gospel of John, where the writer tells of Jesus' struggle with the fear, doubt and mother complex regression in his prayer in the garden on the eve of his betrayal. He prayed with severe agony and difficulty, not wanting to go through with the trial, pain, humiliation and torture on the cross and his eventual death. He prayed to God that this cup of suffering should pass from him.

Perhaps we can say that God allowed Jesus to suffer this agony in his praying to empower Jesus to discover his innermost strength for the coming climax of the suffering of his crucifixion, death and burial. Regardless of why this suffering (evil) occurred, the writer of the gospel makes it clear that the suffering was very real and was part of Jesus' human condition and complete identification with humanity.

Only after what might have been hours of struggle, fully in touch with and honoring his Shadow and the emotions laying within it, Jesus was able to make the conscious decision to move forward. He proclaimed, "Nevertheless, not my will, but yours be done," as his summary prayer.

Jesus taught that health was an integrated ego, persona, and Shadow with the Self, or in Christian language, Christ within. Nothing was to be split off that is part of our created human nature. It is my conviction that Jesus did not address issues of conscious sexuality or gender identity because such questions are most often unnecessary in the quest for wholeness. They are non-issues. They only become issues when who we are is repressed, hidden and unconscious, thus part of our Shadow. He did, however, consistently honor and affirm the gold which dwelt in individuals and small group Shadows, as he knew how society and family could repress what God has created.

One example of honoring the gold in a person's Shadow may be his response to the loud, obnoxious, persistent Phoenician woman whose daughter was demon possessed. Her voice most likely came across loud, obtuse, and angry because she was worn out being the primary caregiver to a mentally ill family member.

Jesus addressed her sense of unconscious animus possession (the negative masculine inner critic) that was openly exposed in her out of control desperate, abrasive shouting for help. Jesus spoke to her Shadow saying, "It is not right to give that which belongs to the children to the dogs." This rebuke allowed her to become conscious, and own her Shadow. She was then able to speak with self-awareness from her gold within, her true treasure of intuitive knowledge, wisdom in humility and faith, saying, "Yes Lord, but even the dogs eat the crumbs that fall under the table of the children."

Jesus then affirmed her inner gold of faith within her Shadow. This relief, and self-awareness on her part allowed the healing to happen and to be complete. "Go, your faith has made you whole. Your daughter is fine," he was able to proclaim to her with certainty and confidence. Her faith was somehow tied up in her need to own the gold in her shadow and move out from the victim mentality that had possessed her.

As in some cases of children having sickness, when the mother brought to consciousness her Shadow unhappiness, her daughter was healed alongside the mother's inner healing. The daughter was no longer having to carry the Shadow of her mother as well as her own.

In Some Ways, St. Paul Was a Stark Contrast to the Self Awareness of Jesus

I am indebted to John A. Sanford for the following insights. The apostle Paul whose writings equaled and, in some cases, surpassed the stories written about Jesus in his influence on the early church may have had very little self-awareness about his persona and his Shadow. While he recognized his own dual nature as described in the Letter to the Romans Chapter Seven, he encouraged what amounted to repression of the Shadow in his teachings. Paul encouraged people to identify themselves with the light-side qualities of love, patience, goodness, and to shun their dark sides of anger, frustration and their need to stay grounded in their humanness. Thus, the acceptance of Paul's writing influenced the early church to repress the Shadow instead of relating to it as Jesus did for himself and others.

We find that Paul, due to either his Stoicism or his Gnosticism and his belief in dualism and denial of all that is natural in humanity, was angry with his opponents at the church in Galatia who felt the Gentile converts needed to be circumcised to become truly Jewish Christians. Paul wrote that he wished the knife they used to cut others for Jewish circumcision would slip and cut their own genitals off! This Paul spoke from his repressed anger in his Shadow through his rage. He was not conscious of his Shadow, thus it revealed itself through his words and vindictive attitude.

Paul refused to accept and integrate his Shadow as an important and legitimate part of his own human nature. He cut it off and labeled it sin. If he had related to it, his Shadow could have given him huge benefits of intuition, feminine relational ability and many other gifts. Instead, because of his inappropriate dualistic view of reality, he drove his Shadow even deeper, cutting off some of his inner gold as well as parts of himself that were not acceptable but could be transformed if he would acknowledge and nurture them into wholeness.

Sanford writes:

Paul acts towards his Christian converts like a parent often does toward their children: anger is reserved as the prerogative of the parent, while the children are expected to be models of perfect behavior. Paul repeatedly urges his Christian congregations to think and behave only out of what we might call their light side. Love, patience, forgiveness, gentleness, reasonableness, and lack of personal ambition are commendable and to be practiced and observed. Hatred, anger, sexual desires or fantasies, and emotions in general are to be denied. The effect of Paul's psychological ethic is the development of a collective persona. And his pressure upon his Christian converts to adopt it resulted in the repression of everything that contradicts this persona.

Paul's attitude towards women and the persona is found in the First Epistle to Timothy. After putting women in a subordinate position inferior to men, Paul adds: "Nevertheless, she will be saved by childbearing, provided she lives a modest life and is constant in faith, and love and holiness." Such a passage makes us wonder what ever happened to salvation through Christ. (Sanford, John A. *Evil: The Shadow Side of Reality.* Crossroads, NY, 1989. p. 58)

Sanford affirms that Jesus was conscious enough to transcend the collective thinking of his time, but Paul was not able to do this. Many in the early church followed in Paul's lack of inner awareness and consciousness and thus did not practice the non-duality in the teachings of Jesus.

This problem Continues in the Church Today

It is my conviction that dualism does not work. Only the unity of opposites can heal and save. How do we accomplish this? What is there to help us who seek to unite our opposites and utilize the energy of our Shadow for positive good? John Sanford's *Evil: The Shadow Side of Reality* has some important answers to this question of what we can do to recognize, confront and stand against evil. This chapter will outline Sanford's ideas in my own language.

One of the more obvious yet often unstated reasons we act out evil within ourselves or allow it in others within our sphere of influence, is that the unconscious decision to do evil leads to our *becoming* evil. While we recognize our Shadow contains the potential to do evil, we cannot ever act on these dark impulses. This is never an answer to the problem of evil within us.

Giving license to the Shadow to act out is not the same as

being aware of our Shadow and making a conscious decision to integrate it into our consciousness. Sanford points out when we recognize our Shadow, we open ourselves to increased compassion, a more authentic self-humility and can engage our sense of humor appropriately. If we do not engage our Shadow, we stay stuck in a collective morality and cannot develop an individuate morality. Such an authentic individuated morality goes hand in hand with the self-awareness of our Shadow.

Another example of evil actions following an unconscious attitude towards life can be found in the following article about the war criminal trial of the Nazi leader Eichmann. Otto Adolf Eichmann was a German-Austrian SS-Obersturmbannführer and one of the major organizers of the Holocaust, referred to as the "Final Solution to the Jewish Question" in Nazi terminology. He was directly responsible for the deaths of millions of victims. In this article from the website *Ways of Thinking*, UK, named *The Unthinkable: Failed Empathy and Hatred of the Other,* we find these observations.

1961, Jerusalem: the year of the Eichmann trial. Hannah Arendt, philosopher, political thinker and journalist, was there.

She subsequently reported on the trial for The New Yorker and her perceptions are important to consider in terms of ways of thinking. She was surprised to find that Nazi war criminal did not look outwardly monstrous or brutal; on the contrary, he appeared bland, ordinary and rather unintelligent. Yet this seemingly unremarkable man had systematically organized the sending of millions of Jews to their death.

Failed empathy is explained as the refusal of another to help in desperate need. Thus the 'idea of man' as a fellow traveler through life, the sense of an 'other' who will be alongside us, is destroyed. In its place is an emptiness, an aloneness, created by the trauma and the sadism of the other in the place of empathy and love.

How was it that such apparent mediocrity belied Eichmann's capability to commit atrocities?

Arendt concluded that it was this very mediocrity that produced the lack of thinking, the 'Thoughtlessness' which led to him blindly following orders from his Nazi superiors. He was unable to reflect and he lacked the ability to think through, critically and independently, the orders he was given. He needed to follow 'routine procedures,' without which he floundered.

Arendt wonders in her book whether our ability to recognize right and wrong is, in fact, directly connected to our ability to think. She comes to believe, as she witnesses Eichmann's behavior, that 'absence of thought' is the cause of evil.

His unthinking, unquestioning submission to the demands of a despotic authority led to the committing of heinous acts. Arendt found no thoughtful profundity in this man, only a 'cliché-ridden language' and a superficiality of evil that spread 'like a fungus on the surface.... Only the good has depth.'

Deborah Lipstatt has also emphasized the central role that Eichmann played in planning the genocide; he was more than a follower of orders. Some critics feel that these new findings contradict Arendt's view that Eichmann was merely unable to think for himself. 'What is most missing is the recognition that a thinking person is not necessarily inoculated against committing evil acts.'

Arendt, it continued, 'grasped an important concept but not the right example.' The concept is indeed important; whether or not it applies to Eichmann is for another discussion, another time.

Yet such 'normalization of the unthinkable' still continues

to this day.
(https://waysofthinking.co.uk/)

There is a difference between saying that one is unconscious and one is not thinking for one's self. I have known of people who are extremely cruel due to what I believe is an unconscious awareness of what they are doing. There are also other people who are very aware of their cruelty who knowingly choose evil acts of cruelty for the purposes of feeling in control because of their personal powerlessness. In the case of Eichmann, it may have been a case of both/and regarding why he carried out the orders to murder multitudes of innocent people.

In the next chapter, we will look at what we can do as individuals to confront evil in our lives and in the lives of others and how our souls can work through such situations without being harmed by the very evil we need to confront.

Chapter Fifteen

What Steps Can We as Individuals Take to Deal with Evil Effectively?

How can we as individuals effectively confront evil in society and make changes for the betterment of humankind? The following ideas are simply suggestions and do not in any manner propose to provide complete answers to these complex questions. Each of us must find what works for us, and what does not.

To begin, I would re-emphasize that collective morality, meaning what a large group designs as a lowest common denominator morality, has only destructive, inflexible utility and needs to be avoided. What is needed is individual, self-aware morality put into practice in pragmatic ways. This is the foremost, most important principle to keep in mind in dealing with evil. When Jung was asked in a BBC televised interview shortly before his death the question:

"Dr. Jung, do you think that humankind will make it?"

Jung, leaned forward with his hands on his knees and replied intensely, "If enough individuals do their inner work, yes, I think we can make it."

We must be very conscious. John Sanford writes:

If we are not (conscious of our Shadow), even those of us who set out unconsciously to do good will try to exceed our capacity for natural goodness and bring about more evil, because our unnatural stance generates an accumulation of darkness in the unconscious.

A writer in the field of sales and marketing, Robert Ringer, wrote decades ago a truth I have found as a priest to be quite true. He writes simplistically and not without some humor in his book, *Looking Out for Number One.* He teaches that there are three types of people.

First is the person who says they are going to hurt you and they go ahead and do it.

A second type is the person who says they are going to help you, but then, consciously, they go ahead and carry out their agenda to harm you.

The third, Ringer wrote without sarcasm, is the most dangerous type of human being to encounter in business, and in my estimation, in life in general. This is the person who truly believes they are good, and they are going to help you, but *they are completely unconscious.* They are intent on destroying you but dishonest with themselves about this. They blindly destroy all that is good.

To practice one's own self-awareness gives us the ability to discern the self-awareness of others. This is the essential first step in dealing with evil. To deal with the evil within ourselves, to be aware of our own tendency to murder, steal, criticize, slander and to destroy others, is the prerequisite to seeing this destructive unconsciousness in others.

When we are conscious of our own evil, we can integrate the aspects of our dark side that can be integrated with our opposites, and we become more whole. What within us is differentiated as potential or actual evil, we can ask for cleansing, forgiveness and removal. We can be intentional about praying for illumination and self-awareness. This is one of the advantages I can see of the traditional Western Christian emphasis on human nature as sinful. Such a teaching can help unconscious people look at themselves perhaps with some moral honesty.

Yet I would go beyond this teaching to say that this sinfulness is not an inherent tendency to be destructive, but is the blindness to our potential within ourselves to be destructive. This blindness creates an overemphasis on the opposite spectrum of being extraordinarily good to the exclusion of our awareness of our own dark side. Only when we are this self-aware can we act in love towards ourselves and to our fellow human beings. This self-mindfulness is the higher morality that Christ called us to and we can attain by the grace of God.

In the words of Episcopal priest and monk Martin L. Smith, Society of St. John the Evangelist:

"Sin is all that is done in the illusory state of estrangement from God"(Smith, Martin L. *Love Set Free: Meditations on the Passion According to St. John*. Cowley Publications, Boston, 1998, p. 68).

This focus on individual self-reflection and mindfulness automatically removes us from the unconscious influence of harmful collective morality which in my experience, is never morally justified or good in any sense of the word. I believe this because collective thinking in us puts us in to a dualistic judgment which is always slanted towards a distortion of truth.

An example from the teachings of Jesus comes to mind. Not long after his public ministry has begun and he had selected his particular disciples from among the crowd that followed him, several of his disciples came to him with a complaint about people outside their immediate, collective group of disciples.

They said to Jesus:

"There is a person baptizing others in your name Lord, who is not one of else. Should we force them to stop this?"

Jesus replied, "No, leave them alone. Whomever is not against us is for us, and no one can give a drink of water to one of these little ones who will not receive their reward."

Jesus made it clear that group, collective thinking, what we might call an "us against them" mentality, was contrary to his message and his divine mission. We must abandon all collective and culturally unconsciously-determined-thinking to uncover our own individual responsible mortality. As Sanford so eloquently wrote:

"A true morality must necessarily go hand in hand with personal knowledge of one's Shadow."

A second step in resisting evil that requires us to relate to our Shadow is this. *We must not identify with our Shadow and live out all its impulses and darkness.* This is not integration, but a shift from one side of opposites to the other, remaining in a split consciousness which is always destructive. This is the nature of the narcissist.

The classic narcissist is a person who demands that others accept all aspects of their Shadow, both the creative and the absolutely destructive aspects of their Shadow. Anyone who refuses to affirm the socially and morally reprehensible aspects of the narcissist's Shadow, do not truly love them; the narcissist demands such blind loyalty. We are never required to accept or affirm the destructive aspects of a person's shadow. Indeed, we are to stand firmly against it.

This insistence on others loving the destructive aspects of the shadow are a direct result of the child not having a close enough bond with the mother, to move from a goddess projection of her to an acceptance of her with all her human limitations. There is no graduate assimilation of the imperfection of the mother, thus the very small child grows with a deep insecurity that nothing can alleviate. The narcissist will not accept that the mother is imperfect, thus they cannot accept their own imperfection.

We can see this aspect of an insistence on others accepting the destructive aspects of our Shadow in the Grail story. At the beginning of Perceval's quest, his treatment of Blancheflor is very unconscious. They sleep together platonically as brother and sister, suggesting innocence. Then upon waking first, Perceval cruelly steals her ring from her finger. The ring was given as a betrothal token by her knight.

As a result of Perceval's greed, stupidity, or both, Blancheflor is rejected by her knight fiancé and suffers immeasurably by this rejection for which she had no responsibility. She is now a flawed woman subject to complete rejection. Perceval has no remorse, no sense of right or wrong; the classic narcissist. I believe he acts this way impulsively because of the domineering relationship by his mother. She was a goddess archetype to him creating in him a disregard for her humanness, thus he projected both the goddess/virgin and the witch/whore onto all the women he would encounter.

This indifferent action by Perceval is evil. It does not matter what his motivation was for stealing the ring. The result was the destruction of a young, innocent and loving person in the character of Blancheflor. Perceval spun from being kind and gentle to an obtuse, selfish narcissist in the matter of a moment. This selfishness can only be described as evil.

I can think of some instances from my work as a parish priest when narcissistic personalities have asked me to love the destructive aspects of their Shadow. Many people in my pastoral care demanded that if I did not love their irresponsible dark side for which they would not take ownership, my lack of accepting their destructive Shadow was a sign that I did not care and love them.

I would suspect this destructive dynamic is behind such a con person as Donald Trump. He insists that people affirm the disparaging, selfish and irresponsible aspects of his dark side. Anyone who resists this is his enemy. I would suggest that many of his followers are people who tend to have a similar lack of self-analysis and control. They may expect others to love and affirm the most grossly arrogant aspects of the dark sides of their personhood. Anything less is seen as a lack of love and acceptance and a type of persecution complex that is completely irrational and irresponsible.

For a greater understanding of Donald Trump's relationship with his mother which explains much of the roots of his narcissism, I recommend a reading of Justin A. Frank's book *Trump on the Couch: Inside the Mind of the President.*

However, I would suggest there is one aspect of difference between Trump and his followers. I believe, based on his personal life history and his actions, that Trump has consciously embraced his own evil and accelerated, even celebrated it, because of his embracing of a demonic power drive. I believe that he, at some point in his adult or teenage life, has made a conscious decision to embrace evil and this has allowed him to *become* evil. Why this is so, I do not speculate. I would not suggest that his followers have done the same. I believe they simply are unconscious, fearful people with great needs for security and find in Trump a savior complex.

However, Trump is a master manipulator, and he arrogantly strokes his audiences with falsehood knowingly because he has consciously "sold his soul to the devil" in some Faustian fashion that only he and his God can know how or why. I would not be surprised if historians one day discover in researching his life that at one point he partook of some kind of semi-private, perhaps religious ritual of embracing an evil archetype or entity in pursuit of his ruthless ambition to have power over others. Usually such a person makes a conscious decision to embrace evil because of extreme feelings of inadequacies and complete powerlessness. In my opinion, even Donald Trump's face has taken on a look of utmost cruelty and ugliness, as he continues his narcissistic path. His eyes changed over the years to a type of serpentine cast.

Confronting Archetypal Evil in Individuals and Groups of Collective Evil

I think there are ways we can confront individual evil in isolated incidents and even in public settings. I think of the wonderful story of Mother Teresa of Calcutta soon after starting her school for girls and the first hospice in Calcutta. She tells the story of how a gang of local mafia young men harassed her and tried to intimidate her to pack up and leave the neighborhood. This taunting went on for many days while she stayed focused on her work.

But finally, I would guess it was not in exasperation, but following a deep intuition as the timing of such confrontations must be right, she went out in front of the hospice building, walked up face to face with the leader of the hooligans. She pointed her crooked finger almost touching his nose and told him in no uncertain terms that he would have to kill her first before the hospice would be shut down or moved.

I would guess that the young man experienced amazement when she confronted him and the spiritual power she emanated convicted him of his evil words and actions. He turned on the spot and ordered his gang to now support, protect and escort Teresa and her workers wherever they went in the city. The enemy was transformed into the supportive friend. The gang would provide this protection for the ministry for years to come. I think it was her days of quiet centeredness that gave her the power, the insight and the intuitive timing to come out, confront him and turn the situation completely around.

A friend of mine many years ago had a similar type of encounter with evil in a public setting. This story also demonstrates the power and effectiveness of listening to one's spiritual intuition.

The town where I lived annually hosted a provincial summer fair which included a large carnival of rides and concessions which usually attracted a large number of very rough people. One afternoon during the fair, just outside the gates to the fairground, a friend of mine while walking to his car, witnessed two of these toughs fighting to the death on the concrete sidewalk. The man who had the upper hand was beating the other man's head against the concrete curb with all his strength. If this continued for many more moments, the man would certainly be killed.

My friend instinctively and quickly trusting his intuition,

leaned his right arm across the top of his car, pointing his finger at the crowd gathered and men killing each other about two hundred feet away across the street. He spoke quietly but firmly, "In the name of Jesus Christ, stop this right now!" The atmosphere in the air suddenly was suspended almost as if time stood still, and the spell on the fighting men was broken. The man in control quickly let go of the other man's head as if he had been struck by lightning. Both men acted dazed, stood up and slinked into the crowd of onlookers. The violence immediately ended.

While my friend acted swiftly and effectively in the moment, I am not sure why I feel that the best strategy may be to not engage collective evil spontaneously. I think it may be better to wait until the spiritual intuition gives specific guidance concerning the content and timing of confrontation. I think it may have something to do with providing evil with an audience. When an audience is not present, the ego needs of an inferiority superiority complex within collective evil are not met.

Collective evil, as in the cases I cite above, as well as instances of individual evil I have encountered have always been about a need to feel powerful because of a huge inner reality of weakness. I think of the Nazi commanders, soldiers, guards, office staff, doctors, and other participants. These people were not only influenced by the general propaganda spewed out by Hitler and his cronies regarding the superiority of the Arian race in reaction to the demoralization of the German people by the consequences of the First World War, but also the hyperinflation and economic collapse of the Weimar Republic. Each of these factors may have contributed to the feelings of powerlessness the German politic must have felt. Additionally, these Nazi perpetrators may have had family system dysfunction in their families of origin that inhibited their moral judgement.

However, these individuals who chose to do Hitler's bidding have been shown by contemporary journalism to believe themselves exceedingly moral in contrast to popular opinion which stated these people were amoral, without conscience. The opposite was true. They were highly morally conscious, believing themselves to be doing the will of God. They felt they were carrying out their righteous duty to eliminate the "inferior" subhuman Jewish race, the Roma, the handicapped, the homosexual, the mentally ill, and birth defected populations that they murdered. The morality of these perpetrators was highly conscious and simultaneously explicitly evil and immoral.

I see parallels to this today among most collective thinking whether it be self-righteous right- or left-wing camps. One cannot say these groups are lacking morals, indeed the debate centers on a high assumptive plateau of righteous morality, thus the antagonism. But there is a spiritual reality behind such rigid moral certainty, a shadow element that portrays itself as a non-rational drivel within the self-righteousness that is ugly, one-sided, blind and delusional, regardless of where the group collective is on the left-right spectrum.

The energy that comes forth is destructive. There is no life to the energy because the self-righteousness itself is based on a lie, the pathological, sociopathic belief that the self-righteous possess the "truth" and all others are wrong. The path of such one-sided blindness is destruction and death, both spiritually, and, in the case of the Nazis, quite literally.

We are each called to live according to truth. Individuals are what make the difference in the larger portrait. We are given the ability to love and cherish God and one another. Anything less is contrary to our human nature.

A Carelessness towards Evil Can Push a Person to Act Evil

Sanford also taught that a carelessness towards evil can predispose a person towards a conscious decision to embrace evil and act upon it. In our Grail story there is an instance of great carelessness that leads to later trouble for our hero in the myth.

When Perceval is in the Fisher King's court for the first time, part of the procession is the display and procession of a semi-broken sword which is given to him by a feminine damsel. She tells him it is important that he heed the sword with care, as it has been weakened and needs to be treated with high awareness of its limitations. Ignoring her, Perceval carelessly sets the sword aside and does not put it on his waist buckle.

Much later in the story, Perceval is chastised for his neglect by another fair damsel, who reminds him that that sword that needed repair cannot be used as if it were complete. Emma Jung in her book *The Grail Legend* retells the symbolism of the sword in medieval Europe. It is a symbol of masculine power, differentiation, categorical, analytical thinking and truth.

I find it very interesting in the Grail story that truth, *philosophically thought of as masculine Logos*, is *mostly spoken and illuminated by female characters*. This again portrays the importance of our cultural need to listen to the feminine wisdom, our intuition and the relationships in which we are involved.

In speaking of the nature of the soul, this sword can represent in us the dominant masculine approach to problem solving which forgets the feminine aspects of remembering, reflection, intuition and relationship. This carelessness in utilizing a broken, in-need-of-repair, masculine focus on truth at the expense of relationship is an excellent metaphor for our current Western cultural sickness and demise. We do not recognize the limitations of our analytical and competitive attitude towards life, and when we apply it with vigor, it most often breaks and creates more disillusionment and chaos in its wake.

Regarding carelessness and the insidiousness of the step by step infiltration of evil in persons and in Western society, I have a very disturbing true story from my early adult life that illustrates this point of Sanford's that carelessness towards evil can lead to extreme spiritual sickness.

Fifty years ago, I was hitchhiking north of San Francisco in the San Rafael area on the Pacific Highway, heading back to my college, Humboldt State, in Arcata, California. I was picked up by a pleasant looking young man who soon wanted to talk about religious subjects. As he talked and I listened, he told me about how three years prior, he and his wife has begun to experiment with the Hasbro Game Company item known as the Ouija Board. They discovered to their delight that when they asked the board personal questions about one another, it would spell out answers that were uncanny in their accuracy.

Over the next year, their skill with the device increased and they began to charge money to friends and acquaintances to practice getting answers to questions from the Ouija board.

One night as they were involved in this activity alone with no one else in the house, a man appeared to them in their living room. He introduced himself as the spirit that has been communicating with them through the occult device. He said he was the Spirit of Jesus Christ sent to help them. He explained that their practice was helping people and that he had revealed himself at this time because he wanted to offer them the opportunity to have greater power, which of course, they would use to help others and provide a better livelihood for themselves.

They readily agreed. Then the spirit said to them. "There is a cost for this gift you will receive. For you must allow me to enter your bodies, and work through you. For this to happen, you must make a small sacrifice to me."

They asked him what it was he required of them. He stated calmly, "Your infant son, who is now three months old, you must kill him. Then I can come in to be inside you and you will have greater powers." After some discussion with his wife, the young man told me that they took a knife and together killed their sleeping infant son.

He told me this story with an uncanny calmness. He did not act fanatical or insane. I was horrified and told him he was deceived, that the Jesus of the Scriptures and of history would never ask them to do such a thing. The young man calmly replied that he had a higher consciousness than I did, and that he and his wife now made a large amount of money helping people get access to great answers directly from the universe.

I was, of course, extremely upset and demanded that he stop the car and let me out, which he calmly did, almost in a detached manner. As I exited the car, he simply said, "God bless you."

I stood by the side of the highway shaking uncontrollably and vomited for about a half hour. I felt dirty and sick over my entire body. I was deeply traumatized by what I had just encountered. I took soil from a field near the road and rubbed it on my face, arms and hands to remove the spiritual contamination as much as possible.

In retelling this shocking story, it is clear that this young man and his wife did not set out to become murderers of their own child. They started this terrible journey somewhat naïvely; they were curious. As time went on they began to feel a sense of spiritual power and earned a lot of money using their occult skill. Their morality, which once may have been sensitive to recognize evil, had been dulled. Eventually they were completely seduced.

This young man did not appear to be a monster. In every respect he seemed like a balanced, reasonable person. However, it is clear that at some point he and his wife crossed a line where they no longer could see clearly, and were deceived into horrible darkness and a deed of outright evil. Thus, *their carelessness descended into an embracing of evil,* all the while believing falsely that they were good and holy people.

A careless attitude towards evil does not have to involve such a dramatic descent into embracing evil and deception. A careless attitude can simply be a denial of things, a bargaining, or a slight diminishing of not naming evil for what it is until one's conscience becomes seared, as in the case above.

Marie-Louise von Franz teaches that a careless attitude towards evil can also be a naïve curiosity towards archetypal evil, a sliding, dishonest type of dabbling, telling one's self that it is to gain knowledge for future insight that one tries to learn too much details about very dangerous and known dark aspects of occult or evil behavior.

An example of this may be what begins as a curiosity going further to a thirst for information in details about what Nazis actually did in experimentation on victims in concentration camps. A similar curiosity that can lead a person to open themselves to darkness is reading novels or watching movies that exhibit only the most depraved aspects of human behavior and cruelty.

Seeking knowledge for knowledge's sake in these dark aspects of human behavior can only have a negative effect on the soul. There are some gifted persons in law enforcement, or government who need to know the darkness of human nature in order to govern and protect the common good. But the maturity level of these persons must be extremely high, and their mature self-awareness must be at a maximum capacity.

The average person must not seek such dark detailed information because if their motive is egocentric, the information they gain will create in them ego inflation, and even, over time, can influence them to either becoming numb to the destruction of others, or even a craving towards utilizing such knowledge for power purposes alone, which can and will destroy the human soul. I believe the example stated earlier in this section about the former Navy Seal assassin is a clear example of someone who allowed curiosity and a power drive to overwhelm his soul, to his own destruction and lost-ness.

Sometimes a careless attitude begins with a laziness or

a desire to escape the tension of one's inner conflicts and a refusal to look at one's shadow honestly that it might properly incorporate that which needs to be integrated. A careless attitude towards evil can lead a person to lose sight that one must make a conscious decision to stay aware of that which is within; that which needs to stay within and never be acted upon.

Religious pretention is one of the most common ways I know for a person to be careless towards the reality of evil, to justify acting upon destructive thoughts from their Shadow. Our ego must be strong enough to say consciously to the destructive aspects of the Shadow, a firm "No," and for all aspects of the Shadow to be subject to what Jung called the Self, or what I as a priest call the Christ within.

Whenever we act in a lazy manner without taking responsibility for our Shadow and facing the tension of the opposites but pretend that all is fine when it is not, then this is a great self-deception, and the development of the personality cannot happen. Maturity waits, and may even be postponed indefinitely. When one tries to escape the struggle of living with the opposites until they are integrated, often their lives lead to spiritual death and not surprisingly, sometimes to a premature, physical death.

Sanford provides this insight in how to understand the uniting of opposites and wholeness:

If we consciously carry the burden of the opposites in our nature, the secret, irrational, healing processes that go on in us unconsciously can operate to our benefit and work towards the synthesis of the personality. This irrational healing process, which finds a way around seemingly insurmountable obstacles has a particular feminine quality to it. It is the rational, logical masculine mind that declares that opposites like ego and shadow, light and dark, can never be united. However, the feminine spirit is capable of finding

a synthesis where logic says none can be found.
(Sanford, John A. *Evil: The Shadow Side of Reality*, NY, Crossroad, 1989, p. 106)

Not only laziness, but any kind of one-sidedness, brought about either by unconsciousness, or an infantile curiosity, a lack of respect for the powers of evil, can lead a person to embody evil.

Marie Louise von Franz speaks of this reality in her book *Shadow and Evil in Fairy Tales*:

In many stories all over the world there is this kind of infantile daring which is not courage. It looks like it, but it isn't. This pseudo-courage, which is infantile daring out of unawareness or lack of respect, is a common feature through which a person steps suddenly into the area of the archetype of evil. In our mountain sagas [Swiss fairy tales] this infantile daring is generally called 'Frevel'. 'Frevel' belongs in the same word group as the English word 'frivolous', but means much more than just a frivolous attitude. In modern German, 'Frevel' means trespassing beyond certain not so much legal, as common rules of behavior. 'Frevel' means stepping over the border, going beyond a respectful attitude toward the numinous powers.
(von Franz, Marie-Louise. *Shadow and Evil in Fairy Tales: Revised Edition*. Shambala Publications, Boulder, CO, 1995, p. 173)

It has been my experience that there are some people who want to approach the spiritual dimension with a conscious immature daring which tells me they are not serious about what they may find when they encounter the spiritual reality. It is a kind of cocky, arrogant, yet, insecure "daring" attitude, which reveals their motives are not sincere. Whether their original motive is to look at their dreams, or to read multiple books about the spiritual realm, the lack of mature commitment proves to be more of a hindrance than a help. Truth demands honesty of us.

The Acts of the Apostles tell the story in Chapter Eight of Simon Magus, a spiritual magician of occult powers who became a Christian under the influence of the apostle Andrew's teaching. After being baptized, Simon watched how people were healed with prayers by Andrew, and then observed as Peter and John put hands upon believers and they received the Holy Spirit. Simon offered Peter and John a large gift of money if they would teach him how to put his hands on people so they would receive the same power.

I would suggest that it is possible he not only misunderstood that Holy power could not be conferred on him by a purchase, most likely because he learned his occult trade and power with a payment of money; I think also he may have had this kind of infantile daring that von Franz mentions above.

This arrogant attitude could have created a disastrous encounter for him with the spiritual dimension. Indeed, Peter confronted him and stated that Simon's heart was in a dark prison, he needed to turn from his sin of treacherous manipulation. He needed forgiveness of this sin of unconscious greed in order to live the life he wanted in honesty with himself, as well as others.

The power motive is strong in all of us. Peter's rebuke helped Simon own his shadow and thus, most likely saved his mortal and immortal life. Complete transparency of motive and integrity is required of us to avoid the insidiousness of evil.

The Superiority of the Feminine Wisdom in the Soul in Discerning the Evil of False Guilt

Feminine Wisdom is not only about wisdom within women. It is a deeper reality that can be and is manifest in all genders. It is not a gender distinction, but a quality of essence and an issue of source.

In our story of the Grail it is the feminine characteristics of the chalice/bowl that adequately hold the tension of the opposites until a balance or interplay is established. How are the opposites shown held together in the story? I think one of the best nuances of the Grail myth is the fact that Perceval is not required to know the answer to the primeval question he is to ask, he only has the responsibility to listen to his intuition and ask the question, "For whom does the Grail serve?"

Needing to ask a question without having any idea of the answer or outcome is a common oppositional situation of great tension that we all face on a daily basis. Examples might be, "Am I really of value?" Another might be, "If I follow my heart and intuition, will I really be alright or am I just fooling myself?"

The inside of the cup is round and concave, it holds, incubates, allows swirling motions, mixture, and balance. The feminine shape of cup or bowl also allows a settling of contents, a separating, like oil and water.

The Grail itself by its shape as a cup, bowl, plate or sphere is a container which has the capacity to hold together the opposites we face each day. This is the power of feminine insight and why masculine rationality alone is insufficient for us to find peace. There are no complete answers in the masculine attitude towards life without the trusting of the unknown and waiting in silence of the feminine. Analytical intelligence, masculine, must be balanced by intuitive, instinctive, feminine intelligence.

The Grail King has an incurable wound. He cannot die from it and he cannot be healed except by the eternal question being asked by a Holy Fool. He must wait patiently. His only solace is fishing on the river or the lake, symbolic of the inner listening of reflecting upon his Shadow and all aspects of his unconscious below the waters.

Another question that concerns us from the story is why has the Grail King been wounded in the first place? Is his wounding a result of evil intent? Another opposite in the story is the ongoing conflict of guilt versus non guilt in the psyche of Perceval, in relationship to the very few women in the story.

First, we can ask, did he abandon his mother, who removed him from civilization to hide him from outside influences deep in the forest in the middle of nowhere? He is confronted several times by women he meets in the story about his guilt of leaving her, and yet, how could he fulfill his destiny as the seeker of the Grail and healer of the wounded King and his Kingdom if he had stayed home and obeyed his mother?

Additional guilt versus non-guilt opposites occur when he is confronted by the ugly old woman in King Arthur's court. In front of the assembled knights and ladies of the court, he is chastised and strongly rebuked by her. She chastises him for the killing of various knights on his travels, suggesting that perhaps his tendency to see each unknown fellow knight as a competitor or obstacle to truth and the serving of "My Lady" the feminine principle, was arrogant, ruthless, or simply foolish and thus, morally wrong.

Are these confrontations by the feminine in the story examples of Perceval's carelessness, which if not checked and confronted may have led him to continued blindness and eventual participation in evil? Was his killing of knights in itself participating in outright evil?

Again and again in the myth, the primary mistake or sin of Perceval seems to come down to a lack of self-awareness or the inability to see both sides of an issue, to be reflective.

Yet, how is it that a lack of awareness is a sin and a sin worthy of the designation of true moral guilt? How can Perceval or any of us grow and learn if not through mistakes and a lack of self-awareness? Is this issue of guilt versus non-guilt a Catch Twenty-Two, an impossible cycle of the fact that one cannot win, that life is a lose-lose situation despite our best efforts to do the best thing?

I would suggest that the Grail itself again provides an

answer to this question of personal guilt versus non-guilt; that regardless of our desire to judge another, it is the individual who must judge one's self and work through each situation to discover if they have truly borne moral guilt or not. This need to live with the tension of the opposites of guilt versus non-guilt is one of the most difficult of all opposites for most human beings to bear. Yet there is no escaping the tension except by outright denial and the continued burying of the self into the Shadow.

As a parish priest, who often heard harrowing stories of induced guilt as people shared in private their stories and burdens, it seemed to me that most people feel guilty about things they probably should not, and conversely, many others *feel no guilt* about things that one may feel they should.

Perhaps the solution lies in allowing the feminine of life to bring to our remembrance our deeds, words, and thoughts, to confront us with them, and then show us intuitively how to differentiate, sort true guilt from false guilt. How can we do this by ritual, by confession, unloading and letting go of the true guilt, so a new beginning can be experienced?

Chapter Sixteen

The Basis of the Evil of Narcissism and Keeping the Soul Wise

The solution to avoiding narcissism is not embracing one's destructive aspects of the Shadow and demanding that others embrace it as well, as a sick and false sign of love and acceptance. The task is for us to honestly face our personal need for a paradoxical ethic. This means we realize that God's purpose in us is to bring about the highest good, our wholeness.

Ladislaus Boros explains the solution in Christian theological language:

> Through contemplative vision a person experiences for themselves something of the perfection inherent in the most insignificant things and events. Thus there develops, out of contemplative vision, that which is entrusted to all persons who have become inward, the kingdom of God: that kingdom of danger and audacity, of eternal beginning and becoming, of the spirit that is open and inward. It is a realm of holiness and uncertainty.
>
> All that is creative stands at the frontier of being, all creation is at risk. The person who does not lose their soul cannot gain it, nor can this one become truly at home in the world. Today such creative vision is perhaps our Christian duty. That is, in and through our vision to create unity out of superficial division, to establish this meaningful unity in the world, and to penetrate ever new and ever more deeply into the depths of things and their transforming power.
>
> (Boros, Ladislaus. *In Time of Temptation*. Herder and Herder, NY, 1968, p. 83)

We have to let go of our insistent, immature, one-sided, black and white ethic and realize that we have the responsibility to live with the tension of the opposites within us. This means we cannot play things safe. We must risk ourselves to live out what we feel we must do and to embrace the consequences of our risk by faith. This is how we come to know who we are.

In other words, when through trial and error we realize some of our actions are truly morally wrong, we can turn about, and ask forgiveness for them. This allows us to move forward embracing what we have learned and passage through to a fuller consciousness of our dark side. We do not let the shadowy urges have their way and live out their energy unobstructed. We recognize and direct them to the higher good. In Jungian language, we submit these dark impulses to the Self, the Christ within. We do not give them leeway to act out their destruction. This requires maturity, great effort and deep, unabashed, honesty.

It is the feminine of life that keeps us honest, that carries memory. In our Grail story, Perceval was confronted with his destructive shadow by the old hag at Arthur's court. She publically chastised him regarding his dismissive attitude towards all that is feminine in his life; his mother's death, his abuse of Blancheflor, his disregard for the fiancée of the knight whom he encountered in the forest, his demand to fight to death every knight he encountered on his journeys. Most of all she confronted him with his immature failure to ask the question of the Grail procession, "For whom does the Grail serve?" thus prolonging the healing of the Fisher King and his kingdom indefinitely.

Fortunately, by this time in the story, Perceval had been confronted enough by women to have gained a stronger ego. Instead of fleeing from the anger of the old hag and the public shaming, he stood still, took her words to heart and vowed to change.

One of the marks of a maturing man is his ability to withstand his woman's anger. A mature man knows that the feminine desires relationship and all confrontation with her is with the goal in mind of relating to another in honesty. He does not run away. He stands and listens and is not shamed, but entreated to reconnect with her and her righteousness.

We find the similar motif when the maturing Perceval, twenty years after his first encounter with the Grail Castle is worn out by his adventures and encounters the pilgrims who remind him that the day was Good Friday. They encourage him to visit the hermit priest down the road to give his formal confession and prepare his soul for receiving the Eucharist on Easter morning. In other words, Perceval had developed enough self-awareness to not only acknowledge that he has missed the mark of his calling, but was willing to take appropriate action to remedy the situation. In this instance, he finds the hermit priest, confesses his sins, and continues his journey, only to encounter the Grail Castle with a second chance to ask the question.

This time, he speaks the question aloud, the king is healed and Perceval himself is able to partake of the Grail blessing, thus receiving his Eucharistic gifts. He is mature enough to transform his shame into humility, and thus is empowered to heal both himself and the others in need. The kingdom of God is openly shown in the Grail Castle and life begins anew.

In my counseling work, I often interact with both men and women who have partners who have not yet reached the maturity level of owning their Shadows, thus an unequal partnership is borne by the other and great unhappiness is the rule. For reasons I cannot detail here, I find that it is mostly men who hold back from owning their destructive tendencies in their Shadow and demand that their partners carry these non-integrated aspects for them. Many men expect their significant others to lug their emotional life on their behalf. This is a great, unjust burden and usually results in a deadening of the relationship.

In my experience, the one thing the burdened partner can do that can speed up the ownership of Shadow of the other is to speak truth consistently and with passion while continuing to refuse to carry the Shadow of the significant other. To continue to carry their Shadow is allowing them to wear Perceval's maternal apron around their waist, thus avoiding their personal responsibility.

In many cases, it is necessary that the relationship be dissolved so the offending party has no choice but to suffer the loss of companionship or own their Shadow and be transformed. In addition, the partner who has been carrying the Shadow of the other must ask themselves what need of theirs is being met by doing so. Often it is a learned codependency, and the need to feel needed.

Some codependent partners actually carry their spouses' shadow simply to gain a feeling of power over the other. Of course, this is destructive and does not work. A new interdependence must be incorporated into the psyche of the partner and the codependency ended.

Jesus used the analogy of the narrow gate to describe this path of individuation and responsibility. He said that only one person at a time can pass through a narrow gate, and it requires humility and persistence. One biblical scholar noted long ago, whom I cannot recall, that when Jesus spoke of the rich having a harder time passing through the narrow gate, he was possibly referring to a small gate known as the Needle through the walls of the ancient city of Jerusalem. When necessary at times the large city gates were closed, yet this smaller gate, easier to guard against enemies, might be used if needed.

This low, narrow gate required that all of the goods had to be removed from a pack animal's back, a camel in this parable. Then the animal was required to move forward on its knees through this low passage and the goods were reloaded. Even so, we in our inner richness, must remove our inner-weighty, egocentric baggage, and then, low to the ground in humility (humus, earthy, grounded) move forward through the gate. This is possible with God's guidance and insight and grace freely given.

Sanford writes that Jesus' ethic, though required of us does not remove our personal freedom. Freedom involves the necessity that we assume the burden of psychological choice and conflict. The greatest ethical value in the teachings of Jesus is to become a free person and to become free we must be conscious. Freedom is of the highest inner value because this alone makes possible the development of realization and unconditional love.

Our Faces Can Reveal if We Are Embracing the Tensions of Opposites or Running from Them

Before continuing the discussion about how we can resist evil with pragmatic steps and processes, I wish to make an observation from my work with people over the years. As previously mentioned, I am hearing impaired from birth. I rely on visual cues, facial expressions, body language, and the tone of voice to discern what a person is communicating.

One thing I have found extraordinary, is that as we age our faces take on how we have lived our lives. Just as in the powerful story by Oscar Wilde of *The Picture of Dorian Grey*, if we choose to remain unconscious and demand that life fulfill itself for us in black and white thinking, our faces become distorted, and in many instances, truly disfigured and ugly as time passes.

When we refuse to embrace the reality of a paradoxical ethic our faces no longer reflect the inner resilience and peace that comes with taking responsibility to let go of either/or thinking. Our faces can take on a rigidness, becoming, perhaps, noticeable in our eyes, but then taking shape in the corners of the mouth, the lines in the cheeks and forehead and eventually, even in our posture.

If a person continues to insist that others accept the dark

destructive aspects of their Shadow as the narcissist does, their faces take on a perpetual angry demeanor. There may exist a slight veneer of persona, but in time, as in Oscar Wilde's story, the face betrays the true colors of the individual who refuses to take responsibility through constant denial of the dark side of their Shadow.

I will give one more example of the insidiousness of evil that can creep into a person's life and how it can affect them from my counseling experience. Many years ago, I was asked by a leading businesswoman to hear her work through a personal problem. I spent a great deal of time and effort listening and giving feedback to the person. She was highly intelligent, and seemingly, completely willing to grow and change.

There came a time when the woman needed to make a decision regarding honesty with herself and her spouse. She basically had to make a choice to both leave her husband and give him half of her financial resources, or continue in a shallow, unfulfilling relationship which gave neither of them pleasure or joy.

The woman chose to keep all of the money and to continue the false pretentious relationship. Even half of her wealth would be more than any person could possibly need or want in ten lifetimes. It was clear that greed and deep insecurity was at the core of all her decision making. Although it grieved me to see this, at this point in the counseling relationship I could see that to continue was pointless and brought things to a close.

Many years later the woman came to a seminar which I was conducting in another part of the country. Her stance had not changed. I was struck by her facial features which at one time had an open, almost childlike quality about them. Now they had changed to a fixed, cruel and sneering countenance that only can be described as a person who has allowed evil to enter and stay in their soul by the choices they made. I was deeply saddened to see the long-term consequences of this unfortunate decision.

Here is another observation regarding how a person can be overcome by evil given by Marie-Louise von Franz in her book *Shadow and Evil in Fairy Tales*. She teaches that when a person takes more from Nature than is necessary, often Nature will retaliate and destroy even that which the person has taken.

I think the above illustration of the woman refusing to be honest in her dysfunctional marriage is an example of someone who has taken way more than necessary from life. It was clear that the insecurity that drove her greed had effectively destroyed her feeling function which contained her values. Taking more from nature than was necessary had detracted, rather than added value to her life.

It is important for each of us to ask of ourselves this question, whether we are taking more from life than is needed, and thus a type of psychic hoarding takes place within us, to our destruction. All gifts of life are to be appreciated and when guidance and common sense dictates to our soul, shared with others.

I have often questioned what motivates us to take more than is necessary from life and try to hoard it. I think it has something to do with supporting a weak ego structure, and a fear and denial of our own self-worth.

Sometimes in counseling when the persona is gently punctured and reveals a person's sadness and insecurities, a question or two can help the person come to terms with their repressed Shadow and begin to heal.

Often attempts at such shadow work results in more denial and suppression. However, the door should always be left open to the one in denial as they may be forced by life's circumstances back into a corner again, and decide the time to come clean with their shadow.

It is my observation that shadow work can be detected on a person's face. When they are in denial, often a constrained anger sits upon the face, with constant frowns, narrow, suspicious eyes watching, and even the body turned tensely sideward when conversing with another person. Each of these gestures of body language suggests defensiveness and a deep need for reconciliation with one's shadow.

Conversely, the person who has honestly acknowledged and gained insight into their Shadow does not have a sudden, negative change of facial expression when asked the pertinent question that pierces beneath the persona. Instead, when an interrelated question is asked, the face relaxes in an honest person with an openness and reveals their innermost gold. Their body language is often open, receptive and anticipatory.

Do We Need to Always Confront Evil Directly to Effective Deal with It?

John Sanford attributes his insights about the following ideas to Marie-Louise von Franz and her work with fairy tales. This question of how and when to confront evil is very important. Marie-Louise von Franz suggested that there is no one way to deal with evil, and I would add, to think and act so, is a black and white dualism that is neither wise nor Christian.

I would suggest that the most important component is for us to be fully conscious and very aware of what we are doing. In many cases we need to recognize and not appease evil but to confront it honestly and firmly. This may mean confronting a dishonest or deceitful person either privately or publically, whatever the case may need at the moment. Sometimes, rare public confrontation is required so the person perpetuating evil cannot continue to try to pull the wool over the eyes of others. Yet, even such a confrontation must be very mindful, because there are situations where such confrontation acts like an affirmation or recognition of the evil-actioned person which bolsters their confidence and can make matters worse.

However, to overlook and not face private or public

evil actions and words often appeases the evil action. True discernment is needed, as Sanford states, "Evil can only be overcome by a superior consciousness." This discernment comes from our inward listening and intuition.

There may be moments when spontaneous confrontation is not the wisest thing to do. I have learned the hard way that reacting to evil with firmness without first listening inwardly for instruction in how to proceed, most often resulted in poor results, or even made the situation worse.

I remember one incident from my parish ministry where I did not first listen to my intuition, but let my instinctive feelings motivate me to act abruptly, which I later regretted. I was chairing a church meeting where a course of action was being discussed. A member of the committee, a known antagonist (who made a habit of creating chaos in group settings) made a snide comment, using words which sounded nice, but with a hypocritical tone of voice that indicated his true motive which was to shame the group. He suggested that prayer is usually what Christians do when they have a problem to solve, so why don't I, as the new priest, lead the group in prayer asking God at that moment to provide us with an answer.

Needless to say, I am a person of prayer and at that time was very experienced in leading group prayer. But I knew this man was a devious person who liked to feel important and to impede progress in this church. He personally was responsible for driving away two previous priests who could not stand up to his manipulative abuse.

Instead of listening first and asking my intuition how to deal with his obvious intent of trying to make me and the group look "unspiritual," I acted on impulse, rose from my chair, walked slowly over to where he was seating, and verbally suggested that since it was his idea, why did he not lead the group in prayer himself. My words were fine, but my body language was not. I was misusing my authority as the parish priest by standing near him and speaking to him in such a way that was wrong. Evil won that evening and the greater good was postponed. This man felt empowered by my action, and continued to destroy the community as he had done for the previous twenty years prior to my coming to the parish.

I know now in retrospect that I could have been quiet, and perhaps in a calm manner made my suggestion to him from where I sat. If he continued to create an argument, I could simply be silent and redirect the meeting. My intent was right in confronting his deception and bullying, but my timing was wrong. I acted from my Shadow where I keep a strong dislike, at times, even a hatred for bullies, due to a childhood of suffering immeasurably because of them. In this instance, I became the bully I so detest in others.

The energy that came forth from my Shadow was unconscious, and perceived by some people who were present as, immature and overactive. It is my contention now that if I had listened to my intuition before I acted impulsively, I would have been able to provide a container for the energy in my Shadow that would have done the needed confrontation, without the diminution of the energy that occurred because of my haste.

I also learned from this experience that I needed to confront evil in this unconscious, manipulative man in the context of a warm human community. I was new to the parish and I had no friends at that time I could trust. I was feeling my way around landmines of great political danger due to two decades of church dysfunction. I was isolated. I could not act but alone, and confronting that which is evil can best be done in community with broad support and prayer. I acted in haste, and had to deal with the consequences.

It is interesting to note that Marie-Louise von Franz also noted that fairy tales from around the world teach that when a person is new to a foreign place, or alone and not in warm community, it is easy to be knocked off balance by evil and evil intent. This is a common problem and one that can be avoided with some precognitive knowledge and self-awareness.

In summary, to listen to one's intuition for direction does not need to take a lot of time, indeed, with practice, we can discern in a moment when to act and when to wait. But developing the habit of listening, and trusting our intuition, can take a long time to learn.

A Positive Example?

Again, using an example involving the same antagonistic person, I will point out a public confrontation *that was effective* in bursting the attention-seeking, lying act behind the unconscious destructive intent of this person.

The setting was a large, all parish, annual business meeting, organized around a set protocol and traditional demeanor. I was asked to lead the meeting and facilitate discussion using Roberts Rules of Order. It took place three years later when I had developed some trust in more than a few members of the church.

At one point we held an election of the financial committee members of the parish. This antagonist loudly interrupted with a pushy confirmation of his desire to speak about a particular aspect of the church budget that was not even in proximity to the items on the printed agenda. I could tell that his motive was to disrupt the proceedings and to attract attention to himself in an egocentric fashion.

This time, thankfully, I *did immediately reflect inwardly*, and felt, what for lack of better language, can only be described as an inward "green light" and quietly, but directly, asked the man to sit down and refrain from speaking, as his concern could be more adequately addressed with myself or one of the elected lay leaders of the church by appointment at a later time. I then moved on with the next item on the meeting agenda, quietly and smoothly. The effect was deafening. The man looked perplexed, hesitated as if to speak again, and then slowly sank down into his chair. He was quiet for the rest of the meeting.

I believe that not only were my actions correct this time, but my manner so conveyed a calmness, an inner spiritual authority not of my office, but something more pertinent, which caught the antagonist off guard. He was used to getting his way in public meetings. In some manner, his system was shocked, distilled, unsettled by the calm action and words that I spoke. I later learned from a leader in the church, that this was the first time in over twenty years that this antagonist was silenced effectively in a public church meeting and that a type of spell he had held over the congregation for years had somehow been broken.

Whether there was any such thing as a controlling demeanor that this man held over the group, I do not know, but apparently the spiritual authority of true, honest confrontation worked to burst the bubble of lying behavior and deceit that lay behind this man's habit of trying to control this congregation with his antagonism.

I do not think this authority had anything to do with my being a priest, but instead, was a deeper, spiritual and psychological authority that could recognize the evil in this man's shadow, and would not accept it to be acted out, thus being an act of love towards him. I remember not feeling anger with him nor with myself, nor self-doubt.

It is as if an energy had come from within my own spirit, possibly my own shadow, but consciously this time. This energy was sufficient to break the control of this lying "spirit" or archetype that had caused so much destruction before. The energy I felt was directed not at him personally, but to the archetype he was embodying. The antagonist did not act hurt nor have an angry look on his face. Instead, I remember glancing at him and seeing a type of surprised astonishment on his face, almost a childlike face of unexpected peace. This man and I would later have a rational conversation where I felt I was talking with a real person, not the archetype that distressed him.

There Are Situations of Evil that Need the Confrontation of Being "Starved to Death."

There is a type of evil that affects some people which I would call an animus or anima possession; they can only be dealt with by walking away from them. I learned this principle from Marie-Louise von Franz in her writings about fairy tales and the natural wisdom she gained from their studies.

There are some people who have a kind of psychological death wish. In men, they have embraced and are possessed completely by a negative mother complex; the aspect of the masculine psyche that finds a reason to regress, an infantile attitude determined not to grow and embrace life.

Similarly, there are women who are so possessed by the negative animus, that everything they do or say boils down to a negative, critical and destructive antagonism against themselves and against all others who will allow it, working everywhere against life itself.

Normally in attempting to bring healing to others as a therapist or priest, one tries to bring Christian love, understanding, and concern to each troubled person. But sometimes, such compassion actually feeds the negative death wish in the troubled person and they get worse. It is as if the normal routes of seeming goodness feeds the destructive spirit within them.

There are some people who do everything they can to cut off life and vitality at every opportunity with jealousy, criticism or cynicism. Marie-Louise von Franz states that this pattern that is against life at every turn is an aspect of very real evil. She states:

It is a spirit in them of no life and no love, which has always been associated with the essence of evil. It is destructiveness for its own sake, which everybody has in himself or herself to some extent. But some people are completely possessed by it. This kind of death-devil is best simply starved to death. One hands back what the person is, what he or she does, and one gives no life. One stretches out a skeleton hand to shake a skeleton hand; one gives no blood, no warmth, nor life, and that makes the devil turn back to where he came from. (Von Franz, Marie-Louise. *Shadow and Evil in Fairy Tales*. Shambala Publications, Boston, 1995, p. 210)

She continues on to say that giving such a person normal Christian love and goodness linked with higher morals can be using the higher path in a wrong way. In other words, we are not to use this higher moral way with other people like this, but only on ourselves. In other words, there are situations where natural moral law, a more primitive morality that allows people to feel the immediate consequences of their actions, needs to prevail so that the person has the opportunity to become conscious through the negative effects of such natural law.

I have learned that unless a person is moving towards me in an attitude of openness and desire to grow; I must use a natural wisdom and allow the other person's refusal to become conscious, letting their repudiation to mature become a burning fire on their heads. This alone may be their saving grace, motivating them to change and open their heart and mind.

As von Franz states:

The refusal of higher development or higher consciousness is one of the most destructive things there is. Someone who has unlived creativity tries to destroy other people's creativity, and somebody who has an unlived possibility of conscious always tries to blur or make uncertain anybody else's efforts towards consciousness. The desire to prevent other people from becoming conscious because one does not want to wake up oneself, is real destructiveness.

(von Franz, Marie-Louise. *Shadow and Evil in Fairy Tales*. Shambala Publications, Boston, 1995, p. 214)

And in my mind, this desire to prevent the consciousness of others is an outright and demonic evil. Sometimes, we are not called to name the shadow in such a person, but to let them come to their own discovery of it by walking away from them. This takes great discernment, so that one does not become the evil which one is opposing in the other.

In the case of the parishioner in the story above, I had stopped trying to treat the man with gratuitous, unusual attention and love. I treated him the same as all the other members, with genuine respect for him as a person. Yet I no longer gave him any of my personal office time to listen to his rants and raves. I spoke to him one time of his need to see a therapist and work on his issues which he angrily rebuffed, and left the situation to work itself out.

Yet the interesting thing was, the public confrontation somehow spoke to him. In the public arena, for the time that I remained in that parish, he no longer had the sway over others than he had enjoyed prior. Somehow the public confrontation performed correctly using my intuition discreetly, took the fire out of his confidence in public disruptions. My prayer was that one day he would seek counsel and heal his wounded heart.

While we cannot help them, people who are so negatively possessed, sometimes we can try to raise awareness in those around them whom they are influencing negatively, by intuitively and using great wisdom, show them by example the power of not empowering the evil with our attention.

Feminine Wisdom in Dealing with Evil: A Partial Conclusion

I have come to believe that the Feminine principle in a person's spiritual life can confront unconsciousness and denial in such a way that is liberating. I am reminded of the Central American native women who have quietly and steadily confronted their governments regarding the disappearances and murders of thousands of their people, and brought about societal changes that are life transforming for their communities.

I think of people like Maya Angelou, who speaks from a place of grounded feminine authority, whose words bring life and illumination. History has many examples of both women and men who have done their inner work and tapped the reservoir of feminine energetic spiritual authority. Perhaps when we listen to the feminine principle speaking through our instinctive intuition, we may find our confrontation of evil in its various forms lose their intensity and even vanish.

Just as Perceval did not have to have the answer to the primal question to bring healing, "To whom does the Grail serve?" but simply was required to ask the opened ended question, perhaps we are to speak our truth and trust that God is speaking through us in our intuition. Maybe trust in the feminine Godhead is the key to inner freedom that can stop the destructiveness of the evil we encounter.

Chapter Seventeen

Having Done All, We Stand

I think it is important to realize that confronting evil is not a dualistic activity. By dualistic, I mean not an either/ or phenomenon. I do not believe that the resistance and confrontation with evil is a dualistic battle that requires a combative attitude. To take on such an attitude may be a sure way to experience failure. A dualistic approach and thinking is a black and white oppositional, masculine approach to the problem that cannot but end in failure.

Instead, as mentioned before in Sanford's writing above, the feminine principle of reconciliation can find a way to confront evil through relationship and honest face to face dialogue. Then with a decision containing great authority there is a releasing of energy, not a combative type of verve.

I see this in the stories of how Jesus encountered evil. In the cases of confronting the evils of hypocritical religious leaders who were so oppressive to the poor and marginalized, he used strong words, even in one case, strong actions (the turning over of the money changers' tables in the Temple in Jerusalem). Yet I sense in the stories that he did not do so in such a way that expended unnecessary energy on his part.

However, in most cases revealed in the gospel stories, Jesus used the relational method of asking clarifying questions of his opponents, not in a combative manner, but in an inquisitive, non-threatening way which invited reflection on the part of the antagonists. For instance, when confronted about Jesus' priorities, attempting him to choose loyalty to the God of Israel or the Roman Emperor by asking him whether they should pay Roman taxes or not, Jesus replied with a question of his own. After asking for a coin, he held it in his hands and said:

"Whose image is this?" The religious accusers answered, "Caesar's." Then Christ replied with a non-dualistic answer by differentiating and dispelling their accusatory questioning, "Render unto Caesar what belongs to Caesar, and to God, what belongs to God." He refused to be drawn into a compromising position by stating the obvious, one pays coinage to Caesar and to God, one's utter devotion.

In confronting evil spirits that possessed or oppressed persons, he only once spent a small amount of time in dialogue with the demonic in the case of the man possessed by a legion of destructive spirits. In that situation, he simply spoke a directive or imperative to the demonic. He was not excited nor overtly spirited in his manner. He was matter of fact in his objective confrontation and the result was the immediate dispelling of the evil stronghold over the person and the man's release into complete freedom.

Another striking case of his calmness and sense of not being hurried or excited by the presence of evil, was the story of the self-destructive boy whose father pleaded with Jesus for help as the man's son constantly threw himself into fire. As the boy fell into what could have been an epileptic seizure on the ground with mouth foaming, Jesus asked the father how long the boy had been acting in this way. The father replied, since birth. Then Jesus asked the father if he had faith for the situation and the father cried out with intense exasperation, "Lord, help me, in spite of my unbelief." Jesus was not dismayed by this emotional outburst nor the boy continuing his convulsions in front of him. Jesus simply spoke to the evil influence, for it to leave and not return and the boy was immediately restored to health.

Jesus used the feminine principles of detachment, wisdom and knowledge, asking relational questions of the father, sizing up the situation, and contemplating his next word or move. Jesus was not pressured by the excitability of the father's plea nor the grotesque behavior of the demonized boy as he thrashed about on the ground in either a tantrum or contortions which are uncomfortable to watch under any circumstances.

A Personal Story

When I was in training for my Music Therapy degree in undergraduate school, I was leading a group of students and a professor in a weekly sing-a-long inside a double locked ward of Stockton State Mental Hospital in California. It was called the Acute Admissions Ward.

I remember one unusual event that happened my first night on the ward. Our teacher, five other students and I were let in by the attendants to the inside of the ward. The place reeked of tension. There were long, shining linoleum floors stretching in each direction. We were surrounded by people who had been picked up on the streets or placed in the institution by family members. Most of them acted heavily sedated. It was a scene straight out of Jack Nicholson's movie *One Flew Over the Cuckoo's Nest*.

Once we were all together inside in a tight unconscious huddle due to the unfamiliar and unhappy environment, I heard a loud, piercing yell coming from far away down one particular hallway. I could see a man with long straggly hair shaking his head side to side in an animalistic fashion. Then, to our horror, the man ran at full speed down the hall approaching our group, came directly up to me and put his face within two inches of mine and then said in a garish intense voice everyone in the vicinity could hear clearly:

"Peter, how long have you been walking in the light of Jesus Christ?"

Stunned, I stepped back and hastily replied, "About four years. Why do you ask?"

The man came up again putting his face in mine, breathing heavily and spoke again with a very loud voice, "That sounds about right. We know who you are, and you know who we are, and we like it this way, so leave us alone, do you understand?" he shouted.

He then abruptly turned, and ran the other direction disappearing into another room out of sight.

I had never been in the hospital before and of course, had never seen this man in my life. Somehow, in spirit, he knew my name and that I was a Christian. If I had known then what I know now, I might have been able to keep my composure and spoken to the spirits in the man and removed them. But hindsight is always easier. It was not to be. Whether this was a true demonic situation or simply the psychological phenomenon called possession syndrome, I do not know. How the man knew my name and my spiritual orientation may have been his intuition using basic telepathy. It matters not how, but the destruction of the man's life was an issue I wished I could have addressed but could not in my inexperience.

I have known similar situations much later in my life as a priest and fortunately have had the wherewithal not to be put off balance, and dealt with the situation with more maturity. These things happen. They are rare but they happen. Certainly, Jesus and other Shamans around the ancient and modern world encountered such experiences and learned how to confront them effectively. In the case of Jesus and the self-destructive boy, the father's son was healed and returned to his thankful family whole and well.

Why Is There Evil?

Jesus did not teach about why evil exists, nor did he try to explain it away. When asked by his disciples why a man was blind from birth, if it was his sin that caused the deformity or the sins of his parents, Jesus responded that the man's condition of blindness had nothing to do with anyone's sin or shortcomings. It was simply a reality which required no explanation. What was needed was healing, not an explanation for why the condition existed. His response to the disciples was that the glory of God would be revealed.

Some readers of the story may say that God permitted the deformity in order for Jesus to prove that he was the Son of God. I reject such a suggestion. To me it makes complete sense that Jesus was just acknowledging that the evil condition existed and the required response was to bring the love and healing of God to bear on the situation. The best books I have read that provide an adequate intellectual discussion of this question of evil is by Jungian psychologist, John A. Sanford, entitled, *Evil: The Shadow Side of Reality* and Marie-Louise von Franz' *Shadow and Evil in Fairy Tales*.

This story of the man born blind is a helpful example to me. Often, I spend energy asking why something is evil or why a person has developed such a warped and insane personality and behavior. While this can be helpful to our understanding it seldom helps us deal with the problem at hand.

Instead, I find it healthier to simply realize that evil exists and focus my attention on how best to deal with it. This is when the inner listening to intuition is imperative. This is when the guidance comes.

The life story of Laurens van der Post gives another helpful hint on how to avoid slipping into an exasperating dualism resulting is ineffective and exhausting fruitless effort in dealing with this reality of evil.

Laurens van der Post was a colonel in the British Army during the Pacific conflict of World War Two in Java fighting the invading Japanese. Early in the war, his group of soldiers were on a hilltop in the jungle surrounded by the advancing Japanese. He and his men had run out of ammunition and were helpless. As the Japanese came close, instinctively, van der Post shouted out in the royal Japanese language a formal greeting to the officer in charge of the oncoming soldiers.

Such was the shock of hearing a greeting in the most formal

style of his language, the officer stopped the advanced and demanded an answer, how could the enemy address him in such beautiful Japanese? Laurens van der Post had lived in Japan for seven years as a young man by invitation of the Japanese Navy. He was a representative of the South African government to the Japanese at a time when all ships had to stop at Cape Town for supplies as the Suez Canal was not yet in existence.

Laurens van der Post replied to the Japanese officer, requesting an honorable surrender, as his men were completely out of ammunition. He politely requested that he and his men not be slaughtered by so noble an adversary. It worked. He and his men spent the next three and a half years in a brutal, sadistic, very cruel Japanese prison camp in Java.

As mentioned before, while telling his continued story, he speaks of his state of soul on the night in a solitary cell in the prison awaiting his ordered execution at dawn the next morning. He knew there was nothing he could do. He looked at the moonlit night sky above and was overwhelmed by a deep sense of joy, love and release, as he knew at the core of his spirit, that God was in control. He knew that the Japanese cruelty and the evil that at times possessed them was not the ultimate end of things. I recommend van der Post's explanation of this type of possession that seized the minds of his captors with monthly rhythm in accordance with the full moon in *The Prisoner and the Bomb*, (William Morrow and Company, NYC, 1971).

We can rest assured to know that life is not a dualism, some kind of ongoing battle of co-equal forces between good and evil. Life is ultimately created, led and empowered in confidence by Love which is God. This is another important aspect of how we are to approach the confrontation with evil in our society and in ourselves.

St. Paul, in the Letter of the Ephesians attributed to him, states that we are to stand in a defensive posture of resolution against evil. There is nothing to do but to stand still in truth, in a protective stance of experiential knowing, *gnosis*. This stance allows us not to fall off balance into a frantic duality that is futile, ineffective and ultimately self-defeating. There is no need for forward movement nor retreat; simply an admonition to stand.

Scott Peck, in his most insightful book about the reality of evil in persons and how to deal with them, *People of the Lie*, states the same principle. He says that all evil is based on lies. To confront lies is to declare and live truth. There is no argument. There is no debate. There is simply a pronouncement of truth. Standing in truth, not chasing after the lies, can be an effective inner stance that does not allow the human spirit to be conquered.

Chapter Eighteen

Finding Language about Evil: Creating a Container for the Questions

We have to find a language that works for us and the world view we live out of. For instance, C. G. Jung wrote in his autobiography, *Memories, Dreams and Reflections*:

I have, therefore, even hazarded the postulate that the phenomenon of archetypal configurations – *which are psychic events par excellence* [emphasis mine] – may be founded upon a psychoid base, that is, upon an only partially psychic and possibly altogether different form of being.

For lack of empirical data I have neither knowledge nor understanding of such forms of being, which are commonly called spiritual. From my point of view of science, it is immaterial what I may believe on that score, and I must accept my ignorance. But insofar as the archetypes act upon me, they are real and actual to me, even though I do not know what their nature is....

Nevertheless, we have good reason to suppose that behind this veil there exists the uncomprehended absolute object which affects and influences us – and to suppose it even, or particularly, in the case of psychic phenomena about which no verifiable statements can be made.

In a personal letter which he wrote to one of my mentors, Dr. Morton Kelsey in October, 1958, Jung wrote the following:

The real nature of the objects of human experience is still shrouded in darkness. The scientist cannot concede a higher intelligence to Theology than to any other branch of human cognition. We know as little of a supreme being as of Matter. But there is little doubt of the existence of a supreme being as of Matter. The world beyond is a reality, an experiential fact. We only do not understand it.

(Kelsey, Morton. *Myth, History and Faith*. Element Books, Rockport, MA. 1976, p. 118)

Each of us must find a language that works for us. As a priest who has been involved in formal prayers for exorcism, I have no trouble at all.

Similarly, the medical doctor and psychiatrist Scott Peck has no trouble using the New Testament language of evil and evil spiritual entities (demonic) to describe what I have experienced. When I teach to a non-spiritual audience, I use the term evil archetype, an acceptable Jungian psychological term.

Other people, such as Dr. Kelsey, may want to use the phrases Destructive Tendencies, or as mentioned above, Evil Archetypes, to describe what they have experienced. It is important for each of us to find language that expresses what we experience in our daily life and work.

As I write these words today, I read a post by theologian Carter Hayward, eminent priest and feminist theological scholar, about the murder of eleven Jewish worshippers at their synagogue in Pittsburg, Pennsylvania, this past weekend.

She named the Trump Administration and the unconscious flagrant followers of Trump, such as the murderer of the congregants in Pittsburg, as Evil. She had no trouble naming what happened and the motivation behind it with a New Testament idiom.

In my view, based on my experience as a businessman, later a priest, and now, as a counselor hearing stories of untold abuse and cruelty, the language of the Bible regarding the word and the naming of evil works. As mentioned above, when I am speaking to a broader, non-spiritual audience, I usually do not use such language, but talk about destructive or negative influences.

Can these spiritual realities be proven in the world view of Logical Positivism? I think not. But neither can they be disproven. This is why it is important for each individual to give a name for that which has caused misery, destruction, and a destroying of life itself, both in their own lives, and in the lives of others.

To deny the existence of this destructive reality is a great disfavor. Do I feel people should be focused in an inordinate way on the reality of evil they perceive? No. Yet to not name it is to deny, minimize, appease, and otherwise give credence to its power. Not naming can only increase the power of evil through falsehood whether that lying is a form of denial, or any other method of avoiding existential truth.

How Do We Bring Spiritual Energy to Bear on this Phenomenon of Evil?

We bring prayer to the forefront first.

John A. Sanford taught specifically that prayer is not a psychological endeavor, but a spiritual practice. Sound psychological teaching makes it clear that we are to use spiritual tools in dealing with spiritual realities. In the Gospel of John which describes a conversation between Jesus with the spiritually-hungry Pharisee leader Nicodemus (later, to be a leader in the early Christian Church in Jerusalem) the writer states that Jesus talked about spiritual rebirth as a necessity for a person to understand intuitively the spiritual kingdom of God.

Jesus taught that spiritual birth is a spiritual issue and natural birth is a natural concern. In response to Nicodemus' question about how a person can be born again Jesus replied "That which is of the spirit is spirit, and that which is of the flesh, is flesh." It is a spiritual rebirth for a spiritual purpose, something which a religious leader of the Jewish tradition would know a great deal about from their spiritual heritage of new beginnings.

Bringing prayer to bear on spiritual, archetypal or destructive evil is an effective tool. How can we do this? To begin we *pray for directions in how to pray and how and when to take action.*

The place to start is to remember that true prayer does not get sucked into an immature dualism as if the prayer itself, even as it endured difficulty and what feels like agony as the aforementioned prayer of Jesus in the Garden of Gethsemane, is not a dualistic endeavor and battle.

Prayer can be difficult because it requires honest reflection and discernment as when and how to pray. This may not be an easy task to discover. Pray is difficult because it demands intense, receptive listening. True prayer requires a laying aside of our egocentric nature in order to discern how best to pray. Once the needed discernment is discovered, praying with this discernment is not problematic. Prayer must also take into account what we know from modern psychology regarding human behavior in order to be effective and focused.

Marie-Louise von Franz, Jungian writer and close associate of C. G. Jung and his wife Emma, wrote about the importance of discernment regarding how to deal with evil. Specifically, as a psychologist, she felt that there was a difference between evil from the realm of purely natural phenomena and that which was theological or spiritual in essence. In her excellent book *Shadow and Evil in Fairy Tales* she speaks about this discernment. I have found her words very helpful in my own work as a priest and counselor.

So you see the problem of evil in the realm of folklore which I am now discussing is unlike a differentiated or specific religious problem of evil. What we call evil on this level differs from theological ideas, for it belongs to the realm of purely natural phenomena. This is tremendously important in psychology, for I think I am not optimistic if I say that in ninety percent of the cases where one has to cope with evil one is confronted with this natural evil on a psychological level, and only very rarely with a more absolute and deep-rooted phenomenon of evil.

It is for this reason that fairy tales are so important. We find in them rules of behavior on how to cope with these things. Very often it is not a shape ethical issue but a question of finding a way of natural wisdom. This does not mean that these powers are not sometimes exceedingly dangerous.

(von Franz, Marie-Louise. *Shadow and Evil in Fairy Tales*. Shambala, Boston, 1995, pp. 191–192)

Marie-Louise von Franz's work in mental health was as a psychologist, thus her view that the vast degree of evil encountered could be understood from a psychological perspective. I share much of this viewpoint. At the same time, as a priest, who networks with psychologists, psychiatrists, clinical social workers and medical doctors to bring healing to people in need, I feel that there is another way to speak about these different levels of evil affecting people.

I would simply say that much of what von Franz would discern as natural phenomena is what I could name *spiritual oppression*, and the ten percent she speaks about, which is a much deeper problem affecting individuals and collective groups having a theological or spiritual basis, I would name *spiritual possession*. This categorical teaching of different levels of evil infiltration is common in Orthodox, Roman Catholic, and in a lesser degree, Anglican theology and pastoral care. In either case, different types of prayer have proven to be successful over the years.

One might say that all of the evil encountered is natural to human capacity or the opposite, that all aspects of evil have a spiritual dimension that can respond to prayers of discernment. Thus, the need for discernment of the one who prayers before embarking on any specific course of action.

So then, from a place of quiet confidence we can first pray and ask God if it is now our time and place to pray against the forces of evil. If we feel we are being called to such prayer, we can then ask for specific guidance on how to do this.

I remember the view of Ernest Baxter, a famous Canadian Neo-Pentecostal evangelist, after a speaking engagement. Baxter spoke at a church I attended while in university. He talked about his being recently in Hawaii and praying, without any reflection or testing of his intuition, against, what he felt were ancient ancestral demonic spirits that were behind the former Native Hawaiian practices of human sacrifice.

He said that after he made a hasty public prayer against what he considered very real demonic powers using his Christian faith and practice, he experienced several near-death experiences of car accidents, and other rare phenomena to him. These occurrences convinced him that he had prayed immaturely against powers he knew little about and acted presumptuously towards.

While I will not focus on his view of ancient Hawaiian human sacrificial practices as being "evil" certainly his explanation is true that he was hasty, non-reflective, and, yes, irresponsible in his public prayer. He may have simply acted from an inflated ego. The near-death accidents lowered his hubris and forced him to self-reflect and examine his motives regarding his role at that time within the public arena. He said that these frightening repercussions, as he viewed them, were very helpful to him.

I do not know the rest of the story and whether Baxter realized or not that perhaps he needed some psychological help to get "grounded" and off his ego inflation, or if he needed to pray against evil as he saw it from a place of true community. The event where he prayed in Hawaii was a conference in which he was the primary speaker. While it may have been a gathering of likeminded and acting colleagues, it was not a true community for him. There was little accountability or nurture provided in such a public and temporary arena. Community it was not. He was similar to a performer with an audience, speaking without their permission on behalf of the gathered community of faith.

He said this experience taught him the value of first listening to his intuition before launching into intense prayer against what he perceived as spiritual evil or archetypal entities.

I believe this was wisdom he gained on his part. Just as Marie-Louise van Franz taught in her teachings from fairy tales; as John Sanford noted, we are not to take a black and white, simplistic approach to dealing with evil. Even so, we are not to pray for every situation in the same way.

The human soul must learn to cooperate with God in this matter of discerning and confronting evil. We need to ask questions of God, just as Perceval was to ask the great question. *This is the feminine relational spiritual orientation we so desperately need in our culture today.* We can pray each time we learn of or encounter evil ourselves, asking God in prayer for discernment and guidance as how to pray and take action. We can listen to our intuition and use the guidance provided.

The teaching that we need to heed God's guidance regarding how and when to pray against evil has been taught extensively in the Orthodox Christian tradition for centuries. I recommend books on this subject by the Episcopal writer Agnes Sanford, specifically her novel *Lost Shepherd.* For contemporary teaching from the Greek Orthodox tradition, I recommend the book by Kyriacos Markides, *The Magus of Strovolos.* Both are listed in the bibliography.

As one who has prayed thousands of times for the healing of mind and body for others, I can attest to the need for calm, reflective prayers to God asking for guidance concerning how to pray.

There is no formulaic approach to such prayers.

At times the guidance is to remove myself from the situation. Either the timing is not right or I am not the best person to deal with the circumstances. But more commonly, I experience a sense of peace and a directive within to speak either aloud or in silence (depending on the social situation, always trying to be appropriate) and confront the evil directly and tell it that I recognize it for what or who it is. I mandate that the evil leave the person or situation and not return. I speak to the evil as if it were an autonomous entity and direct it to the Spirit of the Risen Christ, the judge of all living things, visible and invisible.

I refrain from any judgment or harshness as I know this is not my place nor my role. *There may be no greater need for feminine, relational listening to God and trusting one's feminine intuition than this need to seek God's direction concerning how to proceed in prayer confronting evil.*

I then pray that God's light and peace infill and surround the person or situation, enveloping them in a protective cocoon. I use my imagination to envision these things, knowing that often our imagination is the very tool of the spiritual dimension which God uses to bring about permanent change. For more detailed instructions regarding this type of healing prayer, I refer the reader to my book on generational healing: *A Moment of Great Power: Sacramental Prayer and Generational Healing.*

The Grail story does not give the reader these suggestions in how to combat evil. I think this is basically because the story is about the blinding domination of the masculine energy overpowering and overriding the feminine principle through neglect, custom and cultural norms. Perceval had to fail in his hero's quest, dispose of his worn mother's underwear representing his unconscious desire to stay immature, and then to risk being a fool by asking the correct question, "For whom does the Grail serve?"

Perceval was confronted by the feminine in a manner that was relational and rooted in the reality of earthly life. Perceval was confronted by the Old Hag in Arthur's court regarding his sins of omission. He had to own his destructive naïvetés, his brash cruelty towards Blanchflor and learn to listen to the feminine principles of life. He had to own evil within himself before he could ask the proper question and free the Fisher King.

Finally, at the end of the myth, Perceval became the primary caretaker of the feminine principle by becoming the guardian of the Grail, the new Grail king. Like Merlin of Arthur's court, in old age he would go into the hills, find a hidden cave and live there eternally until the message of the Grail was needed to be brought forth again.

Perhaps this end of the Grail Legend shows that timing is most important in dealing with evil. Thus, the retreat by its Guardian until needed again.

What may be clear is that personal ownership of one's Shadow and coming out of the realm of the negative mother or father complex, is needed by all of us for clarity of thought followed by discerning action. "To whom does the Grail serve?" is another way to ask the question, "Are we submitted and listening to God or to our own ego?"

Marie-Louise von Franz continues this theme of the need for us to use discernment when we encounter evil persons or groups. She says that is it important to hide one's integrity, what she calls our "innocent nucleus of the personality," and not put it out on "display like a fool." I have found this to be very true. When we are dealing with evil in other people, we need to be discerning and wise not to reveal our innermost self, as evil can sense this and will attack or use this openness to defend itself. Also, the person who puts their innocent nucleus out there can be spiritually contaminated and oppressed. This can be avoided with discretion and spiritual discernment.

Specifically, in a group setting, where a group evil is present, we need to hide our best self, and only "very rarely let it come out. One has to draw a veil over a part of one's personality because of the automatic lowering of the ethical level" (von Franz, Marie-Louise. *Shadow and Evil in Fairy Tales*. Shambala

Publications, Boston, 1995, p. 213).

By a lowering of the ethical level, von Franz is referring to what was discussed before about the unconsciousness of collective or group thinking that can easily gravitate to the lowest common denominator regarding ethics, and often evil can be released in such a collective unconsciousness. This happens because of an absence of individual ethical thinking in the group. One must only take a look at the bizarre behavior of people gathered at Donald Trump's rallies to realize this reality.

She states from experience that in less than five percent of group gatherings, a kind of supernatural harmony can prevail with an accompanying numinous quality of Holy presence.

In concluding these teachings about how to deal with evil in order to help people find spiritual and psychological freedom, I would like to share a passage from the Hungarian theologian Ladislaus Boros, in which he describes the ideal conduct of one who prays to bring God's healing to those in need. Boros discusses the need to integrate true Simplicity and Shrewdness.

Simplicity, spiritual poverty, a limited outlook, innocence, and naivety are combined in the biblical symbol of the dove. The saint accepts the gifts from God's hand without question, almost without thanks. When this person uses them, their right hand does not know what their left hand is doing. They do not feel qualified to pass judgment on others or on themselves. With simplicity they fulfill the will of him who gave them courage to dare to love. They do not see anything remarkable in the fact that the interior miracles of God's presence take place in them. They enter into God's friendship simply and unconcerned.

At the same time, however, they test everything and exercise spiritual discernment. Everything on this earth is provisional for them, replaceable and ambiguous. They feel called upon to "plan" grace, and "calculate" divine things.

To do this they have to treat with reserve even the sublimest expression of the spirit. This person regards all emotional enthusiasm with suspicion.

Their worst opponents are fanatics who want to make an absolute of what is finite and conditioned. "Be wise as serpents." – They know how to be careful, and skillfully avoid the attacks of their enemies. They answer the world's malice with well-considered prudence. Their attitude towards life includes a certain element of mistrust and mild skepticism.

Dove and serpent – the saint combines them not merely simultaneously in their own person, but in the single act of serving the transcendent in a world which is narrow and impenetrable and of which only the deceptive surface is visible. Their true location lies far behind these confusing oppositions, at a point where their life is ecstatically absorbed in the divine abyss of love.

(Boros, Ladislaus. *We Are Future*. Herder and Herder New York, 1970, p. 115)

Boros, a Jesuit Roman Catholic priest had to flee for his life from his beloved native Hungary in 1949 at the tender age of twenty-one. He was a true discerner in prayer and pastoral counseling of how to overcome and confront evil. He led a quiet life of deep influence for multitudes as a teacher of philosophy and theology in Berlin and as an editor of the primary Jesuit academic journal in Post-World War Two Europe from his home in the French speaking area of Switzerland.

At age fifty-two he developed throat cancer, and could no longer speak above a whisper. He then requested and was granted by the Pope to step down from his priesthood and devoted his teaching skill to writing full-time until his death at age sixty-two. He married a woman whom he deeply loved. I own twelve of his books that have been translated and published by British and American publishers, including my own denomination's now defunct Seabury Press.

He faced the evils of Soviet Communism in his native Hungary, embraced the loneliness of exile, forced to speak and write in a foreign tongue. He confronted the horrors of cancer, and eventually embraced his death with a courage that knew evil had been overcome by his Christ, once and for all. He lived what he taught by combining the wisdom of the serpent and the simplicity of the dove. Of all the writers and theologians who have influenced my life from the grave, Boros has led the way with the greatest clarity and vision of loving truth. I highly encourage others to read his writings.

The following chapter will teach practical ways one can continue to own the Shadow and to find one's way on the narrow path of listening to God, motivated by love for God and profound love for all humankind.

Section IV

Conclusion

Spiritual Disciplines to Practice to Nurture the Soul

I would suggest that the very nature of the mythological structure of the Grail myth affirms to us the transformative power of images and imagination. I will begin this section on practical things to do to nurture the soul, along with the most important ancient Christian spiritual discipline of working with one's dreams as messages from God for healing and wholeness. I will also teach about the journaling tool used throughout the ages called Active Imagination and provide the best resources for developing this helpful skill that I have been able to find.

I will teach briefly about the significance of making pilgrimage, creating sacred space, the importance of solitude on a daily basis, the value of prayer, especially definitive petition prayer, the consuming of wholesome food, proper cleansing routines for the body, and the importance of adequate and restful sleep.

I will teach about the importance of spiritual rituals and private worship of God as well as ways to enjoy more public or corporate worship with other, like-souled persons. Finally, I will conclude this section with teaching about how to surround one's self with loving, soulful and healthy people, while learning to provide adequate boundaries, and even the complete negation of activities and interactions with destructive individuals.

I hope the reader finds help in these practical suggestions. The list is intentionally not complete, but hopefully this will be a good start for many. Each of these suggestions come from my own experience, not just my study and reading of others which, of course, has contributed greatly to my understanding of their value.

All techniques and tools for nurturing the soul have their foundation in the act of self-emptying which is a feminine activity of the ego and the soul. This means a letting go of expectations and letting ourselves descend to a place of deep trust in the goodness and love of God within.

Self-emptying is our center. Soul work is not a matter of going "up," or trying to "get better" at spiritual disciplines. God is not up. God is right here, within. One might even say God is "down." We discover this reality by a complete self-emptying. This is not an abolition of the ego but a strengthening of it by letting go of all expectations that degrade and weaken the ego.

Rituals that enhance the soul are not about techniques, which is a type of ego-driven striving "up." Self-emptying is a type of movement "down," a decision to be open to relationship where love is given and love is received. We each are invited to a dance of giving and receiving with God which allows us to be completely vulnerable and open to healing.

Ritual is an important way we can remind ourselves to trust God's sovereignty within and outside of us. Each of us contains this treasure of God's providence and sovereignty.

As Ladislaus Boros reminded us in his wonderful book *Hidden God*:

"Once a person is free of an egocentric self, we are open to the world and prepared to love everything and everyone, the real world begins to grow in and around us, and we have the sense of being completely at home" (Boros, Ladislaus. *Hidden God*. The Seabury Press, New York, 1973, p. 106).

The Holy Grail is a feminine container which is both empty and completely full, and simultaneously overflowing with grace. Healing happened for the Fisher King when the ultimate question of purpose and meaning was simply asked by the holy fool represented in us by Perceval.

We do not need to have an answer. It is only in this act of

asking the question which brings the healing. The answer does not even need to be given. By asking the question of ourselves, "Who are we serving?" This letting go creates the dance that brings relational Love which flows from one to the Other and from Other to the one.

Each of the suggestions that follow that may enhance the nurture of the soul are simply tested means and ways that people have learned to let go and ask the question, stepping into the unknown of pleasure, comfort and supreme joy.

With this preface, we begin by addressing the value of listening to and working with one's dreams as the primary way to nurture the modern soul and find spiritual satisfaction and joy.

Restoring Dream Work as a Primary Spiritual Discipline for the Soul

Dreams have long been considered the voice of God from the earliest time in ancient Christianity and most of the oldest spiritual systems of the world. The dream uses images from both our outer life events and the inner archetypal realm to speak to us where we are spiritually and psychologically. The dream is in the arena of the right-brain, non-rational intelligence, intuition, and instinct. The non-rational intelligence works in conjunction and coordination with the more rational, categorical, analytical left-brain aspects of intelligence when we record, analyze and honor the dream.

The spiritual struggle in Western humanity has seen a demise of trust in the non-rational to the detriment and poverty of spirit in the culture. The dream has long been considered one of the primary means by which God speaks to the individual giving guidance, affirmation, comfort, and warning. The power of myth which the grail story carries is the same power of the mythological images and language of the dream. Both have the same source, the collective unconscious, or in Christian terms, the Mind of Christ indwelling all human beings.

I encourage the reader to begin recording their dreams the best they can. Putting out a notepad next to the bed with a pen ready to write is a good way to start. Also praying or giving the mind suggestions before sleep asking to be receptive to the dream, will help one remember content, feeling, emotion and images.

I encourage the reader to read John A. Sanford's *Dreams: God's Forgotten Language.* In my opinion, this work, now over fifty years since its first publication, is still the best book to understand the value of one's dreaming material. My book may also be helpful: *Dreams: A Spiritual Guide to Healing and Wholeness.* It is an eBook available on Amazon.com and Amazon. com.uk.

Two excellent guides for use in interpreting the symbolic images in dreams is J. C. Cooper's *An Illustrated Encyclopaedia of Traditional Symbols,* and Suzanne F. Fincher's *Creating Mandalas: For Insight, Healing and Self Expression.* Both give rich and varied information about how various symbols and images are understood in various cultures around the world and are helpful for sparking ideas regarding what the images may be saying to us in the dream.

As the dreamer relates to the inner images and understands them as parts of one's unconscious or spiritual self, one finds a new sense of connection and meaning within. Dreams use the images of people we know in outer life to help us, through association, to view these images as symbols representing aspects of ourselves. One can simply ask the question, "What characteristics would I use to define these persons I know in my outer life?" These characteristics are then either viewed as parts of our inner being that need to be reconciled and integrated, or simply asking us to become more self-aware of what we already know.

Images of persons in our dreams whom we *do not know* in

outer life are what are known as Shadow figures, aspects of ourselves that have been repressed, ignored, or damaged by trauma, neglect or abuse. Often these images are negative or defective in the dream. However, once we pay attention to and honor them as lost aspects of ourselves they are transformed into positive images who assist us on our journey. Sometimes the unknown persons in our dreams are beautiful, intelligent, witty, and powerful. They represent our lost inner gold, our treasure, our uniqueness. These Shadow images are lost aspects of ourselves that need conscious integration and honoring. The best book for beginning to understand our shadow is Robert Johnson's *Owning Your Own Shadow.*

The actions in dreams portray the direction we are moving in in our outer and inner lives. Dream images involving transportation can provide us with guidance for either affirmation of the direction we are traveling or a confrontation to stop, turn aside, or even turn back and start again.

For example, a dream of traveling in a car driven by an unknown person signifies that an aspect of our Shadow is in control of how we are moving about in our outer life. This shows that we are experiencing an unhealthy unconsciousness. The car is the primary means of transportation in western culture and, thus, is usually understood psychologically as the carrier of the ego.

If an aspect of our Shadow is in control of our ego, we are in deep trouble and we can take this as a warning to take a good, hard look as to what we are attributing to our ego, and bring it down to earth, so to speak. While all of us need a healthy strong ego to get about in our daily life, if we are too identified with the ego, we can become egocentric, inflated, and out of control. Thus, the Shadow as driver in our dream can indicate such a travesty that must be consciously stopped.

Conversely, if one is walking barefoot on a dirt or stone path or sandy beach, we know that the ego is grounded. The bottom of the feet indicating that the soul is in touch with the earth, soil and sand, showing a balance. Movement forward in this manner can be affirmed in us through the dream. Being barefoot is a symbol of the centered, grounded soul, as the bottom of the foot was considered in Western culture since the early Greeks to be the entrance point of the soul into the human body. This is because they believed the loss of sensation in the feet experienced first in the dying process illustrated that the soul passed in and out of the body through the feet. We may get our word sole (soul) from this ancient association.

I want to encourage the reader to record their dreams because even the act of recording brings healing as we are honoring our inner Self or the Christ within. As you seek additional resources about dream work beyond what has already been mentioned, please feel free to email me at the address at the back of this book or here at plfritsch@hotmail.com. Each book listed in the Bibliography has wonderful suggestions for extended reading.

It does not require a huge study of dream resource scholarship to receive an abundance of rewards from one's spiritual discipline of dream work. The key is to begin and to recognize that "the voice speaking to one through the dream is God's voice," as the second-century Christian philosopher and apologetic Tertullian proclaimed. Tertullian wrote a four hundred-page thesis on dream work and was the first to use the term REM or Rapid Eye Movement for the fourth level of sleep while observing the infants of his adult children and friends sleeping over a twenty-two-year time period of study.

The Jewish word for dream, *chalom*, is the same word used to describe a vision, trance or what we might call a daydream or fantasy. It is important that we see each of these common non-rational phenomenon as different ways of describing soul experiences. I encourage the reader to write down and record their daydreams, imaginations, fantasies, and any auditory or visionary messages they have seen or heard. They are not to be taken verbatim, but as images and symbols of the language of the spirit and are usually to be understood symbolically not literally.

As a priest, I have experienced very few visions, only one of the heavenly realm and one of the demonic imposed on the face of another human. I find it interesting that I, as a severely hearing-impaired person from birth, would have an abundance of experiences hearing auditory words and music from the unseen dimension. As a teenager, I once experienced an out of body movement while sitting in a grassy field near my parents' house while contemplating the meaning of my life. These are common human experiences. As a parish priest, I have heard hundreds of such stories from members of my churches. I encourage the reader to honor these numinous experiences and integrate them into their own self-image and life story.

As these phenomena are not unusual, their presence does not signify deep spirituality or holiness. They just happen and need to be taken with care and processed just as one would look symbolically and allegorically at the images from a dream. There is no shame in reflecting on these experiences. Quite the contrary. Such reflection and processing enriches the soul and prepares us to move forward in our sense of call in life. In my pastoral experience, I would guess that about five to eight percent of the population has regular (monthly or at minimum, yearly) visions and experiences involving the spiritual dimension by sight, smell, touch, taste or sound.

For further understanding of the spiritual value of dream work, I recommend Morton Kelsey's books *Encounter with God; Transcend: A Guide to the Perennial Spiritual Quest; Dreams: The Dark Speech of the Soul,* and *God, Dreams and Revelation: A Christian Interpretation of Dreams* along with William James's *The Varieties of Religious Experience* as scholastic works to help the reader familiarize themselves with the various psychic experiences common to all people. Also C. G. Jung's autobiography, *Memories, Dreams, and Reflections*, contains vast reflective material of his dreams, visions, daydreams and auditory spiritual experiences. Familiarizing one's self with these authentic true stories will affirm and enrich one's own awareness of the reality of the spiritual dimension speaking to one's life situations.

Active Imagination

The next most helpful suggestion in practical nurturing of the soul lies in learning the skill of Active Imagination journaling. This form of personal writing has been used for centuries as a way for people to engage their imagination in conversation with images from their dreams or other sources of images from literature, sacred texts, art work and other sources. Plato utilized this technique of writing in his *Dialogues* as did Ignatius of Loyola in his spiritual exercises. One simply engages characters from sacred text, or in our case from our dreams, in active imaginative dialogue.

I have used this form of writing engaging my innermost self for over thirty years and have always found it beneficial at a profound place within. While the practice may seem artificial or contrived by persons who mistrust their imagination, I have found the practice most helpful in reconciling and reconnecting with lost or repressed parts of my soul and memory.

One method of Active Imagination is simply to have a few moments of quiet reflection in an atmosphere of non-distraction and quiet.

One can then take an image or person from one's own dream and simply begin by greeting them (in writing), asking them a question such as how they are, or why they have appeared recently in the dream. Robert Johnson in his excellent book *Inner Work* suggests using the computer with the capital letter lock to distinguish between one's conscious voice and the words that come from the imagination. This way one can write fast and keep track of the separate voices that may appear. This is all done consciously and deliberately.

This form of writing *is not automatic writing,* which is an ancient occult practice. Automatic writing is a form of surrendering the unconscious completely to the spiritual realm or an abandonment of the conscious to the unconscious. Without a strong ego and awareness on the part of the practitioner, automatic writing can be very harmful in exposing a person to spiritual forces and/or contents of the unconscious that can overwhelm the conscious mind in a destructive effect. I have personally known two individuals from my university years in training for Music Therapy at a mental hospital in California who used automatic writing and went into a permanent psychotic-break state from which they did not recover.

Active Imagination journaling is a conscious, controlled interaction with one's inner self and it requires a strong ego without unconscious egocentricity. Robert Johnson recommends that when a person begins this practice, they should limit it to perhaps fifteen to twenty minutes at a time and only one session a day. To do more than this, one can become overly subjective and cause a person to become too introverted and liable to ego inflation. The practice is not to be feared but revered and used with grace and common sense. It may also help the reader who does this exercise to have another person experienced in the practice as an accountable mentor, because the richness of the inner dialogue can be so interesting and enjoyable that it is possible to sidestep one's common life and neglect basic duties to self, family and work.

At first, I found writing the Active Imagination journaling to feel artificial. It felt contrived. However, within minutes of being intentional about dialoguing with inner images from dreams, I found the thoughts had a life energy flowing of their own and the feeling of pretentiousness departed. Sometimes I would get insights into my life situation that might not have come to me otherwise. In every case, the practice helps me connect emotionally with inner parts of myself. Afterwards, I feel a deep sense of peace, concord, and prevailing astuteness of being.

For further information about Active Imagination, I recommend Robert Johnson's book *Inner Work*. It is the best scholastic volume available that I have read and used repeatedly, as well as successfully recommended to others. Other excellent resources regarding Active Imagination is Barbara Hannah's *Encounters with the Soul: Active Imagination as Developed by C. G. Jung* and Marie Louise von Franz' study titled *Alchemical Active Imagination*.

This tool is a wonderful way to engage the inner life authentically and to find new healing as repressed or forgotten parts of ourselves are brought to conscious awareness and connection, bringing new emotional oneness and joy.

Pilgrimage

The next spiritual discipline which nurtures the soul that I encourage the reader to practice is creating a habit of making pilgrimage. What this entails is the intentional process of recapturing memories of one's favorite places and visiting them on a regular basis, perhaps once a year, or once every three years, whatever resources allows.

In our Grail story Perceval's spiritual quest is renewed by his return to the Grail Castle twenty years or more after his first encounter. This can be a metaphor for our own need for pilgrimage, not just for the sake of remembering which is of great value in itself, but for the purpose of deeper interaction with sacred space, place, and time, opening us to more spiritual reality than we have known before.

Most people think of visiting sacred places known to the public arena. But what I am speaking of is a more personal notion, revisiting places that have special meaning for us from childhood or places where our ancestors may have lived and worked.

One of the ways to get in touch with the inner self is to visit the place where one was raised. If there are unpleasant memories about the place it might be best to bypass such a visit unless the inner voice calls one to do so. Otherwise, visiting places where good memories took place can be a very affirming way of connecting and affirming the child within. It is a common phenomenon that when people sleep in the places or towns near to where they grew up, significant dreams occur which can enhance one's sense of self in God. To visit such places with some type of regularity can help solidify a foundation of inner peace and reconciliation.

It is an ancient worldwide belief that places have memory. The earth, soil, rocks, air, buildings, and living plants such as trees and fields have memory that can nourish our souls upon pilgrimage. I believe it is more than just recollection that occurs. I believe, based on my experience and my scholastic studies on the subject, pilgrimage to places from our past allows the spiritual aspects of the places to speak to us in non-rational and intuitive ways and means. Many scientists have studied such sacred places and recorded actual energy that can be measured in the ground, trees and, in some cases, the very stones and buildings of such places. For an excellent introduction to learning more about sacred places I suggest reading the following article by *The World Pilgrimage Guide*: https://sacredsites.com/martin_gray/publications/the_power_of_place_sacred_sites_and_the_presence_of_the_miraculous.html

Some people find it beneficial to visit the gravesites of family members with some regularity. In my new home country of Hungary, Halloween, as Americans celebrate, is not given much credence, but All Soul's Day, the first of November, is very important. It is a meaningful time for many Hungarians to visit the cemeteries and gravesites of their ancestors, bringing flowers, and other gifts as tokens to honor those who have passed to the next life.

Personally, I have not found this form of pilgrimage helpful due to very painful memories of abuse from my family of origin. However, I know for many people this practice is helpful in connecting with a greater sense of belonging or as Fritz Kunkel would say, group soul. However, I have made a pilgrimage to the graves of people who have influenced my life through their writings, such as the grave of C. G. Jung in Küsnacht, Switzerland, and his retreat home, Bollingen, where I found these visits meaningful, powerful and healing experiences.

For me, pilgrimage has been meaningful to revisit childhood nature haunts, forests, rocks, and lakes where I played as a child. These natural surroundings provided safety for me as a child, nurture and abounding re-creation. Recently my wife and I stayed for five nights in an Airbnb house in the neighborhood called Emerald Hills in Redwood City, California, where much of my childhood took place. We hiked the hills, walked to the downtown far away, and visited Hanley's Rock, Emerald Lake, and various footpaths still visible in the tall weeds where I wandered as a child. These experiences not only gave my wife a deeper sense of who I am, but provided me with a dreamlike state of remembrance which awakened within me a sense of profound gratitude.

I did not feel a need to live in this place again. The decades that have passed have created an unrealistic expensive overhead and exorbitant cost of living to a once very affordable place to live. But touching the oak trees, smelling the eucalyptus leaves and swimming in the lake of my youth helped me connect with the child within, the divine spark which lights all of us. What was so nurturing was how my senses perceived the experiences; the sights, sounds, aromas, physical contacts and tastes of my childhood touched me deeply and brought a new type of union with Self.

Pilgrimage to places of the heart is like a labyrinth walk: going back to the center of where life began for us on earth, then moving out again with a freshness of spirit renewed. Additional places to visit are parks, hiking trails, art museums, even favorite bookstores or university campuses. Each of these places has a strong sense of soul. I encourage my readers not to limit themselves to places of pilgrimage for others, such as famous churches, historical sites, or government buildings. I feel it is important for our individual soul to visit the special places of our own personal journey, and to make this a part of our routine.

I recently visited the village of Rockport, Massachusetts, on the north shore of Cape Ann, north of Boston. My mother's family were one of the earliest settlers of the area in 1645. However, the significance of the place does not just lie here with my ancestors.

The major factor of nourishment for my soul regarding Rockport is the memory of childhood freedom, especially the development of entrepreneurship. I spent several weeks each summer between the ages of ten and twelve at the family summer home in Rockport. It is a tourist town.

At that time soda pop was sold in glass bottles processed by the Twin Lights Bottling Company located on Main Street. I would compete with other children to collect the used bottles out of the garbage cans lining the streets and take them in an old squeaky-wheeled wagon up the hill to the bottling company. They paid us good money for recycling them and we always had plenty of pocket money to use at the penny candy counter in the General Store on Bearskin Neck near the house.

This financial freedom motivated me to discover a small rocky cove on Bearskin Neck that used to be the area's garbage dump. Down beneath the granite boulders and smaller rocks were pieces of old green, yellow, white and blue broken bottles worn rough and interesting into unusual "beach glass." I would collect this glass by the hour and then put it in plastic sandwich bags and sell to tourists on the Neck. I also, eventually, created a wall hanging out of driftwood, shells, lobstermen used-rope and seaweed. I sold it for quite a bit of money to a fashionable lady from New York City. This activity would serve me well as a self-employed teenager, young adult and now, as an elder. Pilgrimage to this village helped me affirm my own God-given gifts of creativity, innovation and individuation so necessary for self-development.

There are sacred places that may be common to many people such as temples, churches, gardens (the Chinese Garden in Golden Gate Park, San Francisco, comes to mind) which can nurture the souls of multitudes of people, especially places that have drawn worshippers over time. Often such persons of pilgrimage are sensitive to the role of Spirit in their lives and use these places as sites for meditation and prayer to their gods and goddesses.

There is a white limestone outcropping at a hill called Tettye which overlooks my home city of Pécs, Hungary. Tradition says that since the Roman era people have stood upon the rock and looked out onto the southern rolling plains that stretch today to the Croatian border. The old stories say that this was a place of meditation, reflection and prayer. I learned about the value of this sacred stone from an atheistic, Information Technology technician at the University of Pécs. This man, like many Hungarians, does not believe in the God portrayed by the Christian traditions of Hungary, but nevertheless, was a deeply spiritual person. He trusted the God of his experience within and his awareness of sacred energy was strong.

I decided to find out for myself and sure enough, within moments of standing on this rock, I could feel the sacred energy emanating upwards from the very ground on this rocky ledge, a type of trembling and electrical vibration of energy that I think could be felt by any self-aware person.

Another sacred site where I have experienced the physical sensation of the spiritual dimension, and a speaking voice with a specific message of healing is the basilica in Einseideln, Switzerland, home of a famous Germanic Black Madonna Shrine. The first time I visited there, I went down into the undercroft, a chapel underneath the main sanctuary of the massive building. In that holy place I felt a strong trembling and heard a sound like a quiet, very low rumbling coming up from the floor. I asked the elderly docent standing nearby what the vibration was and the source of the sound. He pointed to the altar and the crucifix on it, and simply indicated with his gesture that it was a spiritual source.

Upon leaving the basilica, joining companions in the outer courtyard facing the village, I heard a distinct voice both in my spirit and with my ears. I heard the message, "Peter, go and begin your life anew." These types of experiences are common in sacred places of pilgrimage and one should not be frightened or surprised if they experienced such phenomena. These experiences are given to us by God to affirm and guide us, and to renew our awareness of the transcendence and immediacy of God's presence.

To be in these places of ancient pilgrimage can affirm what we already instinctively know, that we are spiritual beings, one with the eternal universe, created in, by and for the purposes of Love.

How often should one go on pilgrimage to such a place of sacred memory? I would suggest a minimum of twice a year, perhaps more often as needed. This circling and centering of pilgrimage is vital to our wellbeing and sense of belonging. Everyone yearns for such connectedness. To neglect this need is to be unnecessarily impoverished.

One of the most helpful books I have encountered regarding the spiritual discipline of pilgrimage was written by travel writer Rick Steves titled *Travel as a Political Act*. Steves is a deeply committed spiritual person and writes about the value of visiting countries which most Westerners have been brainwashed to disregard, such as Iran, the former Yugoslavian countries, El Salvador, Turkey, and Morocco. Steves teaches how we can remove our projections and enter into the true spiritual nourishment of these countries and cultures. Most of what I have learned about the true value of travel in the past ten years has come from Rick Steves' insights and encouragements.

Discovering and Creating Sacred Space

One of the most important things we can do is both create and recognize sacred space for ourselves. Similar to the benefits of spiritual pilgrimage, we can create and discover sacred space that nurtures the soul in unexpected places and situations.

One of the realities that is pointed out by Robert Johnson in his excellent volume *Owning Your Own Shadow* is the fact that our emotions do not know the difference between ritual and actual situational facts. Creative ritual is very important to the nurture of our souls.

Johnson gives the following example. He tells us in his writings that he is an extreme introvert by nature. In fact, C. G. Jung told him not to ever join groups of any kind because Johnson was the most introverted person Jung had ever encountered.

Robert tells the story of having a speaking engagement in front of a large audience. He was a keynote speaker alongside Marie Louise von Franz, noted Jungian writer and teacher. He shared with her that he was always feeling weak and afraid when he had to do public teaching. She encouraged him to stand in his motel room, take a bath towel and soak it in the sink, wring it out a degree, then roll it into a tight ball and slam it down on the floor of the bathroom as hard as he could with both hands. He was to repeat this action several times until he realized his energy level was up and strong.

He hesitantly did as she encouraged and to his surprise

discovered the ritual of slamming the wet towel on the floor energized him to the point of feeling as if he had the courage of an African lion! When he strode out on the platform to speak, his timidity was gone and he was able to speak with quiet authority and great clarity.

We can use ritual to release all kinds of needed inner energies. We may be feeling agitated and need to calm down. One could light a candle, listen to soothing music, and meditate on a beautiful photograph or item of peaceful artwork. We can repeat calming words quietly to ourselves. There are many possibilities.

Likewise, as in Johnson's case, when high energy is required of us, we can take a wooden spoon and pretend that it is a blazing sword and use it to fight an imaginary foe in mortal combat. We can repeat warrior cry words or sounds to ourselves, and suddenly find the energy to confront whatever situation we are feeling afraid about.

Here are a few rituals that I use in my daily life that have proven over the years to be helpful. I am a strong introvert like Johnson.

As an Episcopal priest, I must give sermons or give teaching lectures in public settings, often on mornings or evenings when all I want to do is crawl back into bed or sit quietly at home alone with a glass of red wine. What I find helpful in this situation is to stand on my toes and pounce on them, up and down, in a type of boxing stance dance. I do this in my office or in the vesting room when I have privacy before a service.

While I have never taken martial arts and find the movements a bit daunting, I sometimes jab out with my hands or fake an invisible karate chop! While I feel childish doing this, I find in acting out these actions that my hesitance and reluctance to face the people in the audience goes away. I feel strong and able to deliver something of pronounced value in the way of words and gestures to them in the service or lecture. Finally, I surrender the process to God in a silent prayer of thanksgiving and trust, and walk out to begin the service with renewed confidence.

Personal rituals are just that, personal. While it may be helpful in spring-boarding one's imagination to repeat a ritual learned from another, it is best to create one's own ritual specifically suited to one's history, preference, and if possible, one's image of God that works best.

For example, a candle lit on a table or bureau could symbolize God as light. A visit to an ocean or lake pier can reflect the image of God as Matter, Mother, Water, Eve, and the Source of All Living. The same can be said of silent, creative prayers while holding stones, minerals or pieces of natural wood that speak to one of the inner riches and solidarity of the spiritual reality.

Gestures and postures are important in ritual. I find sitting in a comfortable position with the ability to rest my head and close my eyes an important means of connecting with the inner peace of God. Some people prefer to stand or even walk while meditating or contemplating. Some may find kneeling a helpful posture when needing to surrender fear of the unknown and receiving Trust within as a gift of the Spirit. I often open my arms and extend them upwards to both express praise and adoration to God as Mystery. The same gesture also allows me to receive in the open spiritual arms of my soul the gift of unconditional love and affirmation so needed by my thirsty and, often, frightened or sorrowful self.

I encourage the reader to experiment. One may read about long established rituals in various world religions and try them on for size, see if they fit in a way that both stretches and enhances the soul. There is no one posture, one exercise, one and only ritual to do, while much teaching about them may seem this way. Try them all and see what resonates. Only that which truly satisfies and brings a strong sense of connection should be utilized. There is no judgment. There is no right or wrong. Each of us is unique in both our expression of self and in our self-nurture.

While most people find it necessary to have complete privacy and silence to establish nurturing rituals that feed the soul, this is not a hard and fast rule at all. For myself, many years were spent in a crowded and noisy coffee shop, journal on the table or countertop, coffee mug full in one hand, the pen in the other, the heart, open, receptive, receiving. I found the white noise of the busy environment actually helped me focus within. Of course, I had to be careful not to allow too much distraction by the interesting people who came in and out of the establishment, and to stay tuned to the task at hand. I am one who sees God in persons and I read, carefully, their body language, facial expressions, even how their clothes fit or are draped, giving me an idea of how and why and in what way the Holy is being expressed in their being.

Malcolm Muggeridge gives a description of a noisy environment for prayer in his book *Something Beautiful for God* of the concrete chapel at the Sisters of Mercy in Calcutta where he was the guest of Mother Teresa. During the sisters' morning devotion time of the adoration of the reserved sacrament, the nuns were silent, transfixed on their contemplation. Just a few feet outside the open windows were loud exhaust spewing motorcycles, cars, buses and thousands of people on their way to work in the crowded city. The environment was the opposite of what one would hope could induce tranquility, yet the sisters had what they needed despite the distractions because of who they were inside.

This story has spoken to me over the years of the need to not allow outer circumstances to become an excuse for not spending quality time with God.

One of the most meaningful rituals I have ever witnessed was in the notoriously violent, crowded maximum security prison known as Folsom Prison outside of Sacramento in California. A friend of mine had been helping develop a centering prayer movement among the prisoners and the guards. I was invited to tag along and give a short talk at the end of the twenty minutes of silent group meditation.

We passed through the expected entry gate pat-downs and other security measures at the outer entryways to the main prison from the parking lot. Then once inside, we were walked by guards through the maze of corridors to the main cell block, a scene from Dante's hell, if ever there was one.

Cells designed for two were crowded with four to six men each, literally toppled above and below one another. Naked prisoners were showering on the perimeter walls of the cellblock exposed to the gaze and gawk of male and female guards roaming around at will within inches of the men trying to shower. I was embarrassed, ashamed, and appalled at the extremely crowded conditions and total lack of privacy.

At the exit to the cell block we were told by the guards to keep walking alone to the chapel building where the meditation would occur. Only later would I learn that the normal prisoner escorts had been detained for no reason by belligerent guards and we were walking without protection through the most dangerous part of the prison, the outdoor recreation yard. At the entrance to the chapel we met the prisoner leaders of the centering prayer movement and we were escorted into the building.

There were forty of us, the maximum allowed by the warden for the monthly event. Requests had been made by prisoners and guards alike for a weekly opportunity to pray which was consistently denied by the warden. A prisoner explained to me that over eight hundred prisoners and two hundred guards were part of the centering prayer movement at the prison. As a result of the warden's restrictions, prisoners had to wait months before they could take their turn in the chapel gathering. I was told that in the cellblocks and guard stations all the others were praying individually their own centering prayer simultaneously with those of us in the chapel. This experience moved me to the core.

On my left was a young man barely twenty or so in age. He quietly told me that the twenty minutes of prayer as part of this group was the only time in his experience in prison when he felt he could relax at all for fear of his life. We all joined hands together and then prayed in silence. The spiritual energy of God flowed through the hands joining mine and moved upwards into the very air between the circle of men. I will never forget the sense of holiness in that space, time and ritual between these prisoners on either side of me.

As requested, I gave a short talk about how God is present with us especially when we feel God's absence and opened the short session for comments. Ritual with such a dedicated group created a sacred space and time that transcended the rational on drastic contrast to the violent and oppressive ethos in the yard only steps away outside.

Each of us has the opportunity to create sacred space, time and ritual to touch the holy and be touched deeply by it. On a daily basis, each of us needs this to nurture and strengthen the soul.

In the myth of the Holy Grail, the primary ritual portrayed is the procession of the Grail in the Grail Castle to which our hero, Perceval, was exposed. The procession itself was like a labyrinth, a circle, creating sacred space and time, moving in a serpentine path, symbolizing spiritual intuition. The ritual of the procession invoked the needed question within Perceval which was required for the healing of the kingdom. *Ritual can open for us the needed questions in our soul that need to be addressed at the current time and place of our journey. Each of us has the opportunity to take the mythology of ritual and integrate it into our outer and interior life.*

We are all different. No one ritual nor sacred space works for all. I encourage us to experiment with ritual and the creation of sacred space to listen to our own intuition, to be creative and make our own unique ones, no matter how simple or elaborate. We can utilize space, time, sounds, smells, tastes, sight and touch, all of our senses to speak to us from without to within.

For excellent reading about creating sacred space in one's living quarters, I refer the reader to a very valuable book called *Places of the Soul: Architecture and Environmental Design as a Healing* Art by Christopher Day.

The Importance of Revisiting Favorite Childhood Stories

The purpose for adults to rereading and experience anew their favorite childhood stories is to re-experience the immediacy and familiarity of childhood. This may be the most neglected spiritual discipline in modern times that can deeply nurture the soul and keep Her healthy. This immediacy is the essential characteristic of childhood, according to Hungarian Jesuit theologian László Boros in his book *Hidden God*. He writes:

A child's soul can be completely enthralled by happenings, things and feelings, so that it no longer looks inward at itself but loses itself in contemplation of the other. The totality of itself, undivided and unfragmented, comes very close to the totality of the other. It makes no calculations; it justifies nothing, conceals nothing. It is simply "there" with wide-open eyes, caught in an overwhelming experience, in a mood of heightened awareness of which it is not even aware.

We must accept that God reveals himself directly to the child as the meaning and intensity of its life in the world, and its relationship to things. This is to postulate, only hypothetically of course a specific kind of mysticism, different from any other form of experiencing God: a supernatural, existential mysticism that is really given by grace, but is never absent from the child's actual existence; a mysticism that penetrates all other aspects and states of the child's life a fundamental, inescapable element of that life. God is present to the child uninterruptedly, in a direct and non-verbalized relationship, as the background of its life and experience in a way that does not bring God, as object of human thought, into the sphere of the sayable, but only enables the child to receive him unreflectively, perhaps as the "light of vision." (Boros, Ladislaus. *Hidden God.* The Seabury Press, New York, 1973, p. 89)

Reading our most meaningful childhood stories helps us get in touch with the time in our life when we had such an immediacy of experience, and with this, a constant, unarticulated knowledge of God. Rereading the stories engages our imagination, not just as adults, but in the eternal realm that we knew as small children, and this very act allows us to touch the eternal now in our adult introspective state. Thus, this is another way for us to nurture our souls with the immediacy of God's presence in the memories we carry within us.

Another reason to reread and relearn the stories that captivated us as children is for self-understanding. In subtle ways, children are attracted to stories that proclaim their own life journeys and the issues they are dealing with within the family system and the environment fate has given them.

Recognizing this reality helps us be gentler with ourselves as we understand better what we as children had to deal with and work through, often without help or comfort. I will give you an example from a client who has given permission for this to be shared.

A man I work with in spiritual direction years ago discovered during a fairy tale workshop I was teaching that his favorite tale was a Grimm's Brothers tale called *The Tinder Box*. The story is simple.

A soldier, recently dismissed from service, was walking through the forests and came upon an old hag witch standing next to a large tree with a huge hole in its trunk. She asked him to help her by letting her lower him by a rope down inside the tree.

She explained that beneath the tree he would find three doors, and behind each would be a room with a dog with big eyes sitting on a chest. He was to take the witch's apron, put it on the floor of the room, place the dog on it (this would keep the guard dog quiet and still), then take as many coins of copper, silver, and gold from the three chests as he wanted. He was also to take a tinder box he would see there, bring it up and give it to her in exchange for the free coins.

The soldier did as she instructed, allowed himself to be lowered into the depths of the tree, found the three rooms, set the dogs on the apron, safely filled his pockets with first the copper, then the silver, then emptied them again to fill with gold coins. He remembered to grab the tinder box and was hoisted back up out of the tree by the witch.

When she requested that he hand over the tinder box, he asked her why it was important to her. She refused to tell him. He threatened to cut her head off with his sword if she did not tell him. When she again refused, he instantly cut off her head, put the gold coins and the tinder box in his backpack and headed to the nearest town to make a new life for himself.

He lived royally on the gold, and soon became famous also for his generosity. He learned that the princess of the kingdom was beautiful, but no one was able to court her. He very much wanted her but did not know what to do. He quickly used up all his reserve coins until he was almost destitute. In desperation, he took out the tinder box, and struck a spark with it. Suddenly, with one strike the first dog appeared before him. With two, the second dog as well. With three, the third. He ordered them all to bring him bags of copper, silver and gold, which they immediately did, restoring him to his grandeur and affluence.

Then, with a bit of ego inflation, he ordered the biggest dog who guarded the gold, to go fetch the princess and bring her back to his house while she slept. This the dog did and the soldier caressed her and adored her while she slept. She was taken back before morning by the dog, yet all during the daytime, she would remember the soldier, as if in a dream.

The queen soon caught wind of what she felt was some mischief happening. She tied a bag of cornmeal with a small hole in it to the princess while she slept. In the morning, she followed the yellow path to the door of the soldier and had him arrested and thrown in the deepest dungeon.

There he awaited execution by the king's soldiers.

The soldier was pretty much accepting of his fate, but then struck upon an idea. He had one copper coin in his pocket, and seeing a shoemaker's young apprentice on the sidewalk above his head in the jail cell, he called him over, offering him the coin if he would first go to his house and retrieve his tinder box. This the boy did.

Upon the gallows, the soldier asked if he could have one last smoke before the noose was set about his neck for hanging. Granting his request, the executioner gave him his tobacco, pipe and tinder box. He put his pipe to his mouth, and struck the tinder box once, twice, three times! Immediately all three dogs appeared. He ordered them to kill the king and queen, and to rescue him and the princess. The king and queen were tossed out of sight and mind by the powerful dogs and never seen again. The soldier and the princess were married and lived happily ever after.

Why was this story so important to the man in counseling? Well, we learned from his family history that as a very young naïve boy, his mother chained him to her psychologically by forcing him through rigorous training to be her primary caregiver for her frequent troubles caused by severe migraine headaches. From a young age he was responsible to help her manage the pain with medications. He would warm wet washcloths to put on her forehead and generally had to be continually attentive to her or suffer the consequences of her rage and abuse.

The man grew up to have no memories of not being responsible for the care of his mother. This infringement upon his childhood was not broken outwardly until he left to go away to university. But the ongoing tie to his mother and her needs persisted in the form of an internalized regressive, negative mother complex into his adult life. Indeed, this was the issue affecting his relationships with women and with his own self-care which eventually brought him into therapy.

When we examined *The Tinder Box* tale we saw many of the elements of his own spiritual journey there. The oppression of the responsibility to take care of the sick mother represented by the witch (the family was wealthy and could have hired a full-time nurse if necessary), and the emotional incest the man endured from her. Also, as I shared with him Robert Johnson's book *He* which tells the story of Perceval, the counselee saw immediately the parallels of the witch's apron in *The Tinder Box* and the homespun undergarment of Perceval in the Holy Grail myth.

The counselee saw that the mother complex was psychologically holding him back, keeping him infantile and naïve as an adult man. He realized that in the beginning of *The Tinder Box* story the soldier could only access the treasure by first acknowledging the negative mother archetype, represented by the instruction to be safe by placing the dogs on the witch's apron on the floor of the inner rooms. Later, after killing the witch, the soldier would discover he could gain access to the treasure at will by igniting the tinder box and calling the dogs to serve him.

The wealth of spiritual treasure available in the soul of the man represented by the three chests of coins, and his intrinsic, natural intuition which led him to seek therapy to get to the root of his problems was represented by the dogs. One might say also, that the positive, nurturing Mother Archetype could be represented by the great tree with the womb of the hole in its trunk allowing descent to the roots where the true treasures lie. There are many images in the story that the man perceived in rereading the childhood favorite which spoke to him at the non-rational, intuitive level, bringing healing and self-awareness.

The spiritual desire and quest within the man helped him to see that his psychological development coincided with his own innate, yet latent spiritual power represented by the tinder box.

The directee saw in the folk tale story his ego inflation and then the destruction of his hubris at midlife, represented by the soldier's secret rendezvous with the princess while she was unconscious, and getting caught by the queen (another reappearance of the negative mother complex and the witch) and his judgement of death by hanging.

The directee realized that his intuition to ask for therapeutic help was portrayed by the soldier's wise and discerning question; could he have one last smoke before he died? Just as Perceval had to ask one conscious, discerning question at the Grail castle hall, "For whom does the Grail serve?"

The counselee saw in the story how the three dogs quickly turned the apple cart upside down by removing the obstacles of the king and queen who represented his old way of doing things. He felt within himself the possibility of a new beginning, symbolized by the coronation of the new king and queen, himself as the soldier, and the princess symbolizing how he valued and reclaimed his feminine aspect.

Studying this favorite story, the counselee found himself in a place of deeper freedom and self-understanding allowing him to forgive himself, to let go and embrace not only what the future could bring to him but *the freedom of living in the present moment.*

By engaging his childhood imagination, this story allowed his adult self to discover more about his own journey and *give himself permission to live his own authentic life.* This spiritual exercise may help others on their journey in ways they cannot fathom until they use it.

The Importance of Solitude on a Daily Basis

I currently live in the city of San Diego, California. I have discovered, after living here one year that most of the people I meet talk about how they cannot make time for a coffee with a friend because they are too busy. Most are working overload all the time and think it is normal.

I have lived in the San Francisco Bay Area, in the Gold Country of Northern California, in Texas, in the high profiled town of Westport, Connecticut, the sophisticated university cities Springfield, Massachusetts, Eugene, Oregon, Lubbock, Texas and Pécs, Hungary. To date I have not encountered such a lack of quality time for people I know due to what they describe as constant busyness.

What I have learned is that busyness is a personal choice. Yes, it is true that for financial survival, especially the poor, people are working seventy or more hours a week to survive. At the same time, I hear the distress of busyness coming from middle class, highly educated professionals who can schedule their own time and work far less time than the poor. As many observant journalists have pointed out, busyness has become a moral badge of honor. I find this emphasis on the constant pressure to be driving somewhere, increasing one's income and fulfilling an unnecessary obligation to be a personal misuse of our willful choice.

I believe we are convinced this busyness will somehow add value to our lives and make us invaluable to others. In truth, I believe the opposite is the case. When I do get alone time with some of these folks, their complaining makes for bad company and even worse conversation. I end up counseling for free!

I cannot encourage all of us enough to make time for authentic solitude on a daily basis. I do not mean fifteen minutes here or there. I mean one to three hours a day of aloneness. No television, no radio or audio tape blaring, no computer or iPhone. Just quiet without distraction. While this may seem like an elitist thing to say, most of us can carve out an hour if we are conscious of our use of time and communicate our needs for solitude to those with whom we live and find mutual agreement.

This quiet may take the form of bodily movement such as exercise, or a walk. Here in San Diego, even a ride on a surfboard at Ocean Beach in the summer. But solitude, quiet within one's self is essential to the nurture of the soul. Let me suggest some reasons why, and a few ways to create this habit that is paramount to our spiritual health.

Solitude is essential for authentic living. When living with others, solitude can be created by either walking outside, or if that is not desirable due to nighttime or some kind of danger, we can go to a different room in the house or flat. This does not even require a special room for retreat.

My wife and I currently share a very small, one-bedroom flat, about four hundred and fifty square feet, tiny by American standards. It has an open kitchen and eating area combined with the living room and entrance. It has a bathroom, shower room and a small bedroom. To gain solitude, one of us either goes to the bedroom where there is both a bed and a small desk and the other occupies the living room open space. We create a routine for ourselves that gives each of us a great deal of solitude in a small environment. It can be done.

I find walking in the neighborhood another way to find the solitude I seek. I do not make phone calls or listen to music. I try to stay aware of the moment and my surroundings. Doing so allows my mind to contemplate, to pray, to observe, to enjoy, to sense and feel things. I do not need to have my eyes closed as I walk or as I sit at the small desk in the bedroom to find this contemplation. It is a mindful choice we must make to enjoy the solitude.

I have learned from the writings of Eckhart Tolle, the value of seeing my mind as a tool, which I can or cannot use; my mind can be unburdened with a conscious detachment. I can disengage from the thoughts of my mind not by dismissing them, but seeing them as just thoughts, and then choosing to engage them or not. We all have this ability to disconnect from our thoughts. We can go back to them later if we choose or we can engage new thoughts that replace them if that is a better choice in the moment.

Solitude provides us with that renewed sense of personal being, of experiencing the current moment. This solitude is available for us and can be used for our enjoyment. It simply requires a conscious choice.

This choice means not saying yes to every email, phone call, text, or invitation into talk with another. We can say to the technology "I will return to you later," or not. We can say to our loved one or co-worker that we acknowledge their request for communication and that in a little while, we can give them our full attention.

I find it helpful to let my wife know when I am going to use the other room for solitude or to take a walk. It is a common courtesy to do so. It is not difficult. There is no offense taken. Each of us can give ourselves and one another this gift of solitude right in the midst of our daily routines.

Giving ourselves solitude allows us to feel more fully engaged with others when we choose to be with them. We do not resent or unconsciously fight this connectedness with others. It flows.

Perhaps partly why it works well is that we have given ourselves over to the habit of being comfortable in our own skin in times of solitude. We are not afraid of our own thoughts, feelings and impulses. We learn to honor them and listen to them when we are ready and have energy to do so. Thus, being present for others does not hinder or frustrate but enhances our wellbeing.

Just as people can understand if we ask them if we can get back to them with our full attention, our thoughts within act the same way. If treated with respect, we can tell our thoughts we hear them, but first we need to attend to our solitude. Then we will give our thoughts the attention they need. Often, when we return to the thoughts that felt so pressing, we discover to our surprise that they are no longer arduous. They may have even disappeared. Politeness with one's own thoughts goes a long way towards a calmer life.

If one walks for solitude, it is best not to use that particular walk to be with the household pet, usually a dog. The dog requires our presence, attention, and direction. What is needed by us is not the companionship of the dog, but at a different time, perhaps earlier or later in the day, we need time alone with ourselves. We can become our own best friends. Then when we do walk the dog, we can give the blessed animal our full attention for mutual affection.

While I read articles that state that many people are afraid to be alone with themselves, I personally have not observed much of this. I think it is more of a habit to keep ourselves distracted, not of fear, but out of constant pressure to conform to the expectations of others. As business consultant Patrick Lencioni states in his book, *Overcoming the Five Dysfunctions of a Team: A Field Guide* he calls *this state of affairs an adrenaline addiction.* The addiction feeds on itself and can be stopped by conscious awareness and commitment to change.

How to Break this Pattern of Busyness

One of the most important missing elements in the Myth of Perceval and the Search for the Holy Grail is the absence of an additional question. It is not enough to simply ask if one is serving God in all things or not.

Based on my work for over four decades with individuals searching for wholeness, there is an equally important question which is often neglected. I believe this question comes from the very nature of the soul that must be answered by each of us individually, after we have first answered the question asked by Perceval in the Fisher King's court. After we are certain our hearts are clearly focused *on our desire for total companionship and co-creation with God*, we need to ask ourselves the second most important question placed within us by God's Self. It is the question that must be continually asked and answered on a daily basis. This question may feel counter-intuitive as if it was a refutation of the Christian ideal of selflessness. However, I believe the question is the opposite of selfishness. The asking of it is crucial to our spiritual health. The question is the following:

What is it that I want, desire, seek, that will fulfill a sense of calling and purpose in my life which is already dwelling in the heart of God? Put more simply, what is it that I want in my soul that God has placed there?

For reasons unknown, the myth does not address this question. Of course, Perceval as a young, naïve and immature person had superficial desires based on his unconscious projections in his soul. Unaware of his own beauty, royalty, and giftedness, he projects these qualities outwardly and wants to be a knight, the divine hero and to sit at the round table of Arthur with the other eleven knights.

But the deeper, real desires of his heart are simply unfolded to him over time. He is introduced to flesh and blood women but he does not keep any of them as companions for more than a few nights of rest. What is needed for personal meaning unfolds to him, but he does not become conscious of these needs until they are given to him. He can only reflect backwards. Never does he learn to reflect pre-cognitively and with maturity.

After carrying out his duty and healing the Fisher King, he discovers that the Fisher King and the Grail Castle King are both his male ancestors. But this revelation happens to him, he does not seek it. He finds his sense of belonging with a family heritage lost to him in his youth. He takes up the role of the new Fisher King, guardian of the Grail and retreats into an unknown obscurity to await when the Grail will be needed by civilization again. But even once he has matured and become a type of elder, he does not sit down and ask himself thoroughly what it is that he wants from his life. This aspect of the myth is unsatisfactory to us. We end the story wanting more from it. It is incomplete.

The most important aspect of the spiritual discipline of making enough time for solitude is for us to ask this question of ourselves, "What is it that we want?" This must become the heart of the Hunter within, the core of our searching and finding.

The Hebrew Old Testament Psalmist wrote in Psalm thirty-seven verses three and four:

"Trust in the Lord and do well, so you will live in the land and enjoy security.

Take delight in the Lord, and he will give you the desires of your heart."

From a Christian point of view, this verse does not make sense to interpret it as meaning that if we are to have joy, then God will give us want we want. That is a "Santa Claus" God and not the God revealed by Jesus Christ; his life and his teachings. This would be an immature, childish "give me what I want," approach to life, which would be egocentric and harmful to all.

However, it could make sense to interpret this verse simply to say, as we trust God with our life and serve God as our highest priority, we can trust that the actual desires we discover within ourselves regarding our life's purpose, meaning, and fulfillment *have actually been given to our soul by God.*

This is what I mean by asking the second question of equal importance, "What is it that we want?" When our ego is submitted, deferring, completely listening to God, we can trust that our intuition and the working of God's Spirit within us is giving us the very desires that well up from our receptive heart.

This kind of "ego in the right place," the ego strengthened but not in control, a consciousness and awareness of the heart resting in the love of God, this kind of interior position can yield to us the vast inner treasures of God's desires placed there. It is only in our solitude that we can discern the things that God has placed within our awakened hearts.

Only an acute self-awareness can produce the kind of reflective answers to the question of what is it that we want which will bring both life to ourselves and to others. This requires daily solitude for reflection, turning back when we have gone astray where we do not belong and asking for the courage to move forward in the fulfillment of these right desires given to us by God.

At a conference long ago, I heard Dr. Morton Kelsey respond to a question from the audience. It was a question that was on everyone's mind but when it was almost innocently asked by a youthful seeker, the tension in the room rose to the point of being palatable. The question was, "How can I know God's will for my life?" which is a modern way of asking the Perceval question. I held my breath as I waited for Kelsey's answer, which was simply this:

One must make daily time for prayer, listen to and record one's dreams, and journal the responses one hears from God.

I was both thrilled and disappointed by the simple answer because I was already trying to do these things. Later I would learn to appreciate the wisdom of his words. There is no other shortcut, nor need there be, because his answer has proven in my life to be more than enough. Not only this, but the answer is completely true. History shows this wisdom to be timeless.

Many people use solitude and this type of time for reflection only when they are beyond exhaustion and at their wits' end. They have suffered a huge financial setback, a lost career, a lost relationship or a perilous health crisis. In other words:

They do personal reflection by default. They require a trauma to stop and listen to their hearts.

If we take the time and energy to be alone daily and ask God for guidance, to listen and record and work with the messages in our dreams and to write down what we are learning, we will find ourselves "ahead of the game" of life.

Unlike too many professional coaches, teachers and speakers one hears, it is the quiet, non-pretentious, steady people, very often found outside the professional religious and academic worlds, who practice this quality spiritual discipline the best. Humility is a fruit of such a practice. Whenever I hear someone say that God has humbled them, I say to myself, no. If a person is truly grounded and walking in humility, they would never make such a statement.

Humility does not talk about itself but embraces the reality and moves on in silence, patience and trust. Only an insecure, self-justifying egocentric person would make such a statement.

Breaking this addiction to busyness requires this type of care for one's self and a refusal to accept the false guilt that can arise from untrue teaching about priorities. If we are fixated on material wealth in a way that tips our inner balance into a kind of "I deserve this" or "I have to focus on my goal," when we do reach the material or vocational goal it will not be satisfying. The abyss of a lack of meaning will continue.

Once we have created this type of grounded, inner condition of listening to God without pretense or projections, we can move to another step that can bring inner freedom. This is the intentional creating of outer structures that enable the inner life priorities to flourish. Here is one practical idea.

For some people it helps to have a plan on paper to keep them on track. For instance, when I was in seminary in Berkeley, California, for three years, I commuted one week at a time from my home three hours east in the Mother Lode foothills of the Sierras to the San Francisco Bay Area. The homework and term paper writing demands from my classes was atrocious. I agreed with my family that if my weekly homework was not completed, I would not come home for the weekend. Only one time did this happen, my second week of study, and I determined never to repeat it.

I created a plan and worked it every day for the three years through till graduation. I used a three by five index card and made out an every half-hour schedule on it for each day from five in the morning to ten at night, a week in advance. I wrote in when I had to be in class or other commitments. Then I wrote in when I would take solitary walks for exercise, when I would do my work-study task of cooking breakfast for the dormitory students, and when I would be in my room to study. I created time blocks of two hours a day for solitude and quiet. I blocked out four weeks, a week for chaos; unwanted and unplanned events and demands on my time beyond my control. Occasionally I would include social time with classmates, but socializing was not my priority. Getting home to be a husband and father each weekend and graduating seminary were the main concerns.

I also took a nine-month calendar, tore it into sections and taped each month together in a wall hanging. I took the syllabus for each class and determined the length and due dates for each paper required to be written. Then I scheduled the task of writing them so that each week I had a specific plan for research and writing. My goal was to enter the final week of the semester with all the papers completed ahead of their due date and none to do that last week.

By working a plan, what seemed insurmountable became very do-able. My stress was reduced by a commitment to the daily activity plan and the paper-writing schedule. Self-care, described through this planning, was paramount. I survived the three years intact. I was able to return home and relax on the weekends with my family with no homework "hanging over my head."

When a classmate or friend would want me to stay in the cafeteria to talk at length, I would take out the card, point to it, and explain that I was committed to another use of my time and politely excuse myself. No one took offense. The most difficult part of this routine was the unexpected, welcomed invitation for a coffee and conversation, which due to the discipline of the plan I was able to amiably decline.

Having the schedule allowed me to move on to what was necessary. This freed up my time to allow myself the freedom to invite a friend for a coffee at a time that worked well for me. I fostered some of the best friendships of my life during those three years but they were not by accident. They were intentional, by design.

Now that I have much more leisure time, I find that making the schedule card habit continues to be even more valuable. It is now a habit to ask myself what it is that I really want and need at any given moment. I go ahead and meet this need and do not suffer false guilt about these decisions.

My life schedule today includes counseling commitments with others during the day. I block out writing and study time along with planned long walks to the ocean for solitude. Hopefully each of us can create a plan that works for ourselves and enjoy the fruits of it.

For suggestions on how to develop a walking habit that feeds the soul, I encourage people to read Henry Thoreau's little treaty titled *Walking*. In this small book he shows how a person can develop a habit of walking in a different direction from their home each day for a certain amount of time, then returning. He emphasized the importance of walking in a natural setting as much as possible.

For people who feel they cannot contemplate or pray while walking in public due to distractions, I refer you to the reading of *The Autobiography of George Mueller*, an incredible person of effective intercessory prayer. Mueller devoted his life to the care of thousands of orphans in London during the middle of the nineteenth century, enduring a life of almost a total lack of privacy. He communed with God and got guidance in how to pray from his soul by walking the crowded, poverty-stricken streets of one of the most densely populated cities in the world at that time.

While prayer during our normal daily activities is required of us, so too is needed the prayer in solitude. It has been my experience that most people understand and practice praying and listening throughout one's day, as is described in the well-known volume *The Practice of the Presence of God* by Brother Lawrence, most people need the self-nurturing solitude with even greater impunity.

Solitude allows us to sense God's presence within us, and his experience allows us to continually sense God's presence in others. Both aloneness and community are enriched with this spiritual discipline of practical self-care. By asking both Perceval's required questions about our innermost priority and then trusting the desires we find there are given to us by God, this process creates a gnosis, *an experiential knowing* which brings great peace and much happiness.

A classic help to change one's attitude towards constant work and the need for quiet time is the German philosopher Josef Pieper's *Leisure: The Basis of Culture*. Pieper was a strong influence on the Post-World War Two German government as they were recreating a democracy from scratch. The utilitarian, dehumanizing focus of the Fascist Nazi movement had destroyed not only the economy and population of Germany, but in many ways completely devastated the very soul of the country. Pieper's writing helped the new government provide people with a renewed sense of who they could become again. Historians have credited Pieper's words for much of the speed in which Germany was able to rebuild itself. It was not just the Marshall plan and the huge amounts of money from America. The *inner framework* for a new society had to be built so that the money could be used properly to refashion a healthy nation.

This particular book was read by multitudes responsible for rebuilding the culture as it removed utilitarian ideas devoid of soul. Pieper's writings helped replaced them with Christian humanist philosophical realities that could undergird the rebuilding of their society. This small book is one of the most often reread and treasured books in my personal library.

Time in Nature

I was raised in a country setting with trees, fields, a lake, all within moments of leaving my family home. Later in life I would live next to the Pacific Ocean in the village of Yachats on the Oregon central coast, steps from the pounding waves on the volcanic rock shoreline and beaches. It was easy and within close reach. Often all that was required was a looking up and out of the living room window to be touched by the beauty and majesty of nature.

However, as mentioned above, I have lived in huge downtown cities, such as Berkeley, California, Springfield, Massachusetts, and suburban neighborhoods in Auburn, California, and Lubbock, Texas and now, San Diego, California. To my delight I have discovered that closeness to nature can be received by more astute observation.

A walk on a city sidewalk can be more than gazing at concrete or asphalt. One can see nature in the faces of people one is walking towards. Often there are tiny pockets of garden, perhaps only a small potted plant next to a business or residential doorway entrance. When seen with the heart, even these minute aspects of living vegetation can nurture and affirm our oneness with the universe.

While stars are impossible to see in the city at night, perhaps the night air can be felt as nurturing, warm or cool, hot or freezing, creating in us a sense of being alive and vibrant. The smells of cooking food can often be easily detected from an open commercial or home kitchen window capturing our sense of smell and imagination. Even making the effort to feel our feet within our shoes bearing down on the pavement can give us a feeling of connectedness with all of life. Many people find it helpful to walk while carrying a flower, small twig from a tree, or a stone in their hands, occasionally lifting it to the nose to catch its natural aroma. While this may seem extreme, I have found it to be true and very worthwhile. There are no small things. All have great intrinsic value to the nourishment of our souls.

The late theoretical physicist Stephen Hawking strongly encouraged all of us to look at the stars. At age twenty-one, Hawking was afflicted with motor neuron disease. He taught us that no matter our difficulties, literally seeing the stars above us at night could give us a new perspective and self-appreciation of our personal value and life's meaning.

If one can find a place, most preferably within walking distance of the house or workplace, where nature is more readily sensed and opened, we must make the daily commitment to be there and use this natural setting as much as possible.

I currently live on the third floor of a huge apartment building overlooking and hearing a very noisy, crowded street with cars and motorcycles roaring past all hours of the day and night. It is not the easiest place to feel at ease. In either direction for about two or more miles, walking takes me to only more commercial and apartment house establishments with strip malls, auto repair shops, and the constant roar of motorized vehicles, all screeching to get to the next stoplight or destination.

There is no natural beauty near my apartment building. But I discovered early on that the beach at Ocean Beach, San Diego, can be reached with a brisk-paced walk of thirty to forty minutes. When I create an hour or more space in my day, I can walk to the beach, get my feet wet if desired in the salt water, walk the sands, and then return home. I must be intentional about using the closeness of this opportunity.

I have learned that when I make myself get up and move in the most comfortable shoes I own and make the trek, my soul is always delighted. Often on the walk I meet strangers coming towards me. Sometimes, my smile is returned or an acknowledging nod of the head from someone I encounter for a brief moment's eye contact on the sidewalk. Often there will be a flowering bush or leafy tree, sometimes just the majestic Southern California palm, which provides the nurturing gaze needed. We are surrounded by life if we open our eyes to behold.

On each walk, I encounter the homeless poor who have no transportation other than their feet, or at the most, the city bus. I find that making eye contact and acknowledging all whom I come across helps me stay close to human nature, which to me can be the Godliest nurturing of all natural encounters.

One other thought about Nature. We can bring what we can of nature indoors with us in the form of plants, rocks, twigs and limbs of trees, moss, and of course, any kind of animal life that can be accommodated in our living situation. I find that simply holding a smooth stone in my hand while I read or pray or sit quietly has a calming effect, not unlike that of being out in the deep forests alone.

What this requires of us is imagination and the deep appreciation for who we are. We demonstrate this self-appreciation in conscious self-care and delight. Each of us has this choice, to find nature right where we are. We do not need to always drive our car to get what we need. Often all that is required is that we step outside and look up while inwardly digesting the feeling in the very air, the sounds, the sights, and the fragrances about us.

There is much more that can be said about the importance of daily contact with Nature. I simply hope to write a few suggestions to set a small fire to the reader's own imagination. Listening within to elucidations for and in our individual situations is the best problem solving there is.

For further reading I suggest *The Earth Has a Soul: C. G. Jung on Nature, Technology and Modern Life,* edited by Meredith Sabini for more insights directly from Jung about the value of naturalness and health of the soul. Also, a beautifully written book that may help raise awareness for us of this need for Nature's nurture is John O'Donohue's *Eternal Echoes,* and his *The Invisible Embrace of Beauty: Rediscovering the True Sources of Compassion.* Agnes Sanford's final book, *Creation Waits,* is another great resource for the spiritually astute person to gain affirmation of forming the habit of participating in Nature on a daily basis.

The Soul Value of Definitive Petition Prayer

There are many wonderful books on the value of contemplative prayer for the health of the soul. I will not repeat what these resources teach but have included them in the bibliography at the conclusion of the book. However, I do wish to put in a word for the value of an aspect of contemplative prayer that often goes missing in today's writings on the subject. That is the value of petition prayer; asking for a specific need or person as guided by the Holy Spirit's voice discerned in contemplation and active listening to God in prayer.

Petition prayer is not magic. It is not asking God for favors. It is not making deals with God. Petition prayer is a skill that is developed over many years. In order to avoid acting presumptuously, many faith communities are not teaching petition prayer beyond vague, non-specific generalities, which in my experience, are not even close to true petition or intercessory prayer, historically speaking. I wish to teach a few ideas that may be helpful and describe why this aspect of prayer is so important to the nurturing of the soul in contemplation.

Our Grail story provides a very basic guideline regarding specific petition prayer which is asking God to do something definite. We need to ask a specific request so that we will recognize the answer of yes, no, not now, start again or wrong petition, as a direct answer to our appeal. Asking specific requests helps us realize anew the fact that God is intimately involved in the details and minute care of our lives. God often provides us with guidance through petition prayer in this way.

We are to ask questions of God. This is basic. The Grail tale teaches that we are to ask. We are not required to have the answer to prayer, unless we are given specific guidance and assurance of the outcome given to us by a gift of faith, which is not presumption. Healing could not come to the Fisher King unless the Holy Fool spoke aloud what was on his mind. He was curious as to what the Grail procession meant and it was proper for him to ask specifically about this. The advice from his mother and his first mentor were wrong; to remain curious but silent and not ask questions at all were responsible for Perceval's early downfall. Being present but not speaking his mind was not enough to bring healing to the Fisher King. The situation demanded that he speak and verbalize his enquiries.

Our questions in seeking guidance in petition prayer are to be both specific and open ended. We are to ask God how we should pray. We are to ask what God's will is so we can pray persistently and with courage. We do not demand. We ask for guidance, and when our intuition grants us that guidance, we pray accordingly knowing the answer will come. Praying as our intuition leads us is not presumptuous prayer. It is being human, knowing we are not God yet knowing we are co-creators through prayer with God. We are to ask God if the request is to be continued, or if faith has been established that the request is no longer needed; only patient trust for the answer being required of us.

For the best biblical instructions and wonderful guidelines about petition prayer, I encourage others to study in depths the prayer of Jesus for his followers in the Gospel of John Chapter Seventeen. There he enjoins God with a variety of specific petitions about the lives and spiritual growth of his disciples. Jesus was very specific and non-apologetic about what he asked God to do through him in prayer on behalf of his group of followers. I find rereading this prayer for instructions on a semiannual basis to be a source of insight, joy, and affirmation.

Of course, there are many other aspects of prayer that I have not touched on: thanksgiving, adoration, stillness, repentance and others. Petition prayer has often been neglected, or the opposite, abused into a form of blackmailing God, which is not prayer at all but only an extension of the egocentric self. True petition prayer is a holy conversant dialogue. We are guided in prayer within and we pray according to this direction the best we can discern. Then we rest our spirits and let go. We learn to trust. There is great excitement in learning to trust. New worlds open before us.

I encourage the reading of all the books by Agnes Sanford; Norman Grubbs' biography on the life of Rees Howells titled *Rees Howells: Intercessor*; and my own book *Sacramental Prayer and Generational Healing* to develop a deeper life of petition prayer. Chapter Four in Mrs. Howard Taylor's biography of James Fraser titled *Behind the Ranges* gives specific instructions regarding appropriate, effective steps to follow in petition prayers of faith that I have found helpful for over fifty years.

Working with Soil, Rocks, and Plants

As the reader knows, I am writing these words while living on the third floor of an apartment building on a busy commercial street in San Diego. I have no backyard, and my petite balcony faces north and supplies some indirect light through the windows, but no direct sunshine at all. I miss not having a vegetable garden I can tend daily.

When I took my first trip to visit Hungary, I was amazed at the prolific vegetable gardens every village and suburban house contained in the front and back yards. Also, on a trip to South

Korea many years ago, I was astonished how the people created vegetable growing space in the tiniest of plots of earth even between the sidewalk and the street pavement where perhaps one foot of soil was contained.

When I came home from Hungary, I dug up my small, high-maintenance front lawn, negotiated with the family for one half of the backyard lawn, and created space to grow food. The very narrow side of the house faced south, so in Western Oregon, where the sun shines less than clouds that flood year-round, I created a one-foot deep and thirty-yards long flower bed to grow what needed the most heat and sun: paprika and tomatoes.

On my weekly trips to lead Sunday services at two country Episcopal churches driving mountain two-lane highways, I stopped at safe places to pull over where rocks had fallen down from the steep sides of the cutouts for the highway. I loaded the trunk of my small Toyota Corona with as much rock as the car could handle.

Using these rocks, I built raised vegetable beds. I made a compost pile and added material to it daily from the kitchen organic garbage. In the fall I collected leaves in plastic bags from the neighbors set out by them to be picked up by the city workers. Eventually I had a remarkably powerful, luscious composted soil that grew magnificent vegetables of all kinds.

I loved coming home from work or heading out as soon as daylight hit to see what was growing and what was ready to pick. I learned how to clean, dehydrate, can and freeze the produce. I enjoyed this activity very much!

The best part of gardening for me, in addition to the adventurous feeling of seeking and finding ripe fruit, is getting my hands dirty in the soil and water. I so enjoyed picking up the banana slugs and beetles, getting my fingers gooey and green pulling weeds, and planting and replanting new seeds and sprouts. The result was a deep satisfaction of the soul.

I learned another grounding idea that relates in a way to

being in touch with the soil from my mentor John A. Sanford. Jack Sanford was not only a world renowned biblical Greek scholar; he also was an expert on East Coast and Southwest Native American rituals and folklore. He taught me to do the following based on his studies of Native American Shamanistic practices.

Whenever I did a private healing prayer service for a counselee or parishioner, I found it helpful to have a coffee or a meal alone in a café after the service to self-process the event, and then upon returning home, to lay down on the lawn or the soil in the garden. Sometimes I would build a small blaze in the fire pit in my backyard and lay on my side beside the circle of stones and relax my body. I could feel the excess spiritual energy or tension in my body dissipate into the soil. Later, after showering I would feel centered and spiritually rested.

Many other indigenous cultures around the world recommend this practice and I, too, heartily recommend it for everyone who must work with people on a daily basis. The Chinese Christian teacher Watchman Nee taught that all of us pick up the spiritual energies of people we encounter, both positive and, often, negative. We need to honor this reality and find ways to remove it so we can be attuned to our own spiritual vitality.

This requires some privacy and quiet. Something I have found that helps if one does not have a safe place to lie down and relax on soil or sand, is to get some dirt or soft sand and rub it vigorously in the hands or even over the arms for several minutes. This, often, can have the same grounding and healing effect. Then as soon as possible, take a warm shower to remove both the soil and the spiritual contamination accrued and it will wash away.

I am aware this sounds a bit farfetched, but I ask the reader to stay open-minded about it and try it like an experiment. Spirituality is not just about spirit, or "air." It is also about grounding, incarnation, and the thorough integration of matter and spirit.

My favorite spiritual writers have all been workers of the soil. From St. Benedict long ago, to Agnes Sanford the profound teacher of healing prayer in the Episcopal Church, to John O'Donohoe and David Adam the beatific writers of Celtic spirituality, all have been people of rocks, trees, soil, plants, bugs, and creeping things. I encourage the reader to do what they can to get their hands dirty in the soil.

Additional thoughts about these important spiritual practices can be found in the books by John and Paula Sandford *Healing the Wounded Spirit*, and *The Transformation of the Inner Man*. John is Native American and has incorporated some of his ancestral practices into his Christian spirituality that has been helpful to me.

Private Prayer, Meditation and Journaling

I cannot emphasize enough the need for daily solitude for private prayer, meditation and personal reflective writing. There are several techniques for private prayer that have been developed over the centuries, but I want to make a few, simple suggestions that may help the reader.

The primary need is to not be legalistic about the practice. If we think of private prayer as a conversation with a loved One, with time to talk and time to listen to the other, an active listening with our full attention, we cannot go wrong. Some people find it helpful to repeat either aloud or silently a mantra of sort that fits their particular spiritual orientation; this can be effective in quieting the mind.

However, I find that simply being honest with God, expressing any frustration or need for help to quiet the mind so I can settle down is enough. It is possible as Eckhart Tolle teaches in *The Power of Now* to realize the mind is simply a tool, and we can sit back from our thoughts a bit, and see them as simply thoughts. The same can be done with feelings. An objective subjective distancing can be done to draw our attention away from the incessant chatter in our minds, to a quiet observation and disengagement with this chatter, thus becoming more conscious of God's voice speaking within by the silent presence.

I do this by focusing on the word *detachment*, or the phrase *to set back from*, to put an emotional distance and objectivity to my thoughts and feelings. This is not a repression of them nor a denial; but a mature, management, in order to more fully engage them in the best and most appropriate way depending on my personal need and preference at the moment.

For me, meditation simply means a quiet, reflective listening, or focus on an aspect of spiritual reality that I feel I need to think about. I probably spend more time simply in quiet conversation or silence with God and end up calling this meditation. The value seems to be mostly in being reminded by this practice that I am loved and cherished.

The key to effective nurturing prayer is to do it whether we feel like it or not. This is no different from being in close communication with a friend or partner in life. We communicate freely and habitually because that is the relationship, not because we have a feeling of wanting to communicate. At times the feelings of companionship with God are strong, other times the feeling wanes and may even be absent, but true relationship is based on action, not in a rigid, legalistic fashion, but a fluid, quiet steadiness. This action is based on mutual love and affection which allows the feelings to be there, without being paramount nor an obstacle to the relationship that truly nurtures.

Journaling is simply a writing down of personal reflections. When I am unsure of what to write due to a vast array of thoughts competing with one another for my attention, I write down items that are similar to a diary, events and activities. Then, after a short while I can shift over to write about feelings, emotional reactions, and finally, prayer. Much of my prayer life is written down in the journal. I do not know why this is so helpful. Many people find handwritten journaling more beneficial than computer typing. The key is to try different methods and see what works best for one's self.

One more idea to share. If one has a low attention span due to Post Traumatic Stress Disorder or Attention Deficit Disorder, one must be extra patient and loving to one's self. We can realize that five minutes sitting still and being quiet may be a major feat to accomplish. It is most important to not be judgmental of one's self or compare what one does with the apparent successes of others.

Many years ago, I had a three-year time period when I could not focus, meditate or pray for more than ten minutes at a time. I had come out of four years of being in highly toxic work environments, one right after the other. I had quit jobs at two large parishes because of the extreme, constant, daily criticism received by a small, but persistent group of antagonistic parishioners. The stress I experienced was profound.

Prior to these abusive situations, I could sit for two or more hours in silence and enjoy the quiet contemplative activity. However, the trauma was so weighty and my self-confidence destroyed, that it literally took me years to recover. Along with this recovery was a need to be gentle with myself regarding what I could and could not do in respect to contemplative prayer and meditation.

God loves us no matter how well we can respond to this love. There simply is no judgment placed on us at all. Each of us are to do what we can do. I encourage all to simply experiment with prayerful activities and see what works. Over time our spiritual activities change. What worked for us at one time may no longer be viable. We can move on. We are not the same person we were in our past.

Each day is a new beginning to discover afresh that we are loved, cherished and appreciated by God who created us in and for love. Just as there are different styles of communication between introverts and extroverts, so there are many different styles and means of prayer and communion with God. I encourage people to read as many books about prayer from mature sources, and to ask people they know for ideas who exhibit the peace of mind and heart that emanates from a real prayer life.

Public Corporate Worship

Public or corporate worship can also be a helpful spiritual discipline for those who can find a safe, inspiring place to participate. There is no perfect worship environment, so to seek such is a futile exercise. However, if one searches, one can often find a large or small faith community of like-minded folks to join with regularity for worship. It is important to find a place that radiates love and has a sense of the common good and a healthy group soul.

One of the difficulties in finding a public worship service that nurtures one's soul is the fact that the more collective the group, the less healthy and authentic the worship experience may become. At the same time, one would hope that we can discover God, however we perceive of God, in whatever worship experience we find ourselves in. By collective, I mean the more artificial sense of conformity that exists, the more difficult it will be to worship with a sense of belonging. I encourage people to trust their intuition in seeking a faith community for corporate worship and give the process time.

My suggestion is to visit eight or more such group gatherings. I do not mean political meetings, or sport events. Certainly, these have their own heightened sense of the common good and enthusiasm. I would suggest that one visits gatherings of their known religious orientation, if one is Buddhist, to visit as many Buddhist groups as possible. If Christian or any other spiritual persuasion, do the same.

The key is to visit enough times that one's sense of comfort is stretched, and one is not just finding a place where the ego is at ease and comfortable. We must find spiritual comfort with others in a place much deeper than ego needs. We must find a place where our shadow can come out of hiding and be nurtured as well.

As religious institutions continue to decline in influence and attendance in the United States (for various reasons), it may become increasingly difficult to find a place that truly nourishes the soul. However, it is important not to ask that a public worship service meets the needs of the soul that can only be met individually in our own spiritual disciplines of solitude, study, prayer and meditation. Indeed, this expectation of many people is one reason why public worship can become quite void of spiritual power and energy. There is no replacement for the individual responsibility in connecting with the God one experiences and trusts in love.

However, if we are taking good care of ourselves, we will probably be able to find a place to worship publically that works for us if our expectations are not unrealistic.

Why may it be helpful to be part of a worshipping faith community? As someone who struggles with institutional organizations, these words come with reflection and a simple admonition for all of us to use our common sense.

Many people have had some kind of negative or hurtful experience in an organized "religious" situation that they cannot forget. I would simply state that part of trusting the universe and the great Love and Mind behind it is to continue to stay open to finding a faith community where we are encouraged and truly nurtured. The faith community may not be a religious organization. But there is probably some kind of collective activity that we can participate in where a common sense of worship prevails.

Some suggestions might be serving at a homeless shelter or food or clothing closet, giving out necessities to those in want. There is a camaraderie among both those who serve and those who are being served. This acknowledging and working towards a common good can be a kind of worship, because within the activity is a sense of experiencing God in the other person or persons.

I currently walk an hour to the pier at Ocean Beach, California, not only to surround myself with the blue Pacific Ocean, but to greet the poor and the homeless who are allowed to fish off the pier for edible fish without the requirement of a fishing license. Most days I see and greet the same faces at the same locations along the pier. I also have many conversations with folks who are complete strangers, often tourists visiting San Diego. It is common to engage in dialogues that usually end up in joint prayer as we discover a common bond of love for God. But mostly there is eye contact, a nod from the head or some kind of acknowledgment of our common humanity that passes between almost all of us.

Is this a worshipping community of faith? In many ways, the eye contact, the observing of people gazing out onto the ocean, others enjoying the pier just as I do while walking or sitting on a bench, yes, this interaction and common experience can be a type of worship service.

Recently on a trip to the Grand Canyon in Arizona, my wife and I experienced the same phenomenon while walking the South Rim Trail. People from all over the world were in a state of silent awe because of the overwhelming sense of God and the magnificence of creation that the canyon expressed. People were quiet and hushed, no jostling about, even children were required by their parents to be still and to honor the need for silence. Yes, this is a kind of worship service.

While this may not be ideal, I suggest to the reader that if they have not already established such a routine, or found such a place of reverence for all of life in a common bond with others, that they seek it out.

Ideally yes, we want to find a collective group of people who formally worship God in one fashion or another in a church, mosque, synagogue, or temple that fits our spiritual experience. A twelve-step group program may provide such a structure together with other like-hearted people to meet our need for solidarity with others.

The thing is to not give up, and to not look for a "perfect gathering" because in my opinion, such a reality does not exist. Human beings are not even close to perfect! But we can come together in a common bond and experience group soul that can nurture our individual soul in ways that remaining in isolation and solitude cannot bring.

I do know that some people are called by the archetype of the hermit to be alone indefinitely. But the most famous hermits in the spiritual chronicles of history did not stay in this isolation forever. Saint Anthony, considered the father of monasticism in Eastern Christianity, after decades of solitude in the desert, became in his elder years a warm, receptive mentor and counselor for many who lived in the area near his home.

Each of us can trust that we will find like-minded, like-hearted others with whom to enjoy God's presence in some type of community of support and vision.

The Spiritual Discipline of Using Social Media Wisely to Experience Faith Community

I have found the internet a viable way to meet people. I belong on Facebook to a few Jungian and spirituality groups and have asked people to become friends. Some of them have become close acquaintances. It is not just their texts and words, but their posts often help me realize the vast number of loving people there are in the world. I do not restrict myself to people living in the United States or Canada, as most educated people abroad speak and write English very well. Writers, therapists, artists, musicians abound worldwide and can be a source of inspiration and friendship. I have close contact with people in the United States, Europe, Australia, South Africa, Ghana, Tanzania, Canada, Mexico, South and Central America, and China. I love the variety and diversity of interests, insights and perspectives.

While many people I know in San Diego are too busy with work or other responsibilities to reciprocate mutually nurturing friendships, I reach out to those in the retirement community among my peers, Episcopal priests and writers. I have found a few people who have the energy and capacity for reciprocal friendships. I find that it is enough to have one or two people locally and others whom I have known over the world with whom I stay connected by email and video calls.

I have also found it helpful to reach out and initiate with people at least on three repeated occasions. Then, if there is no adequate response, I let them be and move on. My experience over my lifetime regarding the ratio for creating close friendships is about one hundred occasions in reaching out for each, strong-lasting friendship that formed. This may seem extreme, but that is about the reality of it in modern West Coast United States where I live now. There is nothing unusual about this. Every part of the United States where I have lived has been a bit different, but not by much degree. In Hungary, I created four very close friendships in three years, which was much more than expected.

I believe this may be because Americans generally have a strong extroversion, but are weak regarding introversion; and as a rule, Europeans are about opposite. Conversely, many Americans are unconscious of their inferior function, introversion, thus have a more difficult time opening themselves to authentic relationships of the heart and soul. The European friends I cherish, have been polite and non-intrusive, yet over time, as trust is developed, their hearts open wide and engage in friendships that last a lifetime with inner richness.

If one experiences such difficulty in creating nurturing

relationships, I encourage people not to be discouraged. It is a reality of life. Most people limit their friendships to a small familiarity base, usually family members, and one or two others. This is true whether those relationships are nurturing and healthy or not.

In summary, this sense of corporate worship is directly related to our deep need to feel that we belong. I have found that belonging is an inward issue that can be resolved by being one's own best friend. Social media is another effective way to create new, long lasting friendships. But again, belonging is an inward reality. Once we accept and nurture this self-friendship, then we can adjust to whatever outward belonging does or does not manifest.

Finding Our Sense of Belonging in God

One year after I moved to Hungary and the novelty of my being one of a very few Americans in a large university city had worn thin, I moved from my small apartment to a larger one on the fourth floor of a huge, ten-story, impersonal building. There I found complete privacy. I had a balcony I rarely used because of the traffic noise from below. But there was no one glancing in my windows from the street or the backyard which had been the situation in my previous flat.

I was there alone for six months. I did not have a relationship with any of the neighbors. I went to my language lesson twice a week to study with my teacher Péter. I had occasional hiking days with my friends Dezső and István, and coffees with Attila, but basically, I was alone.

I had time to think, to write and to sleep when I needed to rest. In many ways this time of complete privacy was similar to a six-month Sabbath rest. I worked on letting go of the pain from my divorce which had divided my adult children and resulted in the loss of relationship with one of them along with that of my grandchildren, a huge heartache and pain. I had the privacy I needed to learn *and discover that friendship with myself was paramount to how I would live my life in the future.*

I realized I had never lived alone. I left my parents' house to live in a dorm, and then a shared house for my university years. Then in my senior year of studies, I married, and lived in this situation for another forty years.

During the second year of living alone in Pécs, I learned that belonging was available to me with God's presence, and with the inner riches in my spirit and soul. I learned to relax, and to enjoy the presence of others in public places, without the constant, painful yearning for recognition and affirmation from others.

I had dated a few Hungarian women but because of the language and cultural barriers, I found it not very workable. Very few Hungarian women close to my age spoke English fluently. I knew it would be many more years before my Hungarian language skills would be adequate to sustain an intimate relationship.

For the first year I would look at the faces of Hungarian women on the streets or in the Árkád (shopping mall) and wonder if one of them might be my future partner in life. The intense yearning I felt for close companionship increased my loneliness and sense of isolation. However, during the first six-month time period in the second year in Hungary, in the complete privacy of the new, small apartment, I slowly accepted the reality that a future partner may not be my fate for the future. One day at a time, I came to terms with it. Over time, I no longer felt needy, abandoned, or lacking in the quality of my life.

I am grateful for that time. I believe now that this aloneness and coming to grips with the reality that I was to become my own "best friend," prepared me to meet my future wife Mónika, which happened within a year of this time period in my life. Perhaps when I came to accept my aloneness and discover the inner reality of Presence and Belonging within, I no longer radiated this neediness and came to a state where I may have been able to engage in a healthy, non-codependent relationship with another person.

I encourage the reader to take a look at Paul Tournier's book *A Place to Belong*, and John A. Sanford's *The Invisible Partners: How the Male and Female in Each of Us Affects the Other*, to gain insight about becoming one's own best friend. Also, an equally valuable read about environmental changes one can make regarding personal living space that can nurture the soul and provide a deeper sense of belonging is Christopher Day's *Places of the Soul: Architecture and Environmental Design as a Healing Art*.

Additional Means of Nurturing the Soul

There are many other means of caring for one's soul that I have not included in this discussion due to the fact there are other reliable and better resources out there that speak about them. I will simply mention a few more that the reader may want to explore that are not usually discussed in the literature of spirituality.

The exemplary chef Anthony Bourdain provided a rich source of heart-opening television shows and contemplative books. He taught us about the human soul and how we can grow through traveling and maintaining friendships made with people from other cultures differing from our own.

Both Bourdain and Rick Steves provide books and videos that can inspire, nourish and teach the soul. There is such diversity in all of human life created by God. These men share their insights on how God speaks through other cultures and individuals who are making a difference in the world. Each one of the stories they tell can enrich and deepen our awareness of God's presence in all, and affirm God's love in our own bodies and souls that can affect small spheres of influence. I encourage all to use the resources available on the internet on a regular basis to broaden our awareness of the presence of God. Rick

Steves' book *Travel as a Political Act* is an excellent source of information about the spirituality of travel.

In a similar line of thought, I add that John Sanford taught me to indulge in reading lots of biographical, and especially autobiographical material. This is because knowing how a person reflects on their inner journey can teach us a lot about both the diversity and the individuality of human nature, and, of God, as God is expressed through human beings. We also can gain insight from biographical works into the nature of evil, and how it gains inroads into people and what we can do to avoid similar mistakes.

I would include a recommendation of reading the novels of Mildred Walker, especially her autobiographical novel, *Winter Wheat*, about life on the wheat fields of Montana. Another classic autobiography by a woman author that teaches great lessons of soul nurture is Ann Morrow Lindberg's *Gifts from the Sea*, which is particularly helpful for men to read. Frederick Buechner's autobiographical writings are extremely insightful reflections, especially his *A Room Called Remember, Telling Secrets* and *The Eyes of the Heart.*

As a Music Therapist, I was trained in the therapeutic value of music making, listening, and engagement. I have not talked about this because it is such an obvious source of spiritual nourishment for people. At the same time, I encourage others to use the internet to explore a vast repertoire of music from various cultures and time periods, and not restrict themselves to only the venues that are familiar to them.

Learning to play a simple musical instrument can be a way for many people to nurture their souls. The ukulele, guitar and harmonica, can easily be learned well enough to provide much satisfaction to anyone who tries to learn. This exercise is not about performance or playing for other people, but for one's enjoyment. Singing in all its forms, again for self-nurture, can be done by anyone. People who have been told they cannot "carry a tune" often feel restrained in singing but can take singing lessons and quickly learn enough biofeedback to sing very well. I encourage simply singing in the privacy of one's own home regardless of self-criticism.

Artwork, in all its various forms, can be a wonderful way to nurture the soul and provide her with expression. Suzanne Fincher's book *Creating Mandalas: For Insight, Healing and Self Expression* is an excellent read about how to do creative drawings spontaneously that give one awareness of what is going on at our deepest levels. I have been drawing abstract mandalas for decades and find the practice enjoyable and helpful. Any kind of artwork, clay, stone, painting, embroidery, sewing, woodworking, can be used as a spiritual discipline to provide expression to the musings of the soul.

Another invaluable resource in which I have found nourishment for my soul are books on art and especially art history from various cultures, not just Western art. I believe that *intellectual understandings of cultural changes in the ethos of a civilization* usually occur first in the realm of the visual arts, then music, followed by philosophy then the sciences, and last of all to become aware and change is theology.

On this note, one of my favorite reads is Simon Schama's book *Landscape and Memory*. This book shows how artists in Western culture have used landscape archetypes in their artwork to speak about the divine in all of life (Schama, Simon. *Landscape and Memory*. Alfred A. Knoff, NY, 1995). Schama is an art historian professor and prolific writer at Columbia University in New York City. I return often to reread my highlights and notes in the margins from my reading of it over the past thirty years. Not only does his information help me understand natural settings in my dreams and their importance for dream interpretation, but both his insights and the lithographs of the paintings and sculptures speak to the deepest parts of my being.

I encourage the regular reading of art history, art

reproduction books and periodicals to speak non-rationally to our souls which are so hungry for beauty and truth. Each of us, whether we have a background in the visual arts or not, can be edified and built up in soul by soaking our minds and the eyes of our souls with the greatest of artwork. We should not confine our art appreciation to our own culture but read cultures very different than our own to understand the various dimensions of the diversity and the unity of the human mind and spirit.

Most soulful people find solace and guidance in books of poetry. I encourage people to remember their favorite childhood poet, and then, as adults, purchase all they can find of the poet's work, as well as read biographical literature about these literary figures. It is important to know the spirituality and psychology, the life challenges, victories and defeats of the poets that speak to us. Often, people who find sacred texts such as the Bible have become dry for them to read find that when they take up reading poetry the soul is so nourished by it that a return to scripture occurs. They, then, find scripture alive and able to quench their spiritual thirst. I personally find the poetry of Rainer Maria Rilke and Robert Frost to be of great help to my understanding of God and humanity.

An addendum to this idea is to read for enjoyment on a regular basis encyclopedias of traditional world symbolism such as the writings of J. C. Cooper, one of which is listed in the bibliography. Reading short articles about how symbols are understood in various cultures around the world is a terrific spiritual discipline which broadens our understanding of the God that we experience; knowing the more we learn of God, the greater the knowing becomes. God is inexhaustible. This is what Love is.

Here are a few more brief suggestions for personal soul nurture. I believe physical, hands-on books themselves contain the essence of Spirit. I believe that the soul enjoys being surrounded by the physicality of books. They can be on bookshelves or in small piles around one's reading chair. The piles can provide a type of cave, not as a regressive hiding place from life, but a uterus of new beginnings for those who are more introverted. Some people find frequent visits to libraries and used bookstores to provide the same sense of affirmation and presence of supportive Holy Spirit.

The physicality of books, their bindings, colors, pages, smells, textures, typescript, feel and styles, contains spiritual energy. It is important not to retain books that have a bad feeling surrounding them. Only surround one's self with books that emit a positive loving spirituality. The content is also important. Books containing cruelty, or severely degrading language and content do not belong in one's personal library. It is important that our sleeping place, the bedroom, or section of living quarters set aside for sleeping has no electronics nearby. This means replacing electric clocks with their blue or yellow glare and brash sounding alarms with silent illumination by touch activation only, or a wristwatch by the bedside. Also, there should be an absence of televisions, radios, computers, and printers from the bedroom. Darkness is needed for restful sleep so the inner Light can come with dreams, fantasies and intuitive insights without outer distraction. Cell phones can be placed in another room, not on a nightstand. Each of us needs deep, relaxing sleep in order to fully bring freedom and joy to the inner soul.

One of the disciplines I learned by watching old Hungarian men in the co-ed locker room of the Hüllám Fürdö (public swimming facility) in Pécs where I live, is to use excellent skin lotions on my body after bathing on a daily basis. Our skin is one of the most important organs we have and, indeed, needs nurture and protection. As a man, I used to think that putting Aloe Vera lotion on one's skin was a woman's prerogative but living in Hungary has proven me very wrong.

Not only does our skin need the moisture of the lotion, but

our bodies need the physical touch of our own hands in loving appreciation. We often think of the importance of getting a regular professional massage, but less often do we realize the need to caress and honor our own bodies with loving touch and kindness. This kind of nurture feeds the soul and affirms our self-image from within in ways that cannot be done by another person. I highly recommend this practice as a spiritual discipline of love for one's self as a beautiful creation of God.

Another spiritual reality I learned by living in Europe was to reduce the amount of clothing that I own. I learned to let go of clothing that did not help me feel really good about myself or was not comfortable to wear. Instead of buying lots of replaceable clothes, I now buy high quality shoes and clothing that lasts for years. When they need repair or resoling, this is done.

Most Hungarians I know have less than two feet of hanging space for their clothes, yet because of their astute care and the clothing's high quality, a person always looks their very best.

Honoring the body in this way also spiritually nurtures and affirms the soul.

It is not about impressing others with what one wears. It is about learning to honor who we are within, which no one can tell us but ourselves. Most Americans, including myself before I moved to Europe, could get rid of eighty percent of their closet and do just fine. For resources about minimizing, look for websites on the internet that speak of this spiritual discipline.

If a person has a body of water nearby, it is important to partake of its presence. Oceans, lakes, rivers and streams are obvious remedies for the thirsty soul. However, even a shallow bowl or atrium close by with moisture can help nurture the soul. We need wetness. While I currently live in a very crowded apartment complex with cars streaming past on the busy street below day and night, the Pacific Ocean is a half-hour walk away. I partake of this luxury by walking to the nearby sea on a daily basis.

For more fascinating information about the importance of water as a soul journey companion, I encourage others to read the books by the Japanese photographer Masaru Emoto, especially his first book of photographs of frozen ice crystals, *The Message of Water*.

I encourage the re-creation of childhood play. In my case, I used to have a box of wooden train tracks, blocks, and plastic or iron figurines. I would build towns and cities, enact battles, dramas, and other important archetypal scenes. Doing the same now is restorative. For me, this has been done by book arranging on bookshelves, collecting rocks and shells from the beach near where I live and putting them on bathroom counters, dining room tops, nightstands, and periodically playing with them, rearranging them spontaneously. Each of us can remember what we enjoyed playing with as small children and find ways to do the same as adults. Stuffed animals or dolls can also provide a sense of play that activates the imagination in soul nurturing ways.

In *Puer Aeternus*, Marie Louise von Franz teaches that it is important that we make large blocks of time and energy for our inferior function, and that we try hard not to organize activities using our inferior function.

For example, I am a thinking, intuitive type. My inferior or weak side is feeling intuitive or sensing. This means I need a daily and weekly Sabbath rest to do non-rational play using my hands and to get out of my head. I have used mandala drawing, vegetable gardening, rock building work and rock carving as means to do this in order to balance my constant thinking and analyzing habits. The Myers Briggs test can tell us our conscious strengths and unconscious weaknesses, and point out what our inferior functions are. Then we can use common sense to create activities that truly give us balance. Many people do this naturally but many of us need to find new conscious ways to nurture the soul and give her the freedom of balance.

For more insight regarding spiritual practices that enhance the soul I recommend Cynthia Bourgeault's Section Three titled "Christian Wisdom Practices" in her book *The Wisdom Jesus: Transforming Heart and Mind—A New Perspective on Christ and his Message.* Bourgeault provides detailed information about the following traditional spiritual practices: Centering Prayer Meditation, Lectio Divina, Chanting and Psalmody, Welcoming and the Holy Eucharist.

Summary

All of us can learn to honor and treasure who we are as God has created us to be; unique, individual and capable of giving and receiving the deepest of love and thanksgiving. The Myth of the Grail gives us a few ideas as to the nature of the human soul as understood by the Western European medieval times in which the story emerged.

The Myth of the Holy Grail is as pertinent to us now as it was in medieval times. With the advance of climate change and the very survival of the planet at stake, each of us must do all that we can to restore the feminine of life to our individual inner worlds. This will show us how to affect our outer worlds in the same way, but the changes must start within.

When Perceval asked the right question, not only was the Fisher King healed, but the entire Kingdom came to life again. Every institution I know of today has a deep need for such influence by individuals who will do their inner work. There is nothing that can bring about the needed renewal from outside of us. The answer lies within.

Different from Perceval, who long after he became the custodian of the Grail as the new Fisher King and retreated into the vast forests to a cave to live out his days, we have the obligation to partake of the Grail and make it available to all who are hungry to eat and thirsty to drink of its feminine nourishment.

This book is only a beginning of personal sharing. I hope to write more.

I am aware that much effort was placed on discussions of the reality of evil and how to overcome it in practical living. This emphasis comes from a conviction that the current method of masculine attitudes towards evil has failed miserably and will continue to fail. To project outwardly what one is unwilling to own inwardly is destined to destroy and negate life. The feminine principle is the only way we can move forward and remove the power of evil and create a better world.

It is felt that by providing help in this area and not regulating evil and its reality to our collective and individual shadow, that we might see how Love has truly triumphed and removed the deadly sting of evil in regards to the overwhelming of our souls and that of the common good.

Life is not compact, nor can it be compartmentalized. We can only approach all of these questions and concerns with a deep reverence for our lives as deepest Mystery. We can honor the subtlety of who we are and the Mystery that is God however we may decide to describe or name this God.

It is hoped that the suggestions provided for renewing and sustaining the soul are helpful in whatever small way they may be. The best recommendation I can give is for all of us to continue to experiment and see what works best for us; what to set aside and what to use.

Finding fulfillment in life and honoring the soul is not another task we have to add to our To-Do List and undertake. If anything, it is hoped that the suggestions in this book help the reader think of how to simplify and rearrange things so that true joy can flow like an unending artesian spring.

Each of us can find our own way because none of us was created exactly alike nor were we fashioned to fulfill a collective destiny. Each of our individual destinies are coming together to create a new heaven and a new universe. This is my deepest conviction, joy and hope.

The bibliography is intentionally extensive. If I can be of any help to the reader, just feel free to write by email. There are no stupid or silly questions. Each of us is connected one to another. We are here to help each other.

Peter Fritsch

plfritsch@hotmail.com

May God's peace flow in all of us and bring peace from within to all the circumstances of our outer life. As Julian of Norwich wrote and prayed long ago, in the midst of incredible political and societal turmoil.

All shall be well, and all shall be well and all manner of thing shall be well.
(Julian of Norwich. Revelations of Divine Love. Oxford University Press, New York, 2015)

Bibliography

Baigent M., Leigh R., Lincoln H. *The Holy Blood and the Holy Grail*. Bantam Dell, NY, 1982.

Bender S. *Everyday Sacred: A Woman's Journey Home*. HarperSanFrancisco, 1995.

Berger M., Segaller S. *The Wisdom of the Dream: The World of C. G. Jung*. TV Books, New York, 1989, 2000.

Bloom A. *Beginning to Pray*. Paulist Press NY, 1970.

Bloom A. *Living Prayer*. Templegate Publishers, Springfield, Illinois, 1966.

Bly R. *Iron John: A Book about Men*. Vintage Books, NY, 1992.

Boros L. *Meeting God in Man*. Image Books, Garden City, NY, 1971.

Boros L. *Hidden God*. The Seabury Press, New York, 1973.

Boros, L. *Living in Hope*. Image Books, Garden City, NY, 1973.

Boros L. *Christian Prayer*. The Seabury Press, NY, 1973.

Boros L. *The Closeness of God*. The Seabury Press, NY, 1978.

Boros L. *We Are Future*. Herder and Herder, NY, 1970.

Boros L. *In Time of Temptation*. Herder and Herder, NY, 1968.

Bourgeault C. *The Meaning of Mary Magdalene: Discovering the Woman at the Heart of Christianity*. Shambala, Boston, 2010.

Brock S. *The Syriac Fathers on Prayer and the Spiritual Life*. Cistercian Publications, Inc. Kalamazoo, Michigan, 1987.

Brooks, S. *The Art of Good Living: Simple Steps to Regaining Health and the Joy of Life*. Houghton Miflin, Boston. 1990.

Buechner F. *The Sacred Journey*. Harper and Row, San Francisco, 1982.

Buechner F. *A Room Called Remember*. HarperSanFrancisco, 1992.

Buechner F. *The Eyes of the Heart: A Memoir of the Lost and Found*. HarperSanFrancisco. New York, 1999, pp. 12–13.

Campbell J. *The Power of Myth*, with Moyers B. Anchor Books, NY, 1988.

Campbell J. *Thou Art That: Transforming Religious Metaphor*. New World Library, Navato, CA, 2001.

Campbell J. *An Open Life: Joseph Campbell in Conversation with Michael Toms*. Harper and Row, NY, 1989.

Cooper JC. *An Illustrated Encyclaopedia of Traditional Symbols*. Thames and Hudson, London, 1978.

Cousineau P. *The Art of Pilgrimage: The Seeker's Guide to Making Travel Sacred*. Conari Press, York Beach, ME. 1998.

Day C. *Places of the Soul: Architecture and Environmental Design as a Healing Art*. Aquarian/Thorsons, London, 1990.

De Castillejo Claremont I. *Knowing Woman: A Feminine Psychology*. Shambala, Boston, 1990.

De Hueck Doherty C. *Poustinia: Christian Spirituality of the East for Western Man*. Ave Maria Press, Notre Dame, IN, 1975.

Dyer W. *The Shift Film*. https://www.youtube.com/watch?v=7SnWOTDykAc

Eisler R. *The Chalice and the Blade: Our History, Our Future*. Harper and Row, San Francisco, 1987.

Eliade M. *Cosmos and History: The Myth of the Eternal Return*. Harper and Row, 1954.

Emoto M. *The Message of Water*. Beyond Words Publishing, Hillsboro, Oregon, 2004.

Fincher S. *Creating Mandalas: For Insight, Healing, and Self Expression*. Shambala Publications, Boston, 1991.

Frank JA. *Trump on the Couch: Inside the Mind of the President*. Avery, division of Penguin Random House, NY, 2018.

Freedman R. *Life of a Poet: Rainer Maria Rilke*. Northwestern University, Evanston, IL, 1996.

Fritsch PL. *A Moment of Great Power: Sacramental Prayer and Generational Healing*. Life Compass, Yachats, Oregon, 2003.

Fritsch PL. *Dreams: A Spiritual Guide to Healing and Wholeness*. Life Compass, Inc. Eugene, Oregon, eBook on Amazon.com, 2003.

Fritsch PL. *Hungary: Finding a Place to Call Home*. Life Compass,

Inc. eBook on Amazon.com.us and uk, 2015.

Griffith JE. *To Believe Is to Pray: Readings from Michael Ramsey*. Cowley Publications, Boston, 1996.

Grubb N. *Rees Howells: Intercessor*. Christian Literature Crusade, Fort Wayne, PA, 1952.

Guardini R. *The Art of Praying: The Principles and Methods of Christian Prayer*. Sophia Institute Press, Manchester, New Hampshire, 1957.

Hannah B. *Encounters with the Soul: Active Imagination as Developed by C. G. Jung*. Sigo Press, San Francisco, 1981.

James W. *The Varieties of Religious Experience*. Penguin Books, 1988.

Johnson EA. *She Who Is: The Mystery of God in Feminist Theological Discourse*. Crossroad, NY, 1994.

Johnson RA. *Inner Work: Using Dreams and Active Imagination for Personal Growth*. HarperSanFrancisco, 1986.

Johnson RA. *Inner Gold: Understanding Psychological Projection*. Koa Books, Kihei, Hawaii, 2008.

Johnson RA. *The Fisher King and the Handless Maiden: Understanding the Wounded Feeling Function in Masculine and Feminine Psychology*. HarperSanFrancisco, 1993.

Johnson RA. *Owning Your Own Shadow: Understanding the Dark Side of the Psyche*. HarperSanFrancisco, 1991.

Johnson RA. *Lying with the Heavenly Woman: Understanding and Integrating the Feminine Archetypes in Men's Lives*. HarperSanFrancisco, 1994.

Johnson RA. *Femininity Lost and Regained*. Harper and Row, NY, 1990.

Johnson RA. *Balancing Heaven and Earth: A Memoir of Visions, Dreams, and Realizations*. Harper Collins, NY, 1998.

Jung CG. *Man and his Symbols*. Dell, Random House, NY, 1964.

Jung CG. *Dreams*. Bollingen Series XX, Princeton University Press, Princeton, NJ, 1974.

Jung CG. *The Red Book: Liber Novus: A Reader's Edition*. Edited

Sonu Shamduasani, Norton and Company, NY, 2009.

Jung E, von Franz M. *The Grail Legend*. Princeton University Press, Princeton, NJ. 1998.

Keating T. *Intimacy with God*. The Crossroad Publishing Company, NY, 1998.

Kelsey M. *Encounter with God*. Bethany Fellowship Inc., Minneapolis, MN, 1992.

Kelsey M. G*od, Dreams, and Revelation: A Christian Interpretation of Dreams*. Augsburg Press, Minneapolis. 1991.

Kelsey M. *Discernment: A Study in Ecstasy and Evil*. Paulist Press, NY, 1978.

Kelsey M. *Dreams: The Dark Speech of the Spirit*. Doubleday Press, Garden City, NY, 1968.

King KL. *The Gospel of Mary of Magdala: Jesus and the First Woman Apostle*. Polebridge Press, Santa Rosa, CA, 2003.

Lawrence Brother. *The Practice of the Presence of God*. Spire Books, Old Tappan, New Jersey, 1969.

Leider RJ, Shapiro DA. *Repacking Your Bags: How to Live with a New Sense of Purpose*. MJF Books NY, 1995.

L'Engle M. *The Small Rain: A Novel*. The Noonday Press, NY, 1945.

Leloup J. *The Gospel of Mary Magdalene*. Inner Traditions, Rochester, Vermont, 1997.

Lencioni P. *The Five Dysfunctions of a Team*. Jossey-Bass, San Francisco, 2002.

Leppmann W. *Rilke: A Life*. Fromm International Publishing Corporation, NY, 1981.

Lindberg Morrow A. *Gift from the Sea*. Pantheon Books, NY, 1955.

Loomis Sherman R. *The Grail: From Celtic Myth to Christian Symbol*. Columbia University Press, NY, 1963.

Louf A. *The Cistercian Way*. Cistercian Publications, Kalamazoo, MI, 1989.

Louf A. *Teach Us to Pray*. Cowley Publications, Boston, 1992.

Macy J., Barrows A. *Rilke's Book of Hours: Love Poems to God*.

Riverhead Books, NY, 1996.

Markides KC. *The Magus of Strovolos: The Extraordinary World of a Spiritual Healer*. Penguin Books, London, 1990.

Markides KC. *Gifts of the Desert: The Forgotten Path of Christian Spirituality*. Doubleday, NY, 2005.

Markides KC. *The Mountain of Silence: A Search for Orthodox Spirituality*. Image Books, NY, 2001.

Markides KC. *Riding with the Lion: In Search of Mystical Christianity*. Viking Arkana, Penguin Group, New York. 1994.

Máté F. *The Wisdom of Tuscany: Simplicity, Security and the Good Life. Making the Tuscan Lifestyle Your Own*. Albatross Books, Norton and Company, NY, 2009.

May R. *The Cry for Myth*. Dell Publishing, NY, 1991.

May R. *The Courage to Create*. Norton and Co., NY, 1976.

Muggeridge M. *Something Beautiful for God*. HarperOne, NY, 2003.

Muller G. *The Autobiography of George Muller*. Whitaker House, New Kensington, PA, 1984.

Muller W. *Sabbath: Finding Rest, Renewal, and Delight in our Busy Lives*. Bantam Books, NY, 1999.

Nee W. *Sit, Walk and Stand*. Christian Literature Crusades, London, 1949.

Nee W. *The Norman Christian Life*. Christian Literature Crusades, London, 1948.

Neumann E. *The Great Mother: An Analysis of the Archetype*. Bollingen Series, Princeton University Press, Princeton, NJ, 1955.

Norton H. (M.D.) *Letters to a Young Poet*. Norton and Company, NY, 1934.

Nouwen HJM. *The Inner Voice of Love: A Journey through Anguish to Freedom*. Darton, Longman and Todd, London, 1997.

O'Donohue J. *The Invisible Embrace of Beauty: Rediscovering the Truth Sources of Compassion*, Serenity, and Hope. HarperCollins, NY, 1994.

O'Donohue J. *Eternal Echoes*. HarperCollins, NY, 2000.

Pagels E. *Adam, Eve and the Serpent*. Vintage Books, NY, 1988.

Pagels E. *The Gnostic Gospels*. Vintage Books NY, 1981.

Pagels E. *Beyond Belief: The Secret Gospel of Thomas*. Vintage Books, NY, 2003.

Pasick R. *Awakening from the Deep Sleep: A Powerful Guide for Courageous Men*. HarperSanFrancisco, 1992.

Pieper J. *Leisure: The Basis of Culture*. Ignatius Press, San Francisco, 2009.

Pieper J. *The Concept of Sin*. St Augustine's Press, South Bend, Indiana, 2001.

Peck S. *People of the Lie: The Hope for Healing Human Evil*. Simon and Schuster, NY, 1983.

Ponca C. *Working the Soul: Reflections on Jungian Psychology*. North Atlantic Books, Berkeley, CA, 1988.

Ramsey A.M. *Sacred and Secular: A Study in the Otherworldly and This-Worldly Aspects of Christianity*. Harper and Row Publishers, NY, 1965.

Ramsey AM. *The Gospel and the Catholic Church*. Cowley Publications, Cambridge, MA, 1990.

Rilke RM. *Diaries of a Young Poet*. Norton and Company, NY, 1942.

Rohr R. *Quest for the Grail*. The Crossroad Publishing Company. New York, 1999.

Sabini M. *C. G. Jung on Nature, Technology and Modern Life*. North Atlantic Books, Berkeley, CA, 2008.

Sandford J., Sandford P. *Healing the Wounded Spirit*. Bridge Publishing, Inc. South Plainfield, New Jersey, 1985.

Sandford J., Sandford P. *The Transformation of the Inner Man*. Bridge Publishing, Inc. South Plainfield, New Jersey, 1982.

Sanford A. *The Healing Light*. Ballantine Books, NY, 1947.

Sanford A. *Lost Shepherd*. Logos International, Plainview, NJ, 1953.

Sanford A. *Oh, Watchman!* The International Order of St. Luke's,

Keokuk, Iowa, 1950.

Sanford A. *Creation Waits*. Logos International, Plainview, NJ, 1982.

Sanford JA. *The Kingdom Within: The Inner Meaning of Jesus' Sayings*. J.B. Lippencott, NY. 1970.

Sanford JA. *Dreams: God's Forgotten Language*. HarperSan Francisco, 1968, 1998.

Sanford JA. *The Invisible Partners: How the Male and Female in Each of Us Affects Our Relationships*. Paulist Press, NY, 1980.

Sanford JA. *Jung and the Problem of Evil: The Strange Trial of Mr. Hyde*.

Sanford JA. *Evil: The Shadow Side of Reality*. Crossroad, NY, 1989.
Sanford JA. *Mystical Christianity: A Psychological Commentary on the Gospel of John*. Crossroad, NY, 1994.

Sanford JA. *Healing Body and Soul: The Meaning of Illness in the New Testament and in Psychotherapy*. Westminster/John Knox Press, Louisville, KY, 1992.

Sanford JA. *Soul Journey: A Jungian Analyst Looks at Reincarnation*. Crossroad, NY, 1991.

Sanford JA. *Fritz Kunkel: Selected Writings*. Paulist Press, NY, 1984.

Schama S. *Landscape and Memory*. Alfred A. Knoff, NY, 1995.

Segal RA. *Jung on Mythology*. Princeton University Press, Princeton, NJ. 1998.

Skinner BF. *Part I: Particulars of my Life,* New York: Alfred A. Knopf, 1976, *Part II: Shaping of a Behaviorist,* New York: Alfred A. Knopf, 1979, *Part III: A Matter of Consequences* New York: Alfred A. Knopf, 1983.

Smith ML. *Love Set Free: Meditations on the Passion According to St. John*. Cowley Publications, Boston, 1998.

Spidlik T. *The Spirituality of the Christian East*. Cistercian Publications, Kalamazoo, Michigan, 1986.

Starbird, M. *The Woman with the Alabaster Jar: Mary Magdalen and the Holy Grail*. Bear and Company, Rochester, Vermont. 1993.

Steves R. *Travel as a Political Act*. Nation Books, NY, 2009.

Steindl-Rast D. *Gratefulness, the Heart of Prayer: An Approach to Life in Fullness*. Paulist Press, NY. 1984.

Taylor Guinness G. *Behind the Ranges: The Story of James Fraser*. Moody Press, Chicago, 1964.

Thoreau HD. *Walking*. The Atlantic Monthly, Boston, MA, 1862.

Tolle E. *The Power of Now: A Guide to Spiritual Enlightenment*. New World Library, Novato, California, 1999.

Tournier P. *A Place for You*. Harper and Row, NY, 1968.

Van der Post L. *The Face Beside the Fire*. Chatto and Windus, London, 1985.

Van der Post L. *The Heart of the Hunter: Customs and Myths of the African Bushman*. Harcourt Brace Jovanovich Publishers, San Diego, CA, 1961.

Van der Post L. *A Mantis Carol*. Island Press, Washington DC, Covelo, CA, 1975.

Van der Post L. *A Walk with a White Bushman*. Chatto and Windus, London, 1986.

Van der Post L. *The Rock Rabbit and the Rainbow*. Daimon Verlag, Einseideln, Switzerland, 1998.

Van der Post L. *The Prisoner and the Bomb*. William Morrow and Company, New York City, 1971.

Van Der Veer J. *November Grass: A Novel*. Santa Clara University, Santa Clara, California Legacy, 1940.

Von Franz M. *Puer Aeternus: A Psychological Study of the Adult Struggle with the Paradise of Childhood*. Sigo Press, 1970. Alchemical Active Imagination. Shambala Press, Boston, 1997.

Von Franz M. *Alchemical Active Imagination: Revised Edition*. Shambala, Boston, 1997.

Von Franz M. *Shadow and Evil in Fairy Tales*. Revised Edition. Shambala, Boston. 1995.

Walker M. *Winter Wheat*. University of Nebraska Press, Lincoln, Nebraska and London, 1944.

Woodman M. *The Pregnant Virgin: A Process of Spiritual Transformation.* Inner City Books, Toronto, Canada, 1985.

Woodman M. *Dancing in the Flames: The Dark Goddess in the Transformation of Consciousness.* Shambala, Boston, 1997.

Zweig C, Abrams J, (Eds). *Meeting the Shadow: The Hidden Power of the Dark Side of Human Nature.* Jeremy P. Tarcher, Inc. Los Angeles, 1991.

CHRISTIAN ALTERNATIVE
BOOKS

THE NEW OPEN SPACES

Throughout the two thousand years of Christian tradition there
have been, and still are, groups and individuals that exist in
the margins and upon the edge of faith. But in Christianity's
contrapuntal history it has often been these outcasts and
pioneers that have forged contemporary orthodoxy out
of former radicalism as belief evolves to engage with and
encompass the ever-changing social and scientific realities. Real
faith lies not in the comfortable certainties of the Orthodox,
but somewhere in a half-glimpsed hinterland on the dirt track
to Emmaus, where the Death of God meets the Resurrection,
where the supernatural Christ meets the historical Jesus,
and where the revolution liberates both the oppressed and
the oppressors.

Welcome to Christian Alternative... a space at the edge where
the light shines through.
If you have enjoyed this book, why not tell other readers by
posting a review on your preferred book site.
Recent bestsellers from Christian Alternative are:

Bread Not Stones
The Autobiography of An Eventful Life
Una Kroll
The spiritual autobiography of a truly remarkable woman
and a history of the struggle for ordination in the Church of
England.
Paperback: 978-1-78279-804-0 ebook: 978-1-78279-805-7

The Quaker Way
A Rediscovery
Rex Ambler
Although fairly well known, Quakerism is not well understood.
The purpose of this book is to explain how Quakerism works as
a spiritual practice.
Paperback: 978-1-78099-657-8 ebook: 978-1-78099-658-5

Blue Sky God
The Evolution of Science and Christianity
Don MacGregor
Quantum consciousness, morphic fields and blue-sky
thinking about God and Jesus the Christ.
Paperback: 978-1-84694-937-1 ebook: 978-1-84694-938-8

Celtic Wheel of the Year
Tess Ward
An original and inspiring selection of prayers combining
Christian and Celtic Pagan traditions, and interweaving their
calendars into a single pattern of prayer for every morning
and night of the year.
Paperback: 978-1-90504-795-6

Christian Atheist
Belonging without Believing
Brian Mountford
Christian Atheists don't believe in God but miss him: especially
the transcendent beauty of his music, language, ethics, and
community.
Paperback: 978-1-84694-439-0 ebook: 978-1-84694-929-6

Compassion Or Apocalypse?
A Comprehensible Guide to the Thoughts of René Girard
James Warren
How René Girard changes the way we think about God and the
Bible, and its relevance for our apocalypse-threatened world.
Paperback: 978-1-78279-073-0 ebook: 978-1-78279-072-3

Diary Of A Gay Priest
The Tightrope Walker
Rev. Dr. Malcolm Johnson
Full of anecdotes and amusing stories, but the Church is still a
dangerous place for a gay priest.
Paperback: 978-1-78279-002-0 ebook: 978-1-78099-999-9

Do You Need God?
Exploring Different Paths to Spirituality Even For Atheists
Rory J.Q. Barnes
An unbiased guide to the building blocks of spiritual belief.
Paperback: 978-1-78279-380-9 ebook: 978-1-78279-379-3

Readers of ebooks can buy or view any of these bestsellers by clicking on the live link in the title. Most titles are published in paperback and as an ebook. Paperbacks are available in traditional bookshops. Both print and ebook formats are available online.

Find more titles and sign up to our readers' newsletter at
http://www.johnhuntpublishing.com/christianity
Follow us on Facebook at
https://www.facebook.com/ChristianAlternative